Morbidity and disability among workers 18 years and older in the Agriculture, Forestry, and Fishing sector, 1997–2007

David J. Lee[1] Ph.D., Evelyn P. Davila[1] Ph.D., William G. LeBlanc[1] Ph.D., Alberto J Caban-Martinez[1] D.O., Ph.D., Lora E Fleming[1] M.D., Ph.D., Sharon Christ[1] M.S., Kathryn McCollister[1] Ph.D., Kris Arheart[1] Ph.D., John P. Sestito[2] J.D., M.S.

[1]University of Miami, Miller School of Medicine, Miami, Florida, USA,

[2]NIOSH Division of Surveillance, Health Evaluations and Field Studies, Cincinnati, Ohio, USA

DEPARTMENT OF HEALTH AND HUMAN SERVICES
Centers for Disease Control and Prevention
National Institute for Occupational Safety and Health

This document is in the public domain and may be freely copied or reprinted.

Disclaimer

The contents of this report are based on deliverables received from the University of Miami (Contract No. 211-2008-26814) except for editorial and format changes. The findings, and conclusions expressed herein should not be construed to represent any agency determination or policy. Mention of any company or product does not constitute endorsement by the National Institute for Occupational Safety and Health (NIOSH). Citations or links to Web sites external to NIOSH do not constitute NIOSH endorsement of the sponsoring organizations of their program or products. NIOSH is not responsible for the content of these Web sites.

Ordering Information

To receive documents or other information about occupational safety and health topics, contact NIOSH

Telephone: 1-800-CDC-INFO (1-800-232-4636)
TTY: 1-888-232-6348
email: cdcinfo@cdc.gov

or visit the NIOSH website http://www.cdc.gov/niosh/

For a monthly update on news at NIOSH, subscribe to NIOSH eNEWs by visiting http://www.cdc.gov/niosh/eNEWS/ .

DHHS (NIOSH) Publication No. 2012-154
October 2012

Contents

Foreword iv

List of Figures v

List of Tables x

Acknowledgements xx

Guide to the figures and data xxi

Background and introduction 1

Previous NHIS Occupational Morbidity Studies 2

Methods 3

    The National Health Interview Survey (NHIS) 3

    Survey Years 1997–2007 3

    Morbidity and disability prevalence measures 4

Employment and NORA Sector 9

Statistical Methods 9

Limitations 9

Summary of Estimates for the Workers in the Agriculture, Forestry, and Fishing sector 10

Figures 13

Tables 41

References 99

Appendices 105

    1. Detailed Matrix of Morbidity and Disability Questions from the NHIS asked
consistently 1997-2007 105

    2. Description of Conversion of 1986–2004 National Health Interview Survey
(NHIS) Industries into NORA Sectors 112

    3. Conversion of 1986–2004 National Health Interview Survey
(NHIS) Industries into NORA Sectors (flowchart) 115

Foreword

The National Institute for Occupational Safety and Health (NIOSH) is the Federal agency responsible for occupational safety and health research. In collaboration with its many partners, NIOSH is committed to the collection, analysis, dissemination, and use of data describing the prevalence of disease and health risk factors among workers in the United States. The National Academies has urged greater use of injury and illness data at the national level to identify priorities, focus resources, and evaluate prevention program effectiveness.

The Occupational Research Group at the University of Miami is illustrative of an extramural partnership which complements NIOSH intramural programs of surveillance and research. Using population health data collected through the Centers for Disease Control and Prevention's (CDC) National Center for Health Statistics (NCHS), they have successfully undertaken a broadly based research program that describes employed worker's disability, disease, health care access, health behaviors and mortality among occupational groups and industry sectors. With the second decade of NORA, NIOSH is developing strategies and programs to better move research to practice within workplaces, using an industry sector-based approach to define high priority needs. The Occupational Research Group at the University of Miami has since completed extensive analyses describing the prevalence of disability, morbidity, mortality, and injury & disease burden among workers employed within the eight NORA sector groups identified in 2006: Agriculture, forestry and Fishing; Mining; Construction; Manufacturing; Wholesale and Retail Trade; Transportation, Warehousing, and Utilities; Services; and Healthcare and Social Assistance.

This report is one of a series of reports developed to describe the prevalence of disability and morbidity among current workers within these eight sectors. Survey data from the years 1997–2007 were used to describe the five aspects of worker's health, including (1) health status, (2) physical activity limitations or disability, (3) prevalent chronic conditions (cancer, hypertension, heart disease, asthma, diabetes, and severe psychological distress); (4) access to and use of health care services; and (5) health risk factors or behaviors. The report was developed as a descriptive resource to supplement ongoing research, and guide occupational health research and research-to-practice activities within industry.

Additionally, the information in this report will facilitate a Total Worker Health™ approach to occupational safety and health research. NIOSH increasingly sees the value of integrating occupational safety and health programs that safeguard workers from work-related hazards and programs that promote overall well-being. This report provides data on characteristics of workers health that must be better understood to fulfill the mandate to assure safe and healthful working conditions and to preserve our human resources. I invite you to learn more about the NIOSH Total Worker Health™ program at http://www.cdc.gov/niosh/TWH/default.html.

John Howard, M.D.
Director
National Institute for Occupational Safety and Health
Centers for Disease Control and Prevention

List of Figures

Health status among workers in the NORA Agriculture, Forestry, and Fishing sector

Prevalence of a **reported decline in health** when compared to health status 12 months prior estimated for workers 18 years and older

    Figure 1a. Workers 18 years and older by **NORA** sectors, National Health Interview Survey, 1997–2007 .... Page 13

    Figure 1b. Workers 18 years and older, **Agriculture, Forestry, and Fishing sector** and **All NORA** sectors, National Health Interview Survey, 1997–2007 .... Page 13

Prevalence of **fair or poor self-rated health status** estimated for workers 18 years and older

    Figure 2a. Workers 18 years and older by **NORA** sectors, National Health Interview Survey, 1997–2007 .... Page 14

    Figure 2b. Workers 18 years and older, **Agriculture, Forestry, and Fishing sector** and **All NORA** sectors, National Health Interview Survey, 1997–2007 .... Page 14

Mean number of **bed disability days** during the past 12 months estimated for workers 18 years and older

    Figure 3a. Workers 18 years and older by **NORA** sectors, National Health Interview Survey, 1997–2007 .... Page 15

    Figure 3b. Workers 18 years and older, **Agriculture, Forestry, and Fishing sector** and **All NORA** sectors, National Health Interview Survey, 1997–2007 .... Page 15

Prevalence of having **2 or more bed disability days** during the past 12 months estimated for workers 18 years and older

    Figure 4a. Workers 18 years and older by **NORA** sectors, National Health Interview Survey, 1997–2007 .... Page 16

    Figure 4b. Workers 18 years and older, **Agriculture, Forestry, and Fishing sector** and **All NORA** sectors, National Health Interview Survey, 1997–2007 .... Page 16

Mean number of **work loss days** during the past 12 months estimated for workers 18 years and older

    Figure 5a. Workers 18 years and older by **NORA** sectors, National Health Interview Survey, 1997–2007 .... Page 17

    Figure 5b. Workers 18 years and older, **Agriculture, Forestry, and Fishing sector** and **All NORA** sectors, National Health Interview Survey, 1997–2007 .... Page 17

Prevalence of **6 or more work loss days** during the past 12 months estimated for workers 18 years and older

    Figure 6a. Workers 18 years and older by **NORA** sectors, National Health Interview Survey, 1997–2007 .... Page 18

    Figure 6b. Workers 18 years and older, **Agriculture, Forestry, and Fishing sector** and **All NORA** sectors, National Health Interview Survey, 1997–2007 .... Page 18

Physical activity limitations among workers in the NORA Agriculture, Forestry, and Fishing sector

Prevalence of health problems requiring the **use of special equipment** estimated for workers 18 years and older

    Figure 7a. Workers 18 years and older by **NORA** sectors, National Health Interview Survey, 1997–2007 .... Page 19

    Figure 7b. Workers 18 years and older, **Agriculture, Forestry, and Fishing sector** and **All NORA** sectors, National Health Interview Survey, 1997–2007 .... Page 19

Prevalence of any **functional limitations** estimated for workers 18 years and older

    Figure 8a. Workers 18 years and older by **NORA** sectors, National Health Interview Survey, 1997–2007 .... Page 20

    Figure 8b. Workers 18 years and older, **Agriculture, Forestry, and Fishing sector** and **All NORA** sectors, National Health Interview Survey, 1997–2007 .... Page 20

Prevalence of **hearing difficulty** estimated for workers 18 years and older

    Figure 9a. Workers 18 years and older by **NORA** sectors, National Health Interview Survey, 1997–2007 .... Page 21

    Figure 9b. Workers 18 years and older, **Agriculture, Forestry, and Fishing sector** and **All NORA** sectors, National Health Interview Survey, 1997–2007 .... Page 21

Prevalence of **visual impairment** estimated for workers 18 years and older

    Figure 10a. Workers 18 years and older by **NORA** sectors, National Health Interview Survey, 1997–2007 .... Page 22

    Figure 10b. Workers 18 years and older, **Agriculture, Forestry, and Fishing sector** and **All NORA** sectors, National Health Interview Survey, 1997–2007 .... Page 22

Health and chronic conditions among workers in the NORA Agriculture, Forestry, and Fishing sector

Prevalence of **cancer** estimated for workers 18 years and older

    Figure 11a. Workers 18 years and older by **NORA** sectors, National Health Interview Survey, 1997–2007 .... Page 23

Figure 11b. Workers 18 years and older, **Agriculture, Forestry, and Fishing sector** and **All NORA** sectors, National Health Interview Survey, 1997–2007 .... Page 23

Prevalence of **hypertension** estimated for workers 18 years and older

Figure 12a. Workers 18 years and older by **NORA** sectors, National Health Interview Survey, 1997–2007 .... Page 24

Figure 12b. Workers 18 years and older, **Agriculture, Forestry, and Fishing sector** and **All NORA** sectors, National Health Interview Survey, 1997–2007 .... Page 24

Prevalence of **heart disease** estimated for workers 18 years and older

Figure 13a. Workers 18 years and older by **NORA** sectors, National Health Interview Survey, 1997–2007 .... Page 25

Figure 13b. Workers 18 years and older, **Agriculture, Forestry, and Fishing sector** and **All NORA** sectors, National Health Interview Survey, 1997–2007 .... Page 25

Prevalence of **asthma** estimated for workers 18 years

Figure 14a. Workers 18 years and older by **NORA** sectors National Health Interview Survey, 1997–2007 .... Page 26

Figure 14b. Workers 18 years and older, **Agriculture, Forestry, and Fishing sector** and **All NORA** sectors, National Health Interview Survey, 1997–2007 .... Page 26

Prevalence of **diabetes** estimated for workers 18 years and older

Figure 15a. Workers 18 years and older by **NORA** sectors, National Health Interview Survey, 1997–2007 .... Page 27

Figure 15b. Workers 18 years and older, **Agriculture, Forestry, and Fishing sector** and **All NORA** sectors, National Health Interview Survey, 1997–2007 .... Page 27

Prevalence of **severe psychological distress** estimated for workers 18 years and older

Figure 16a. Workers 18 years and older by **NORA** sectors, National Health Interview Survey, 1997–2007 .... Page 28

Figure 16b. Workers 18 years and older, **Agriculture, Forestry, and Fishing sector** and **All NORA** sectors, National Health Interview Survey, 1997–2007 .... Page 28

Health care utilization among workers in the NORA Agriculture, Forestry, and Fishing sector

Prevalence of not having seen a **primary health care provider** during the past 12 months estimated for workers 18 years and older

Figure 17a. Workers 18 years and older by **NORA** sectors, National Health Interview Survey, 1997–2007 .... Page 29

Figure 17b. Workers 18 years and older, **Agriculture, Forestry, and Fishing sector** and **All NORA** sectors, National Health Interview Survey, 1997–2007 .... Page 29

Prevalence of **dentist contact** of one year or greater estimated for workers 18 years and older

Figure 18a. Workers 18 years and older by **NORA** sectors, National Health Interview Survey, 1997–2007 .... Page 30

Figure 18b. Workers 18 years and older, **Agriculture, Forestry, and Fishing sector** and **All NORA** sectors, National Health Interview Survey, 1997–2007 .... Page 30

Prevalence of **surgery** during the past 12 months estimated for workers 18 years and older

Figure 19a. Workers 18 years and older by **NORA** sectors, National Health Interview Survey, 1997–2007 .... Page 31

Figure 19b. Workers 18 years and older, **Agriculture, Forestry, and Fishing sector** and **All NORA** sectors, Health Interview Survey, 1997–2007 .... Page 31

Prevalence of **hospital emergency room visit** during the past 12 months estimated for workers 18 years and older

Figure 20a. Workers 18 years and older by **NORA** sectors, National Health Interview Survey, 1997–2007 .... Page 32

Figure 20b. Workers 18 years and older, **Agriculture, Forestry, and Fishing sector** and **All NORA** sectors, National Health Interview Survey, 1997–2007 .... Page 32

Health risk factors or behaviors among workers in the NORA Agriculture, Forestry, and Fishing sector

Prevalence of **current smokers** estimated for workers 18 years and older

Figure 21a. Workers 18 years and older by **NORA** sectors, National Health Interview Survey, 1997–2007 .... Page 33

Figure 21b. Workers 18 years and older, **Agriculture, Forestry, and Fishing sector** and **All NORA**sectors, National Health Interview Survey, 1997–2007 .... Page 33

Prevalence of **current alcohol drinkers** estimated for workers 18 years and older

Figure 22a. Workers 18 years and older by **NORA** sectors, National Health Interview Survey, 1997–2007 .... Page 34

Figure 22b. Workers 18 years and older, **Agriculture, Forestry, and Fishing sector** and **All NORA** sectors, National Health Interview Survey, 1997–2007 .... Page 34

Prevalence of **obesity** estimated for workers 18 years and older

    Figure 23a. Workers 18 years and older by **NORA** sectors, National Health Interview Survey, 1997–2007 .... Page 35

    Figure 23b. Workers 18 years and older, **Agriculture, Forestry, and Fishing sector** and **All NORA** sectors, National Health Interview Survey, 1997–2007 .... Page 35

Prevalence of not meeting **CDC recommended leisure time levels of physical activity** estimated for workers 18 years and older

    Figure 24a. Workers 18 years and older by **NORA** sectors, National Health Interview Survey, 1997–2007 .... Page 36

    Figure 24b. Workers 18 years and older, **Agriculture, Forestry, and Fishing sector** and **All NORA** sectors, National Health Interview Survey, 1997–2007 .... Page 36

Prevalence of **lifetime HIV test** estimated for workers 18 years and older

    Figure 25a. Workers 18 years and older by **NORA** sectors, National Health Interview Survey, 1997–2007 .... Page 37

    Figure 25b. Workers 18 years and older, **Agriculture, Forestry, and Fishing sector** and **All NORA** sectors, National Health Interview Survey, 1997–2007 .... Page 37

Prevalence of not receiving an **influenza vaccination** during the past 12 months estimated for workers 18 years and older

    Figure 26a. Workers 18 years and older by **NORA** sectors, National Health Interview Survey, 1997–2007 .... Page 38

    Figure 26b. Workers 18 years and older, **Agriculture, Forestry, and Fishing sector** and **All NORA** sectors, National Health Interview Survey, 1997–2007 .... Page 38

Prevalence of never receiving a **pneumococcal vaccination** estimated for workers 60 years and older

    Figure 27a. Workers 60 years and older by **NORA** sectors, National Health Interview Survey, 1997–2007 .... Page 39

    Figure 27b. Workers 60 years and older, **Agriculture, Forestry, and Fishing sector** and **All NORA** sectors, National Health Interview Survey, 1997–2007 .... Page 39

List of Tables

Table 1. Estimated U.S. worker population and sample size for workers 18 years and older, All NORA industry sectors and **Agriculture, Forestry, and Fishing sector**, National Health Interview Survey, 1997–2007 .... Page 41

Table 2. U.S. Health Status, Disability and Morbidity Prevalence (percent) estimates for workers 18 years and older, NORA industry sectors, National Health Interview Survey, 1997–2007 .... Page 42

Health status among workers in the NORA Agriculture, Forestry, and Fishing sector

Table 3. Prevalence of a **reported decline in health** when compared to health status 12 months prior estimated for workers 18 years and older, **All NORA sectors**, National Health Interview Survey, 1997–2007.. Page 44

Table 4. Prevalence of a **reported decline in health** when compared to health status 12 months prior estimated for workers 18 years and older, **Agriculture, Forestry, and Fishing sector**, National Health Interview Survey, 1997–2007 .... Page 45

Table 5. Prevalence of **fair or poor self-rated health status** estimated for workers 18 years and older, **All NORA sectors**, National Health Interview Survey, 1997–2007.. Page 46

Table 6. Prevalence of **fair or poor self-rated health status** estimated for workers 18 years and older, **Agriculture, Forestry, and Fishing sector**, National Health Interview Survey, 1997–2007... Page 47

Table 7. Mean number of **bed disability days** during the past 12 months estimated for workers 18 years and older, **All NORA sectors**, National Health Interview Survey, 1997–2007 .... Page 48

Table 8. Mean number of **bed disability days** during the past 12 months estimated for workers 18 years and older, **Agriculture, Forestry, and Fishing sector**, National Health Interview Survey, 1997–2007 .... Page 49

Table 9. Prevalence of having **2 or more bed disability days** during the past 12 months estimated for workers 18 years and older, **All NORA sectors**, National Health Interview Survey, 1997–2007.. Page 50

Table 10. Prevalence of having **2 or more bed disability days** during the past 12 months estimated for workers 18 years and older, **Agriculture, Forestry, and Fishing sector**, National Health Interview Survey, 1997–2007 .... Page 51

Table 11. Mean number of **work loss days** during the past 12 months estimated for workers 18 years and older, **All NORA sectors**, National Health Interview Survey, 1997–2007.. Page 52

Table 12. Mean number of **work loss days** during the past 12 months estimated for workers 18 years and older, **Agriculture, Forestry, and Fishing sector**, National Health Interview Survey, 1997–2007 .... Page 53

Table 13. Prevalence of **6 or more work loss days** during the past 12 months estimated for workers 18 years and older, **All NORA sectors**, National Health Interview Survey, 1997–2007 .... Page 54

Table 14. Prevalence of **6 or more work loss days** during the past 12 months estimated for workers 18 years and older, **Agriculture, Forestry, and Fishing sector**, National Health Interview Survey, 1997–2007 .... Page 55

Physical activity limitations among workers in the NORA Agriculture, Forestry, and Fishing sector

Table 15. Prevalence of health problems requiring the use of **special equipment** estimated for workers 18 years and older, **All NORA sectors**, National Health Interview Survey, 1997–2007 .... Page 56

Table 16. Prevalence of health problems requiring the use of **special equipment** estimated for workers 18 years and older, **Agriculture, Forestry, and Fishing sector**, National Health Interview Survey, 1997–2007 .... Page 57

Table 17. Prevalence of any **functional limitations** estimated for workers 18 years and older, **All NORA sectors**, National Health Interview Survey, 1997–2007 .... Page 58

Table 18. Prevalence of any **functional limitations** estimated for workers 18 years and older, **Agriculture, Forestry, and Fishing sector**, National Health Interview Survey, 1997–2007 .... Page 59

Table 19. Prevalence of **hearing difficulty** estimated for workers 18 years and older, **All NORA sectors**, National Health Interview Survey, 1997–2007 .... Page 60

Table 20. Prevalence of **hearing difficulty** estimated for workers 18 years and older, **Agriculture, Forestry, and Fishing sector**, National Health Interview Survey, 1997–2007 .... Page 61

Table 21. Prevalence of **visual impairment** estimated for workers 18 years and older, **All NORA sectors**, National Health Interview Survey, 1997–2007 .... Page 62

Table 22. Prevalence of **visual impairment** estimated for workers 18 years and older, **Agriculture, Forestry, and Fishing sector**, National Health Interview Survey, 1997–2007 .... Page 63

Health and chronic conditions among workers in the NORA Agriculture, Forestry, and Fishing sector

Table 23. Prevalence of **cancer** estimated for workers 18 years and older, **All NORA sectors**, National Health Interview Survey, 1997–2007 .... Page 64

Table 24. Prevalence of **cancer** estimated for workers 18 years and older, **Agriculture, Forestry, and Fishing sector**, National Health Interview Survey, 1997–2007 .... Page 65

Table 25. Prevalence of **hypertension** estimated for workers 18 years and older, **All NORA sectors**, National Health Interview Survey, 1997–2007 .... Page 66

Table 26. Prevalence of **hypertension** estimated for workers 18 years and older, **Agriculture, Forestry, and Fishing sector**, National Health Interview Survey, 1997–2007 .... Page 67

Table 27. Prevalence of **heart disease** estimated for workers 18 years and older, **All NORA sectors**, National Health Interview Survey, 1997–2007 .... Page 68

Table 28. Prevalence of **heart disease** estimated for workers 18 years and older, **Agriculture, Forestry, and Fishing sector**, National Health Interview Survey, 1997–2007 .... Page 69

Table 29. Prevalence of **asthma** estimated for workers 18 years and older, **All NORA sectors**, National Health Interview Survey, 1997–2007 .... Page 70

Table 30. Prevalence of **asthma** estimated for workers 18 years and older, **Agriculture, Forestry, and Fishing sector**, National Health Interview Survey, 1997–2007 .... Page 71

Table 31. Prevalence of **diabetes** estimated for workers 18 years and older, **All NORA sectors**, National Health Interview Survey, 1997–2007 .... Page 72

Table 32. Prevalence of **diabetes** estimated for workers 18 years and older, **Agriculture, Forestry, and Fishing sector**, National Health Interview Survey, 1997–2007 .... Page 73

Table 33. Prevalence of **severe psychological distress** estimated for workers 18 years and older, **All NORA sectors**, National Health Interview Survey, 1997–2007 .... Page 74

Table 34. Prevalence of **severe psychological distress** estimated for workers 18 years and older, **Agriculture, Forestry, and Fishing sector**, National Health Interview Survey, 1997–2007 .... Page 75

Health care utilization among workers in the NORA Agriculture, Forestry, and Fishing sector

Table 35. Prevalence of not having seen a **primary health care provider** during the past 12 months estimated for workers 18 years and older, **All NORA sectors**, National Health Interview Survey, 1997–2007 .... Page 76

Table 36. Prevalence of not having seen a **primary health care provider** during the past 12 months estimated for workers 18 years and older, **Agriculture, Forestry, and Fishing sector**, National Health Interview Survey, 1997–2007 .... Page 77

Table 37. Prevalence of **no dentist contact** during the past year estimated for workers 18 years and older, **All NORA sectors**, National Health Interview Survey, 1997–2007 .... Page 78

Table 38. Prevalence of **no dentist contact** during the past year estimated for workers 18 years and older, **Agriculture, Forestry, and Fishing sector**, National Health Interview Survey, 1997–2007 .... Page 79

Table 39. Prevalence of **surgery** during the past 12 months estimated for workers 18 years and older, **All NORA sectors**, National Health Interview Survey, 1997–2007 .... Page 80

Table 40. Prevalence of **surgery** during the past 12 months estimated for workers 18 years and older, **Agriculture, Forestry, and Fishing sector**, National Health Interview Survey, 1997–2007 .... Page 81

Table 41. Prevalence of **hospital emergency room visit** during the past 12 months estimated for workers 18 years and older, **All NORA sectors**, National Health Interview Survey, 1997–2007 .... Page 82

Table 42. Prevalence of **hospital emergency room visit** during the past 12 months estimated for workers 18 years and older, **Agriculture, Forestry, and Fishing sector**, National Health Interview Survey, 1997–2007 .... Page 83

Health risk factors or behaviors among workers in the NORA Agriculture, Forestry, and Fishing sector

Table 43. Prevalence of **current smokers** estimated for workers 18 years and older, **All NORA sectors**, National Health Interview Survey, 1997–2007 .... Page 84

Table 44. Prevalence of **current smokers** estimated for workers 18 years and older, **Agriculture, Forestry, and Fishing sector**, National Health Interview Survey, 1997–2007 .... Page 85

Table 45. Prevalence of **current alcohol drinkers** estimated for workers 18 years and older, **All NORA sectors**, National Health Interview Survey, 1997–2007 .... Page 86

Table 46. Prevalence of **current alcohol drinkers** estimated for workers 18 years and older, **Agriculture, Forestry, and Fishing sector**, National Health Interview Survey, 1997–2007 .... Page 87

Table 47. Prevalence of **obesity** estimated for workers 18 years and older, **All NORA sectors**, National Health Interview Survey, 1997–2007 .... Page 88

Table 48. Prevalence of **obesity** estimated for workers 18 years and older, **Agriculture, Forestry, and Fishing sector**, National Health Interview Survey, 1997–2007 .... Page 89

Table 49. Prevalence of not meeting **CDC recommended leisure time levels of physical activity** estimated for workers 18 years and older, **All NORA sectors**, National Health Interview Survey, 1997–2007 .... Page 90

Table 50. Prevalence of not meeting **CDC recommended leisure time levels of physical activity** estimated for workers 18 years and older, **Agriculture, Forestry, and Fishing sector**, National Health Interview Survey, 1997–2007 .... Page 91

Table 51. Prevalence of **lifetime HIV test** estimated for workers 18 years and older, **All NORA sectors**, National Health Interview Survey, 1997–2007 .... Page 92

Table 52. Prevalence of **lifetime HIV test** estimated for workers 18 years and older, **Agriculture, Forestry, and Fishing sector**, National Health Interview Survey, 1997–2007 .... Page 93

Table 53. Prevalence of not receiving an **influenza vaccination** during the past 12 months estimated for workers 18 years and older, **All NORA sectors**, National Health Interview Survey, 1997–2007 .... Page 94

Table 54. Prevalence of not receiving an **influenza vaccination** during the past 12 months estimated for workers 18 years and older, **Agriculture, Forestry, and Fishing sector**, National Health Interview Survey, 1997–2007 .... Page 95

Table 55. Prevalence of never receiving a **pneumococcal vaccination** estimated for workers 60 years and older, **All NORA sectors**, National Health Interview Survey, 1997–2007 .... Page 96

Table 56. Prevalence of never receiving a **pneumococcal vaccination** estimated for workers 60 years and older, **Agriculture, Forestry, and Fishing sector**, National Health Interview Survey, 1997–2007 .... Page 97

Acknowledgements

This document is one of eight documents prepared by NIOSH, each based on the March, 2010 report NORA Morbidity and Disability: The National Health Interview Survey (NHIS) 1997–2007 prepared under contract with the Department of Epidemiology and Public Health, University of Miami School of Medicine. NIOSH has supplemented the original report with additional figures, and reformatted the contents to conform to NIOSH publication guidelines.

The contract report and each of NIOSH documents received technical reviews. We extend our thanks to the reviewers for their thoughtful and insightful comments. We acknowledge the contributions of: John Mendeloff, Ph.D., RAND Center for Health and Safety in the Workplace; Eve Powell-Griner, Ph.D., Division of Health Interview Statistics, National Center for Health Statistics; Gordon Smith, M.D., Department of Epidemiology and Preventive Medicine, University of Maryland School of Medicine; Doug Trout, M.D., M.H.S., K. Ann Berry, Ph.D., MBA., Roger R. Rosa, Ph.D., Tanya Headley, M.S., David Utterback, Ph.D., James Helmkamp, Ph.D., Linda McWilliams, M.S., Casey Chosewood, M.D., and Anita Schill, Ph.D., National Institute for Occupational Safety and Health.

The report is composed of text, color figures, and tables. Color choices were influenced by the work of Cynthia A. Brewer, Pennsylvania State University, based on colors from ColorBrewer.org. Color image templates were created and evaluated using http://www.visicheck.com, a visual simulation tools for color blindness.

Editorial and Production Support

Editor

John P. Sestito, J.D., M.S.

Graphics Development and Editing

John P. Sestito, J.D., M.S.
Evelyn Davila, Ph.D.

Document Design and Desktop Publishing

Greg Hartle, General Infomatics (CTR)

Guide to the figures and data

Data are presented on pages 13–39 using two horizontal bar charts to summarize NHIS estimates for 27 morbidity and disability measures. The first bar chart\figure presents overall summary estimates for All NORA Sectors (i.e., all workers) and workers employed within each of the eight NORA sectors.

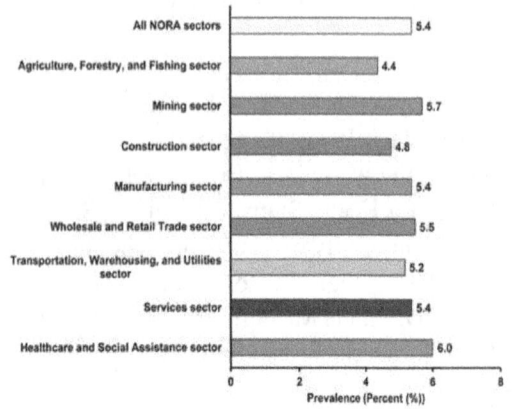

The horizontal bar for Agriculture is assigned a different color to contrast with other entries.

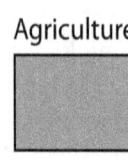

Agriculture   All NORA Sectors

The second bar chart\figure presents estimates by population subgroups (all subgroups, gender, race, ethnicity, age, education and insurance status) for the Agriculture, Forsetry, and Fishing Sector and the All NORA Sectors category.

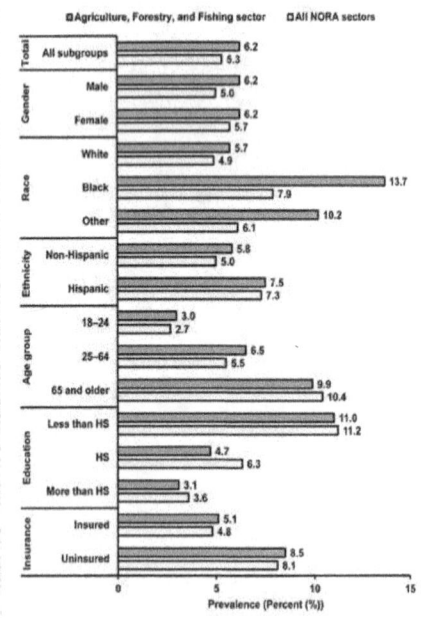

The horizontal bar for Agricluture is assigned a different color to contrast with All NORA Sectors.

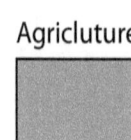

Agricluture   All NORA Sectors

The majority of the figures present prevalence (percentage) values reflecting non-zero estimates. For a small number of figures, the response values displayed may include symbols indicating (1) no data available, which occurs where the population subgroup sample is zero; (2) the computed quantity or value is greater than 0.0 but less than 0.05% (symbol (0.0)); and (3) there were no cases in that particular cell, and thus the response value estimated (symbol (–)) as zero quantity. These values are distinguished in the figures with the following symbols:

(---) No data available indicating the population subgroup sample is zero

(0.0) The estimated prevalence value is greater than 0.0 but less than 0.05%

(–) No cases in this cell, thus the response value is estimated as zero quantity

Background and introduction

The ongoing collection, analysis, dissemination and use of population health data has been an integral part of the National Institute for Occupational Safety and Health (NIOSH) research program since the 1970s. In collaboration with its many partners, NIOSH has established programs to describe the magnitude of occupational hazards, diseases, and injuries in the United States. These activities document the nation's progress in reducing the burden of work-related diseases and injuries. These activities have continually identified new areas that require additional research and prevention efforts. Despite these accomplishments, occupational health surveillance in the United States remains fragmented, with substantial data gaps.

NIOSH conducts a range of efforts in the area of research, guidance, information, and service. To better coordinate these efforts, NIOSH has adopted aspects of matrix management to both organize and manage its research portfolio. In 2005 NIOSH solicited the involvement of both intramural staff, and extramural partners and stakeholders, to develop the National Occupational Research Agenda (NORA) goals to advance the prevention of occupational injuries and illnesses for eight targeted sectors of U.S. industry. The eight sector programs, with their corresponding North American Industry Classification System (NAICS) 2-digit codes, are identified below:

NORA sectors	NAICS codes
Agriculture, Forestry, and Fishing	11
Mining	21
Construction	23
Manufacturing	31–33
Wholesale and Retail Trade	42, 44–45,
Transportation, Warehousing, and Utilities	48–49, 22
Healthcare and Social Assistance	62; 54194
Services	51–56, 61, 71–72, 81, 92

As an integral part of the NIOSH Program Portfolio, the NIOSH Surveillance program has developed five strategic goals. These goals outline the major elements of a long-range plan for a comprehensive occupational surveillance program. These national goals seek to both strengthen and balance national and state-based partnerships, and support a comprehensive intramural program of illness, injury, and hazard surveillance activities.

Occupational health surveillance is challenged to narrow many substantial data and information gaps. To this end, the NIOSH surveillance program promotes increased coordination and information exchange within NIOSH and among our many external partner organizations. One such organization is the Occupational Research Group at the University of Miami. This Group was funded in the past by NIOSH to study the U.S. employed population's morbidity and mortality using statistical resources publicly available through the National Center for Health Statistics (NCHS) of the Centers for Disease Control and Prevention (CDC).

The focus of this report is to describe the prevalence of morbidity and disability among employed workers in the Agriculture, Forsetry, and Fishing sector. This report is based on work products from comprehensive analyses performed by the Occupational Research Group at the University of Miami using an established methodology to assess predictors of acute and chronic disability morbidity for U.S. workers by the National Occupational Research Agenda (NORA) sectors using the 1997–2007 National Health Interview Survey (NHIS) data [Fleming et al. 2004; Fleming et al. 2005; Fleming et al. 2007a].

The National Health Interview Survey (NHIS) is a continuous multipurpose and multistage probability area in-person survey of the U.S. civilian non-institutionalized population living at addressed dwellings [NCHS 2000]. Each week a probability sample of households is interviewed by trained personnel to obtain information about the characteristics of each member of the household. Data from the NHIS include a range of measures of population health, acute and chronic disability, health care access, and individual risk factor and health behavior collected for all participants. After adjustment for sample weights and design effects, prevalence measures were estimated for workers ages 18 years and older for each of the eight NORA sectors; as well as by population subgroups categorized by age, gender, race, ethnicity, health insurance, and education. Additional information has been made available to allow for extrapolation to the entire U.S. worker population during the 1997–2007 study period.

Previous NHIS Occupational Morbidity Studies

Previous studies have used the NHIS data to explore a range of occupational health issues, including: injury, smoking characteristics, health characteristics in the longest held occupation and industry, injuries in racial subgroups, cardiovascular disease and working women, impairments and chronic diseases in farmers, back injury and disability, workplace accommodations, AIDS knowledge among health care workers, and carpal tunnel syndrome [Behrens et al. 1994; Biddlecom et al. 1992; Brackbill et al. 1994a,b; Cooper et al. 1993; Guo et al. 1999; Hurwitz and Morgenstern 1997; La Rosa JH 1988; Nelson et al. 1994a,b; NIOSH 1980; Sterling and Weinkam 1989, 1990; Tanaka et al. 1995; Wagener and Winn 1991; Zwerling et al. 1997, 1998, 2003].

NIOSH colleagues Kaminski and Spirtas [NIOSH 1980] analyzed NHIS data and produced proportionate morbidity ratios (PMRs) from the 1969–74 NHIS surveys to examine the morbidity, disability, and reported health care use patterns for 498,580 individuals by industry. They did not look at trends over this relatively short time period. The highest specific disease conditions were reported for agriculture, furniture manufacturing, metal fabrication, railroad transport, repair services, amusement and recreational services, state and local government workers, and new workers; the highest disabilities were found for forestry and fisheries workers, certain manufacturers, medical and health services workers, and federal government employees; the greatest use of medical services was among metal industries, specific manufacturers, and railroad workers; the greatest morbidity was reported by private household service workers although they had less disability and use of medical services; overall manufacturing industries had the largest proportion of workers with work injuries and the service industries had the smallest. The authors pointed out that although some of the results confirmed previous studies, other results of their study revealed new associations of morbidity with particular industry/occupations of U.S. workers. These observations were possible because the NHIS survey design is not limited to a particular industry, occupation, or geographic area. Therefore, Kaminski and Spirtas [NIOSH 1980] suggested that NHIS data be used for surveillance of disease morbidity and mortality for U.S. workers, and recommended that its use for this purpose be explored further.

The Occupational Research Group at the University of Miami used the NHIS data from 1986–2007, with mortality follow-up through 2002, to evaluate various issues of health disparities among all U.S. workers, particularly among poor and minority worker subpopulations predominantly by occupational subcategory [Caban et al. 2005; Caban-Martinez et al. 2007a,b; Christ et al. 2007; Fleming et al. 2003; Fleming et al. 2007b; Gómez-Marin et al. 2004, 2005; Lee et al. 2004; Lee et al. 2006a,b; Lee et al. 2007a,b; McCollister et al. 2010]. They have evaluated occupational health disparities in terms of health behaviors, health insurance, obesity and exercise, occupational segregation, morbidity, and mortality in all U.S. workers, as well as morbidity and mortality in particular occupations and industry sectors. Overall, they have found that minority and blue collar workers are less likely to reported having health insurance, health screening (such as cancer screenings), and receiving health prevention information from their health care providers. At the same time, these workers are more likely to be obese, less likely to exercise, more likely to reported morbidity, and more likely to report risky drinking and smoking behaviors (See http://www.umiamiorg.com/ for online monographs and other documentation).

Methods

The National Health Interview Survey (NHIS)

Since 1957, the National Center for Health Statistics (NCHS) has administered the NHIS as a continuous multipurpose and multistage area probability in-person survey of the U.S. civilian non-institutionalized population living at addressed dwellings [Botman and Jack 1995; NCHS 1989, 2000]. The survey was authorized by Congress to obtain national estimates on disease, injury, impairment, disability, and related issues on a uniform basis for the U.S. population. The NHIS Survey has evolved over the years with a significant redesign in 1997.

Survey Years 1997–2007

The NHIS was completely redesigned in 1997 to collect key health information from a single randomly selected adult household member. In case the randomly selected household member is not home when the interviewer goes to the home, then the interviewer returns at a different date to interview this person. This strategy greatly enhances the reliability of acute and chronic condition assessment.

Data exist in three separate files: the Person, Sample Adult, and Sample Child. These files include both household and individual level information on various demographics and aspects of health. However, the data that exist in each of these files differ. For example, the Sample Adult file contains information on health conditions, physical and social activity limitations, psychological distress, and chronic conditions important risk factors (such as tobacco and alcohol use) among the adult randomly selected to be interviewed, while the Person file contains information on functional status and access to health care of all NHIS participants. Data on occupation and industry is only available in the Sample Adult file. For the survey years 1997–2007 of the NHIS, there were 196,924 adult participants currently employed at the time of the household interview (see table below). Annual response rates to the 1997–2007 adult core survey ranged from 69% (in 2005) to 80% (in 1997) [NCHS 2002a,b; NCHS 2003a,b; NCHS 2004a,b; NCHS 2005; NCHS 2006a,b; NCHS 2007].

Sample size for gender and age-group by ethnic or race subgroups
National Health Interview Survey, 1997–2007

Subgroup	Females		Males	
	18-59 years	60 years and older	18-59 years	60 years and older
Hispanic origin				
Hispanic/Latino	14,908	679	17,526	807
Not Hispanic/Latino	76,281	7,288	72,391	7,044
Race				
White	70,250	6,734	73,358	6,698
Black/African American	15,248	963	10,238	813
Unknown/multiple races	5,691	270	6,321	340
Total	91,189	7,967	89,917	7,851

Morbidity and disability prevalence measures

The tables below summarize the questions administered consistently from the NHIS for the period 1997–2007. A comprehensive summary of these questions is found in Appendix 1.

These questions include:

Demographic subgroups	
Variable	Question(s)
Gender	Are you male or female?
Age	How old are you? (years)
Race	What races do you consider yourself to be?
Ethnicity	Do you consider yourself to be Hispanic or Latino? Hispanic includes: Puerto Rican, Cuban, Dominican, Mexican, Central/South American, other Latin American, other Hispanic
Insurance	Are you covered by health insurance or any other health care plan?
Education	What is the highest level of education that you have completed?

As noted under Statistical methods below, estimates are provided for population subgroups based on responses to these questions on gender, age, ethnicity, insurance coverage and education.

Since the 1970s health planners have used various metrics to gauge population health status. In recent years, both Healthy People 2000 and 2010 have included measures that seek to characterize the quality of life, and efforts within CDC seek to track health days as measured by the NHIS and the CDC's Behavioral Risk Factor Survey [CDC 2000]. This report provides data on self-reported health status, which is supplemented with data on bed day disability and lost work days among the employed U.S. population.

Health status	
Variable	Question(s)
Health Last Year	Compared with 12 MONTHS AGO, would you say your health is (better, worse, or about the same)?
Self Rated Health	Would you say health in general is excellent, very good, good, fair, or poor?
Bed Day	During the PAST 12 MONTHS, that is, since [12 month ref date], ABOUT how many days did illness or injury keep you in bed for more than half of the day? (Include days while an overnight patient in a hospital).
Lost Work Day	During the PAST 12 MONTHS, that is, since [12 month ref date], ABOUT how many days did you miss work at a job or business because of illness or injury (do not include maternity leave)?

The NHIS provides NIOSH with the opportunity to describe working populations relative to more subtle aspects of physical activity limitations or disability. These questions permit us to examine a proportion of employed workers who labor under physical limitations; require the use of special equipment; or have hearing or visual impairment.

Physical activity limitations	
Variable	Question(s)
Special Equipment	Do you now have any health problem that requires you to use special equipment, such as a cane, a wheelchair, a special bed, or a special telephone?
Limitations	NHIS recode based on all the 12 NHIS questions on activity limitations: How difficult it is for you to: o walk ¼ mile w/o special equipment? o Climb 10 steps w/o special equipment o Stand 2 hours w/o special equipment o Sit 2 hours w/o special equipment o Stoop, bend or kneel w/o special equipment o Reach over w/o special equipment o Grasp small objects w/o special equipment o Lift/carry 10 lbs w/o special equipment o Push large objects w/o special equipment o Go out to events w/o special equipment o Participate in social activities w/o special equipment o Relax at home w/o special equipment
Hearing Impairment	Which statement best describes your hearing (without a hearing aid): good, a little trouble, a lot of trouble, deaf?
Visual Impairment	Based on two questions: o Do you have trouble seeing, even when wearing glasses or contact lenses? and o Are you blind or unable to see at all?

Establishment-based surveys of occupational illness provide limited insight on the prevalence of many chronic diseases and mental health problems. For the years 1997–2007 the NHIS permits one to pool data so as to estimate and describe the prevalence of cancer, hypertension, heart disease, asthma, diabetes, and severe psychological distress.

\multicolumn{2}{c}{Health and chronic conditions}	
Variable	Question(s)
Cancer	Have you EVER been told by a doctor or other health professional that you had cancer or a malignancy of any kind? (yes/no)
Hypertension	Have you EVER been told by a doctor or other health professional that you have had hypertension, also called high blood pressure?
Heart Disease	Have you EVER been told by a doctor or other health professional that you had heart disease? Based on NHIS questions of specific diseases: o Coronary heart disease o Angina o Heart attack o Any kind of heart condition or heart disease
Asthma	Have you EVER been told by a doctor or other health professional that you had asthma?
Diabetes	Have you EVER been told by a doctor or other health professional that you have diabetes or sugar diabetes?
Severe Psychological Distress	Based on 6 NHIS questions: "During the past 30 days how often did you feel…?" o so sad that nothing could cheer you up? o nervous? o restless or fidgety? o hopeless? o that everything was an effort? o worthless?

The health of workers depends on access to and use of health care services, both of which are essential to maintaining the productive capabilities of the labor force. These questions provide important data on access to primary medical and dental care, and the use of hospital emergency rooms and surgical procedures.

Health care utilization	
Variable	Question(s)
Seen Primary Health care Provider	During the past 12 months, have you seen a primary health care provider (any of the following): o Ob/GYN o general doctor
Dental	About how long has it been since you last saw or talked to a dentist? Include all types of dentists, such as orthodontists, oral surgeons, and all other dental specialists, as well as dental hygienists.
Surgery	During the PAST 12 MONTHS, have you had SURGERY or other surgical procedures either as an inpatient or an outpatient? This includes both major surgery and minor procedures such as setting bones or removing growths.
Emergency Room Visit	During the PAST 12 MONTHS, HOW MANY TIMES have you gone to a HOSPITAL EMERGENCY ROOM for your health?

Health promotion and disease prevention for many chronic diseases emphasize the importance of smoking cessation, and moderating alcohol consumption. Few would question that regular physical activity is important for maintaining a healthy body, enhancing psychological well-being, and preventing premature death. Yet, while we have statistics that estimate more than half of adults in the United States are overweight or obese, we have limited data on how these factors vary among employed workers and industry. Immunizations can prevent disability or severe health effects from infectious diseases among individuals and help control the spread of infections within communities. Recent campaigns in the U.S. have focused on the importance of the spread of influenza by and among selected high-risk occupational groups, as the workplace is recognized as an element of community-based immunization programs. The NHIS permits one to pool data so as to estimate and describe the prevalence of these factors among population subgroups within industry sectors.

| Health risk factors or behaviors ||
Variable	Question(s)
Smoking status	Is the individual a never smoker, former smoker, or current smoker? Based on the NHIS questions: o Have you smoked at least 100 cigarettes in your entire life? o Do you now smoke cigarettes every day, some days, or not at all?
Drinking status	Based on three questions related to historical and current alcohol use patterns: o In your ENTIRE LIFE, have you had at least 12 drinks of any type of alcoholic beverage? o In ANY ONE YEAR, have you had at least 12 drinks of any type of alcoholic beverage? o In the PAST YEAR, how often did you drink any type of alcoholic beverage?
Body Mass Index (BMI) (obesity)	NHIS Recoded variable based on NHIS variables: o Self-reported weight without shoes (pounds) (AWEIGHTP) o Self-reported total height in inches (AHEIGHT)
Leisure Time Physical Activity	Did the individual meet CDC Health People 2010 recommendations for leisure time physical activity (i.e. engaged or light-moderate activity for ≥ 30 minutes ≥ 5 times/week or "vigorous activity" ≥ 20 minutes ≥ 3 times per week or both). Based on NHIS questions: o Frequency of light/moderate activity (times per week)? o Duration of light/moderate activity (in minutes)? o Frequency vigorous activity (times per week)? o Duration of vigorous activity (in minutes)?
HIV/AIDS Test	The next questions are about the test for HIV. Have you ever been tested for HIV?
Influenza Vaccine	During the past 12 months, have you had a flu shot? A flu shot is usually given in the fall and protects against influenza for the flu season.
Pneumococcal Vaccine	Have you ever had a pneumonia shot? This shot is usually given only once or twice in a person's lifetime and is different from the flu shot. It is also called the pneumococcal vaccine.

Employment and NORA Sector

Beginning in 1997, employment was defined as having worked during the week prior to the NCHS survey and asked of all Sample Adult NHIS participants 18 years and older. This definition includes paid as well as unpaid work. The NHIS employs U.S. Census Occupational and Industrial Codes to classify workers [NCHS 1993a]. NCHS then recoded the Census Occupational Codes into 13 broad categories, and 41 more specialized categories.

For this analysis employed workers were aggregated by codes into eight industrial sector classifications corresponding to National Occupational Research Agenda (NORA) sectors [Soderholm 2006]. Of note, these industrial groupings are heterogeneous in that each group may include workers engaged in both blue- and white-collar occupational activities. Sector definitions follow the North American Industry Classification System (NAICS), which has replaced the U.S. Standard Industrial Classification (SIC) system. More information about NAICS can be found on the U.S. Census Bureau [http://www.census.gov/eos/www/naics/]. NAICS provides definitions for 20 sectors which NIOSH aggregated into eight sector groups (see Background and introduction).

For survey years NHIS 1997–2004, the industry codes do not translate directly into the NORA sectors. A conversion process was developed to translate the codes, the details of which are provided in Appendices 2 and 3.

Statistical Methods

Because of the multi-stage sampling design, all analyses were performed with adjustment for sample weights and design effects using the SUDAAN and SAS statistical packages [Research Triangle Institute 2004]. These analyses also took into account relatively minor sample design modifications implemented in 2006 due to smaller sample size recruitment targets [NCHS 2008]. The sample weights used were those required for the analysis of data from combined survey years and were calculated as originally specified by Botman and currently recommended by the NCHS [Botman and Jack 1995; NCHS 2008]. Sample weights are also used to estimate the number of workers in the U.S. with various health conditions. In some cases these values will be underestimates due to either (1) the presence missing data for the condition of interest (e.g., respondent did not respond to a chronic disease question), or (2) in the case of stratified analyses, there are missing values for the stratification variable (e.g., educational attainment).

Estimates are presented in a table format for All U.S. workers and all workers employed in the Agriculture, Forsetry, and Fishing sector (and are available for each of the remaining seven NORA sectors). Within each table, estimates are presented for all workers identified with the NORA sector subpopulation, and then by subgroups of age, gender, race, ethnicity, health insurance status, and education. Each table provides the NHIS sample size and the estimated employed U.S. worker population by each of these subgroups. Estimated standard errors (SEs) are included in these tables, which can be used to compute confidence intervals.

Limitations

The NHIS data are collected cross-sectionally every year, thus causal inference is difficult. Nevertheless, the fact that the NHIS collects data from a representative sample of the U.S. civilian population annually makes it a powerful surveillance tool to look at pooled data for a range of factors in all U.S. civilian workers.

The data from the NHIS are entirely self-reported which can lead to biases of both under- and over-reporting. For example, weight and height were collected in a self-reported or proxy fashion, which could have led to less precision in the calculation of the BMI. Previous research has suggested that people tend to under-report their weight and over-report their height, leading to the underestimation of BMI; additionally, the degree of under- and over-reporting varies as a function of age, gender, race, ethnicity, and social class [Caban et al. 2005; Engstrom et al. 2003; Kuczmarski et al. 2001; Spencer et al. 2002].

Some of the NORA sectors, particularly Mining and to a lesser extent Agriculture, Forestry and Fishing, have relatively few workers. Consequently, small sample sizes may limit one's ability to produce estimates for less prevalent chronic conditions (e.g., cancer, psychological distress) or impairments, as well as inferences and conclusions users derive from these estimates. This is most apparent where one stratifies by the different demographic subgroups (e.g., race, ethnicity, or age group).

The figures display and reflect the tabulated prevalence (percentage) values for these population samples. For a small number of figures, the response values displayed may include symbols indicating (1) no data available, which occurs where the population subgroup sample is zero (symbol (---)); (2) the computed quantity or value is greater than 0.0 but less than 0.05% (symbol (0.0)); and (3) there were no cases in that particular cell, and thus no response value estimated (symbol (–)) is zero quantity.

The NHIS does not consistently collect data on occupational exposure or direct occupational health effects with the exception of work loss days. Of note, NCHS has collaborated and conducted occupational supplements in the past [NCHS 1990,1993b]. NIOSH sponsored an Occupational Health Supplement to the 2010 NHIS. An advanced statistical report of these data is expected in the 3rd quarter of 2011.

Summary of Estimates for the Workers in the Agriculture, Forestry, and Fishing sector

Population and demographic Overview for 1997–2007

All U.S. Workers

From 1997–2007, 196,924 U.S. workers age 18 years and older (representing an estimated 126,898,030 U.S. workers annually) participated in a probability sampling of the entire non-institutionalized U.S. population (see Table 1, page 41). Of the U.S. workers, there were approximately equal percentages of men (54.0%) and women (46.0%) during this time period. The majority of the U.S. workers self-identified as White (83.0%) with 11.1% Black and 5.9% "Other" race, while 11.8% were Hispanic and 88.2% Non-Hispanic. The majority (83.5%) of U.S. workers were in the 25–64 year old age group with 13.4% in the 18–24 year old age group and 3.1% in the 65 years and older group. The majority (59.4%) of U.S. workers had more than a high school education, with 11.7% having less than a high school education and 28.4% having completed high school. Although 83.8% of U.S. workers reported having health insurance, 16.0% did not have health insurance.

Agriculture, Forestry, and Fishing

From 1997–2007, an estimated 2,694,267 U.S. workers age 18 years and older worked annually in the Agriculture, Forestry and Fishing sector (see Table 1, page 41). Of the total U.S. workforce, approximately 2.1% work in the Agriculture, Forestry and Fishing sector. Within Agriculture, Forestry and Fishing sector the majority of workers were men (77.5%) with only 22.5% women. The majority of the workers self-identified as White (91.4%) with 3.5% Black and 5.1% "Other" race, while 25.2% were Hispanic and 74.8% Non-Hispanic. The majority (78.7%) of workers were in the 25–64 year old age group with 14.5% in the 18–24 year old age group and 6.8% in the 65 years and older group. In this sector, 35.7% of workers had more than a high school education, with 32.1% having less than a high school education and 31.3% having completed high school. Although 66.3% of workers in this sector reported having health insurance, 33.2% did not have health insurance.

The following summary statements on population, disability, and morbidity measures are based on data found in Table 1 (page 41) and Table 2 (page 42–43)

Health Status

An estimated 4.4% or about 118,000 NORA Agriculture, Forestry, and Fishing sector workers reported their health status was worse when compared with 12 months prior.

An estimated 6.2% or about 167,000 NORA Agriculture, Forestry, and Fishing sector workers reported their self-rated health status in general was fair to poor.

NORA Agriculture, Forestry, and Fishing sector workers reported an estimated mean of 1.4 bed disability days during the past 12 months; 18.1% or about 487,000 workers reported 2 or more bed disability days.

NORA Agriculture, Forestry, and Fishing sector workers reported an estimated mean of 3.6 work loss days during the past 12 months; 8.8% or about 237,000 workers reported 6 or more work loss days.

Physical Activity Limitations

An estimated 1.2% or about 32,000 NORA Agriculture, Forestry, and Fishing sector workers reported having a health problem that required the use of special equipment.

An estimated 20.3% or about 547,000 NORA Agriculture, Forestry, and Fishing sector workers reported experiencing any functional limitations in any of 12 activities.

An estimated 16.4% or about 442,000 NORA Agriculture, Forestry, and Fishing sector workers reported some degree of hearing impairment.

An estimated 5.7% or about 154,000 NORA Agriculture, Forestry, and Fishing sector workers reported some degree of visual impairment.

Health and Chronic Conditions

An estimated 3.9% or about 105,000 NORA Agriculture, Forestry, and Fishing sector workers reported ever being told by a doctor or other health professional that they had cancer or a malignancy of any kind.

An estimated 16.5% or about 445,000 NORA Agriculture, Forestry, and Fishing sector workers reported ever being told by a doctor or other health professional that they had hypertension.

An estimated 5.9% or about 159,000 NORA Agriculture, Forestry, and Fishing sector workers reported ever being told by a doctor or other health professional that they had heart disease (including Coronary heart disease, Angina, Heart attack, or any kind of heart condition or heart disease).

An estimated 6.5% or about 175,000 NORA Agriculture, Forestry, and Fishing sector workers reported ever being told by a doctor or other health professional that they had asthma.

An estimated 3.4% or about 92,000 NORA Agriculture, Forestry, and Fishing sector workers reported ever being told by a doctor or other health professional that they had diabetes (or sugar diabetes).

An estimated 0.5% or about 13,000 NORA Agriculture, Forestry, and Fishing sector workers reported experiencing symptoms of severe psychological distress in the previous 30 days.

Health Care Utilization

An estimated 46.1% or about 1.2 million NORA Agriculture, Forestry, and Fishing sector workers reported not having seen a primary health care provider during the past 12 months.

An estimated 50.3% or about 1.4 million NORA Agriculture, Forestry, and Fishing sector workers reported not having seen or talked to a dentist during the past year.

An estimated 8.4% or about 226,000 NORA Agriculture, Forestry, and Fishing sector workers reported having surgery or other surgical procedures as an inpatient or outpatient during the past 12 months.

An estimated 14.6% or about 393,000 NORA Agriculture, Forestry, and Fishing sector workers reported having made one or more hospital emergency room visits during the past 12 months.

Health Risk Factors or Behaviors

An estimated 23.1% or about 622,000 NORA Agriculture, Forestry, and Fishing sector workers reported being current smokers.

An estimated 65.8% or about 1.8 million NORA Agriculture, Forestry, and Fishing sector workers reported being current alcohol drinkers.

An estimated 21.5% or about 579,000 NORA Agriculture, Forestry, and Fishing sector workers reported a combination of height and weight consistent with obesity.

An estimated 73.5% or about 2.0 million NORA Agriculture, Forestry, and Fishing sector workers reportedly did not achieve CDC recommended leisure time levels of physical activity.

An estimated 24.7% or about 665,000 NORA Agriculture, Forestry, and Fishing sector workers reported ever being tested for HIV.

An estimated 85.8% or about 2.3 million NORA Agriculture, Forestry, and Fishing sector workers reported not receiving an influenza vaccination during the past 12 months.

An estimated 69.2% or 216,000 NORA Agriculture, Forestry, and Fishing sector workers 60 years and older reported never receiving a pneumococcal vaccination.

Figures

Prevalence of a reported decline in health when compared to health status 12 months prior estimated for workers 18 years and older

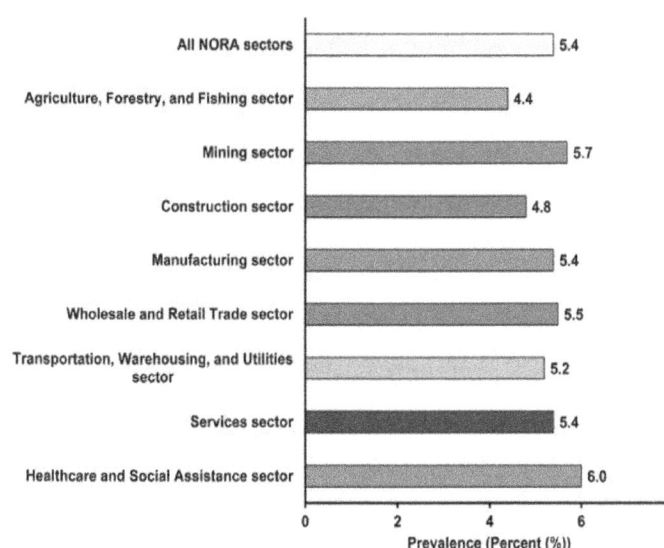

Figure 1a. Workers 18 years and older by NORA sectors, National Health Interview Survey, 1997–2007.
An estimated 5.4% of all employed U.S. workers reported their current health was worse when compared to their health status 12 months prior (see Table 2, page 42, and Tables 3 and 4, pages 44–45). Among the NORA sectors, Healthcare and Social Assistance sector workers reported the highest decline in health status compared 12 months prior (6.0%), while Agriculture, Forestry, and Fishing sector workers reported the lowest (4.4%).

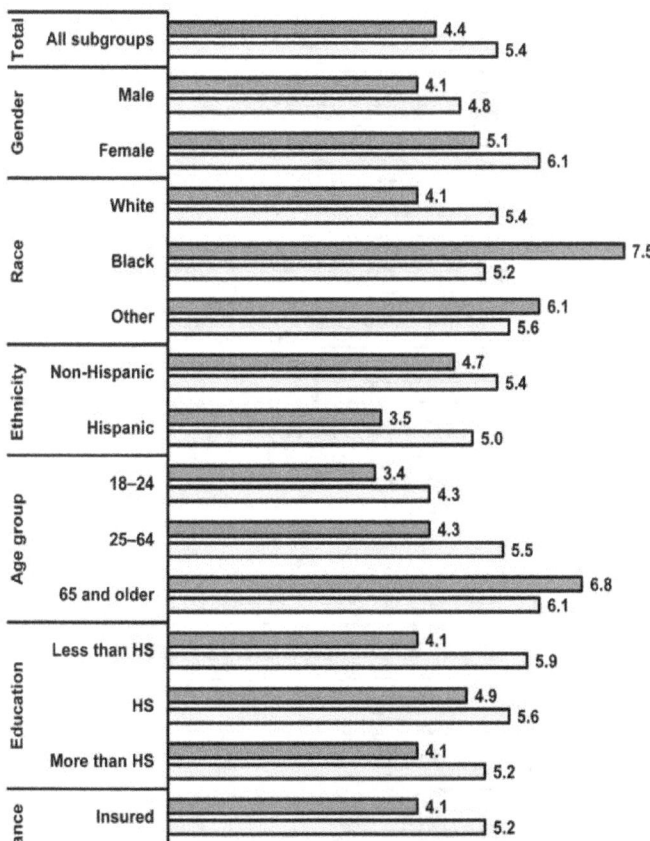

Figure 1b. Workers 18 years and older, Agriculture, Forestry, and Fishing sector and All NORA sectors, National Health Interview Survey, 1997–2007.
An estimated 4.4% of workers employed in the Agriculture, Forestry, and Fishing sector reported their current health was worse when compared to their health status 12 months prior. Among the subgroups, Black workers reported the highest prevalence of a decline in health status compared 12 months prior (7.5%), while workers 18–24 years of age reported the lowest (3.4%) (see Table 4, page 45). Among all U.S. workers, uninsured workers reported the highest prevalence of a decline in health status compared 12 months prior (6.6%), while workers 18–24 years of age reported the lowest (4.3%) (see Table 3, page 44).

Prevalence of fair or poor self-rated health status estimated for workers 18 years and older

Figure 2a. Workers 18 years and older by NORA sectors, National Health Interview Survey, 1997–2007. An estimated 5.3% of all employed U.S. workers reported their self-rated health status was fair or poor (see Table 2, page 42, and Tables 5 and 6, pages 46–47). Among the NORA sectors, Mining sector workers reported the highest prevalence of fair or poor self-rated health status (6.5%), while Services sector workers reported the lowest (4.9%).

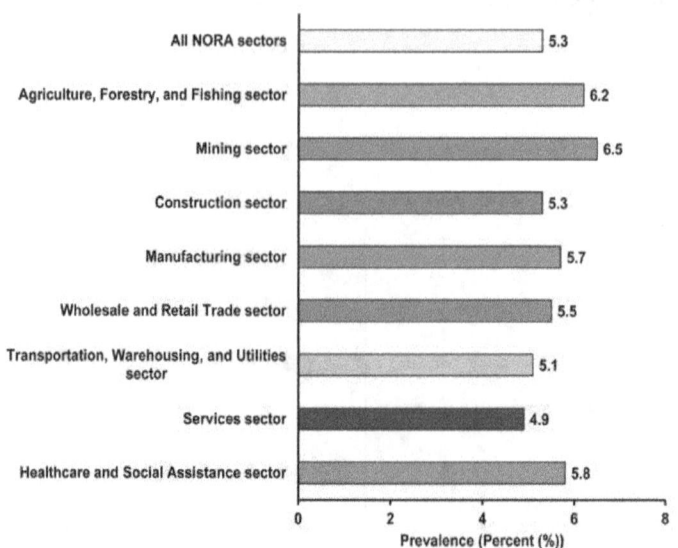

Figure 2b. Workers 18 years and older, Agriculture, Forestry, and Fishing sector and All NORA sectors, National Health Interview Survey, 1997–2007. An estimated 6.2% of workers employed in the Agriculture, Forestry, and Fishing sector reported their self-rated health status was fair or poor. Among the subgroups, Black workers reported the highest prevalence of fair or poor self-rated health status (13.7%), while workers 18–24 years of age reported the lowest (3.0%) (see Table 6, page 47). Among all U.S. workers, those with less than a high school education reported the highest prevalence of fair or poor self-rated health status (11.2%), while workers 18–24 years of age reported the lowest (2.7%). Uninsured workers reported nearly twice the rate of fair or poor self-rated health status relative to insured workers (8.1% vs. 4.8%) (see Table 5, page 46).

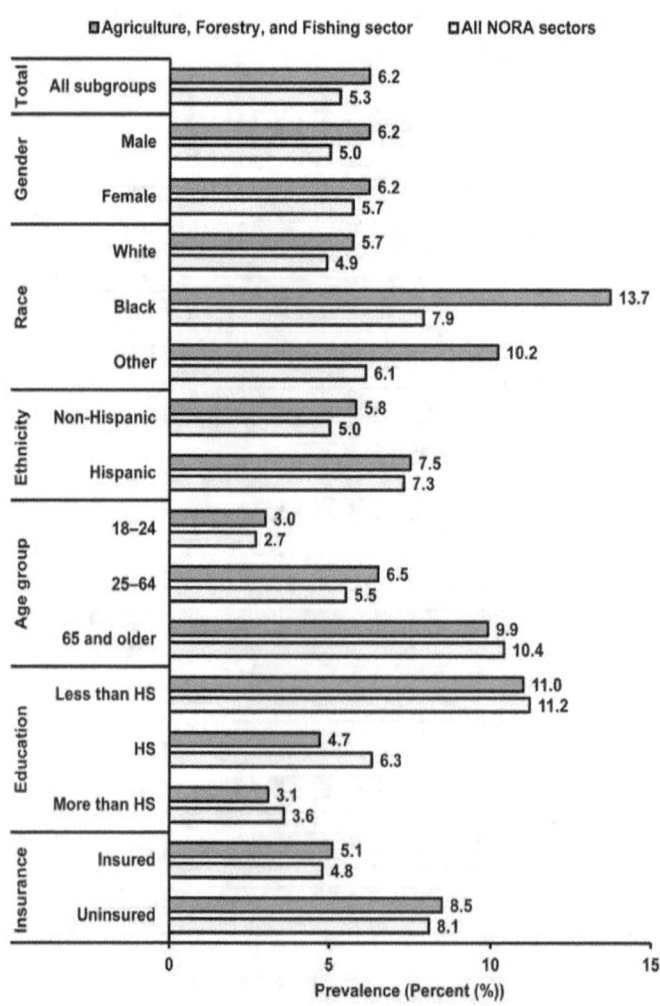

Mean number of bed disability days during the past 12 months estimated for workers 18 years and older

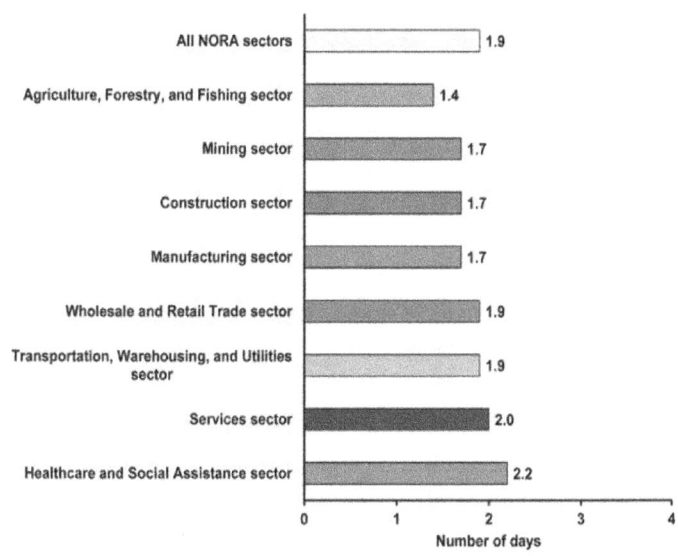

Figure 3a. Workers 18 years and older by NORA sectors, National Health Interview Survey, 1997–2007. Employed U.S. workers reported an estimated mean of 1.9 bed disability days during the past 12 months (see Table 2, page 42, and Tables 7 and 8, pages 48–49). Among the NORA sectors, Healthcare and Social Assistance sector workers reported the highest mean number of bed disability days during the past 12 months (2.2 bed disability days), that is days in bed for half a day or longer because of illness or injury, while Agriculture, Forestry, and Fishing sector workers reported the lowest (1.4 bed disability days).

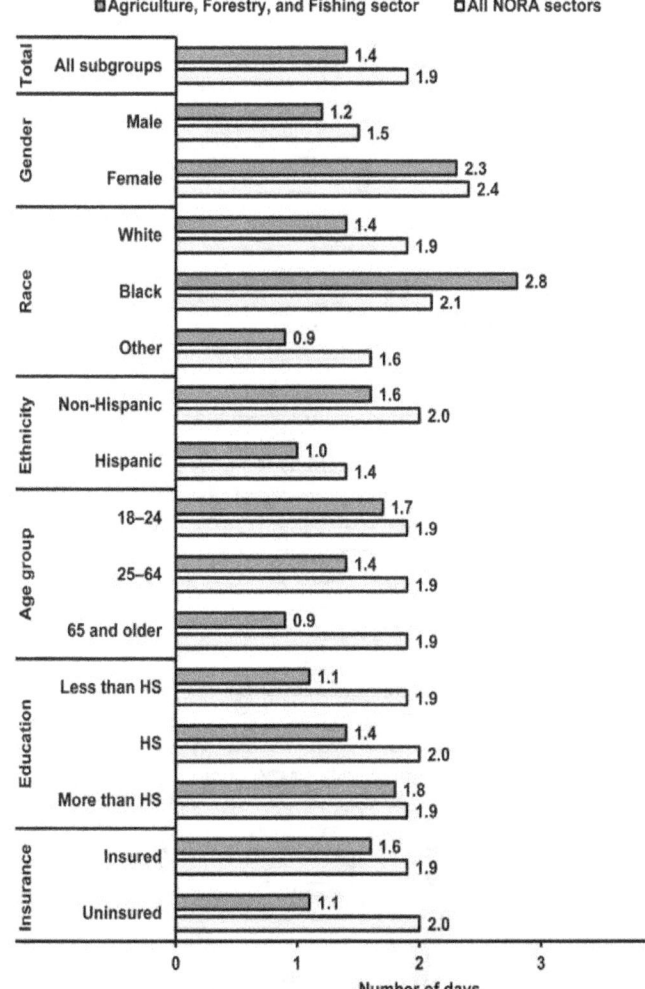

Figure 3b. Workers 18 years and older, Agriculture, Forestry, and Fishing sector and All NORA sectors, National Health Interview Survey, 1997–2007. Workers employed in the Agriculture, Forestry, and Fishing sector reported an estimated mean of 1.4 bed disability days during the past 12 months. Among the subgroups, Black workers reported the highest mean number of bed disability days during the past 12 months (2.8 bed disability days), while workers 65 years of age or older and workers of "Other" race reported the lowest (0.9 bed disability days) (see Table 8, page 49). Among all U.S. workers, female workers reported the highest mean number of bed disability days during the past 12 months (2.4 bed disability days), while Hispanic workers reported the lowest (1.4 bed disability days) (see Table 7, page 48).

Prevalence of having 2 or more bed disability days during the past 12 months estimated for workers 18 years and older

Figure 4a. Workers 18 years and older by NORA sectors, National Health Interview Survey, 1997–2007.
An estimated 25.3% of employed U.S. workers reported having had at least 2 or more bed disability days during the past 12 months (see Table 2, page 42, and Tables 9 and 10, pages 50–51). Among the NORA sectors, Healthcare and Social Assistance sector workers reported the highest prevalence of two or more bed disability days during the past 12 months (28.5%), while Agriculture, Forestry, and Fishing sector workers reported the lowest (18.1%).

Figure 4b. Workers 18 years and older, Agriculture, Forestry, and Fishing sector and All NORA sectors, National Health Interview Survey, 1997–2007.
An estimated 18.1% of workers employed in the Agriculture, Forestry, and Fishing sector reported having had at least 2 or more bed disability days during the past 12 months. Among the subgroups, female workers reported the highest prevalence of 2 or more bed disability days during the past 12 months (25.1%), while Hispanic workers reported the lowest (12.0%) (see Table 10, page 51). Among all U.S. workers, female workers reported the highest prevalence of 2 or more bed disability days during the past 12 months (30.5%), while workers 65 years of age and older reported the lowest (17.5%). Rates for these older workers 65 years and older were lower than the rates for younger workers, 18–24 years [27.2%] and 25–64 years [25.2%], respectively (see Table 9, page 50).

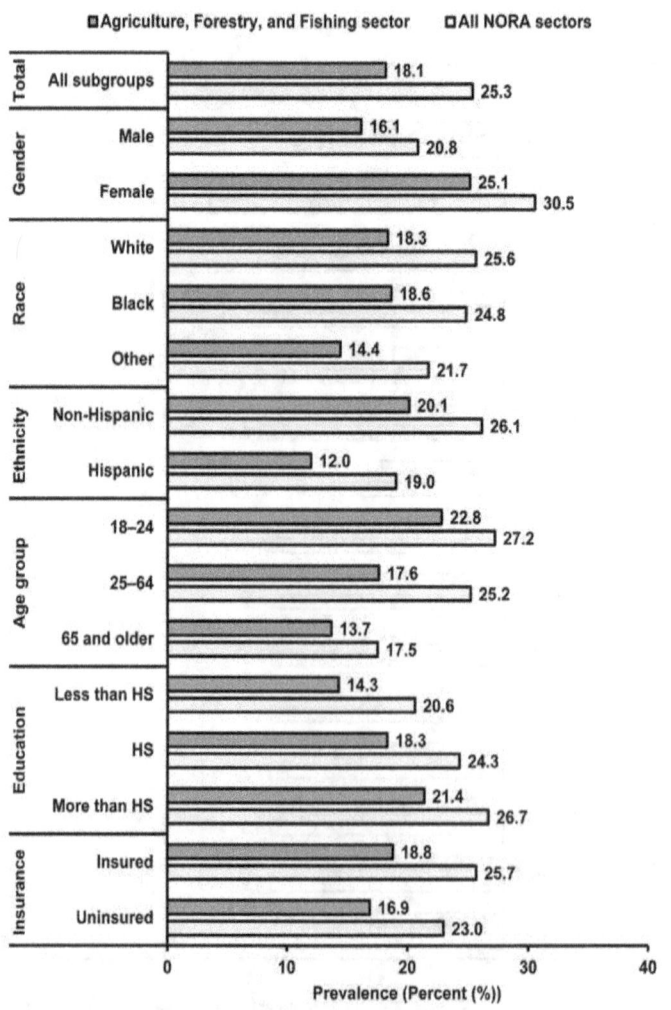

Mean number of work loss days during the past 12 months estimated for workers 18 years and older

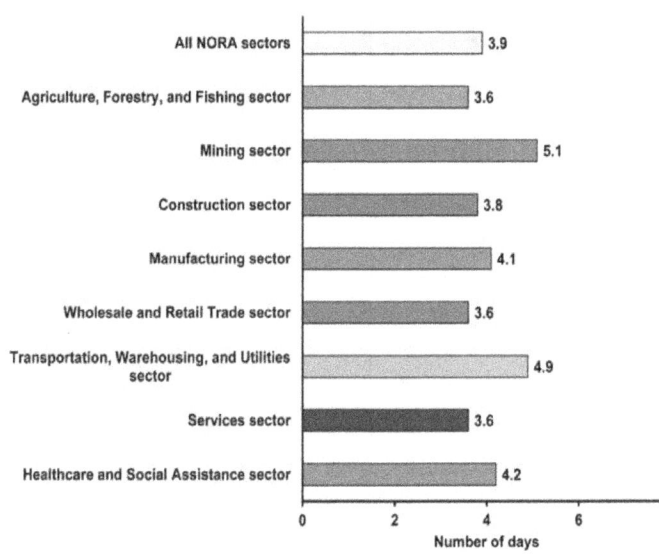

Figure 5a. Workers 18 years and older by NORA sectors, National Health Interview Survey, 1997–2007. Employed U.S. workers reported an estimated mean of 3.9 work loss days during the past 12 months (see Table 2, page 42, and Tables 11 and 12, pages 52–53). Among the NORA sectors, Mining sector workers reported the highest mean number of work loss days during the past 12 months (5.1 work loss days), while Agriculture, Forestry, and Fishing sector workers, Services sector workers, and Wholesale and Retail Trade sector workers reported the lowest (3.6 work loss days).

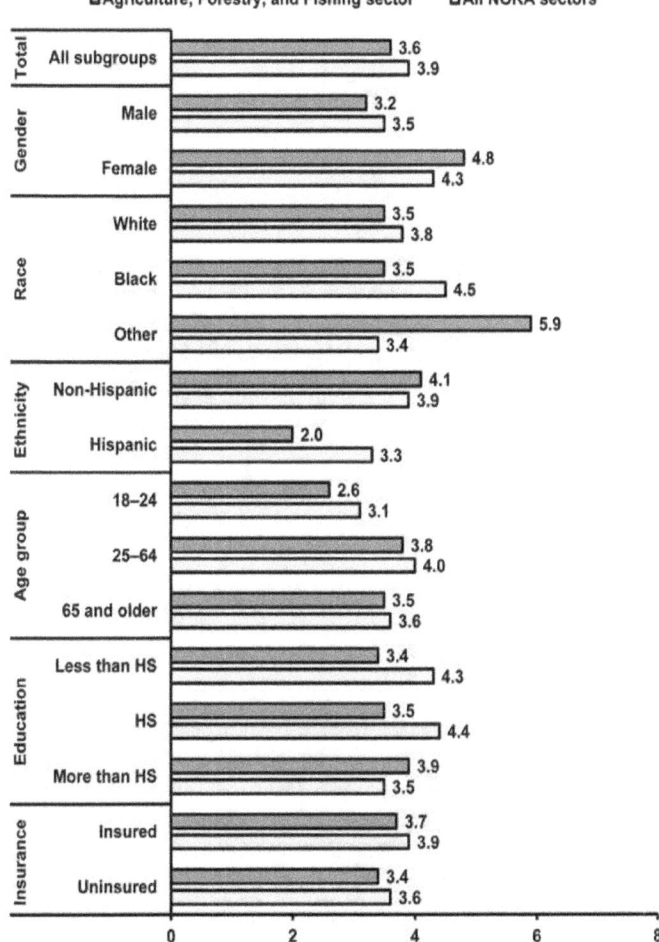

Figure 5b. Workers 18 years and older, Agriculture, Forestry, and Fishing sector and All NORA sectors, National Health Interview Survey, 1997–2007. Workers employed in the Agriculture, Forestry, and Fishing sector reported an estimated mean of 3.6 work loss days during the past 12 months. Among the subgroups, workers of "Other" race reported the highest mean number of work loss days during the past 12 months (5.9 work loss days), while Hispanic workers reported the lowest (2.0 work loss days) (see Table 12, page 53). Among all U.S. workers, Black workers reported the highest mean number of work loss days during the past 12 months (4.5 work loss days), while workers 18–24 years of age reported the lowest (3.1 work loss days) (see Table 11, page 52).

Prevalence of 6 or more work loss days during the past 12 months estimated for workers 18 years and older

Figure 6a. Workers 18 years and older by NORA sectors, National Health Interview Survey, 1997–2007.

An estimated 11.1% of employed U.S. workers reported having had > 6 work loss days during the past 12 months (see Table 2, page 42, and Tables 13 and 14, pages 54–55). Among the NORA sectors, Transportation, Warehousing, and Utilities sector workers reported the highest prevalence of > 6 work loss days during the past 12 months (13.1%), while Agriculture, Forestry, and Fishing sector workers reported the lowest (8.8%).

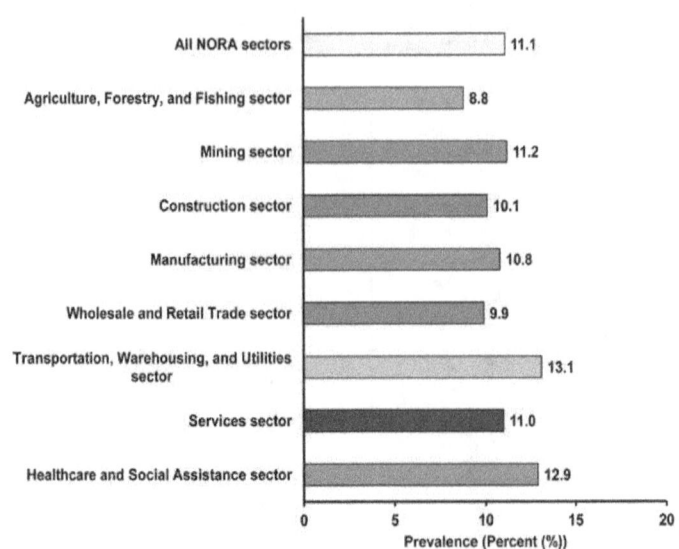

Figure 6b. Workers 18 years and older, Agriculture, Forestry, and Fishing sector and All NORA sectors, National Health Interview Survey, 1997–2007.

An estimated 8.8% of workers employed in the Agriculture, Forestry, and Fishing sector reported having had > 6 work loss days during the past 12 months. Among the subgroups, Black workers reported the highest prevalence > 6 work loss days during the past 12 months (11.0%), while Hispanic workers reported the lowest (5.5%) (see Table 14, page 55). Among all U.S. workers, female workers reported the highest prevalence of > 6 work loss days during the past 12 months (13.0%), while Hispanic workers reported the lowest (9.2%) (see Table 13, page 54).

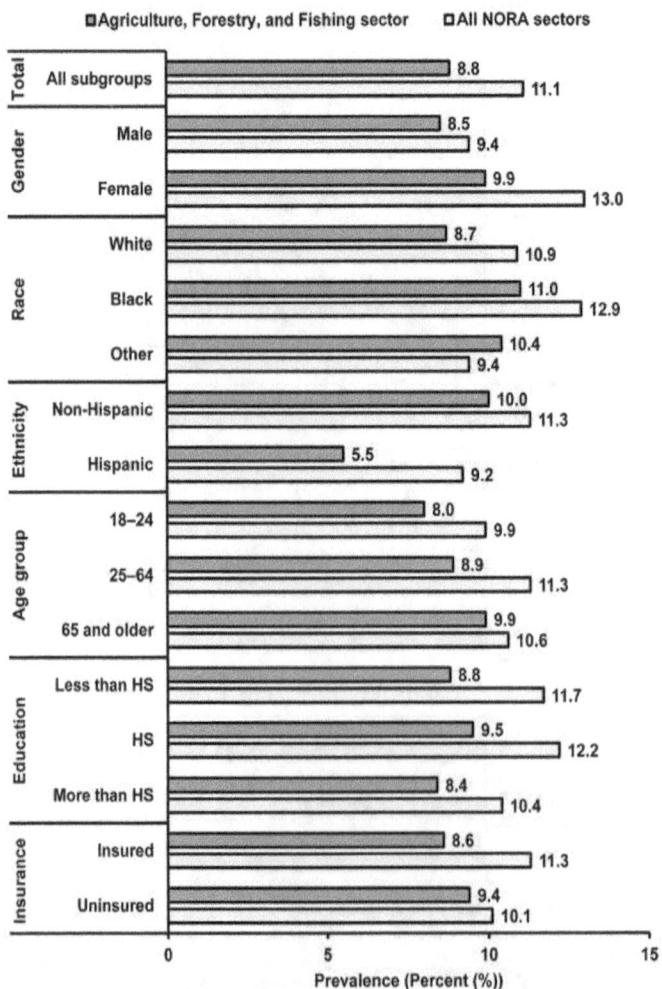

Prevalence of health problems requiring the use of special equipment estimated for workers 18 years and older

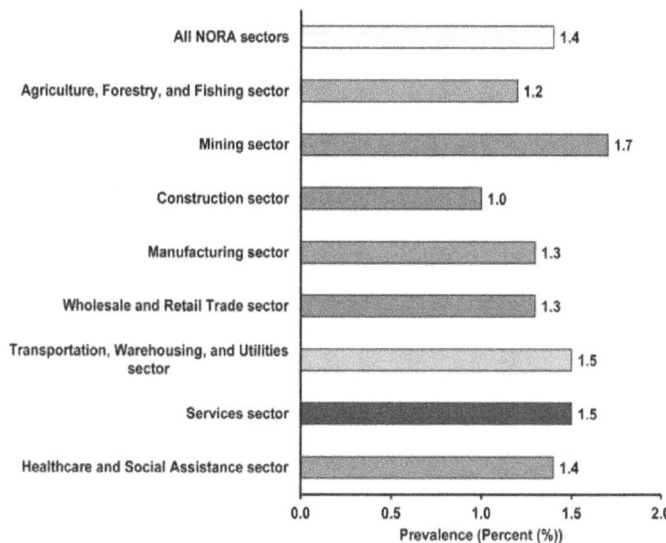

Figure 7a. Workers 18 years and older by NORA sectors, National Health Interview Survey, 1997–2007.

Health problems that require the use of special equipment (such as a cane, a wheelchair, or a special telephone) are uncommon in the U.S. workforce as a whole, with a prevalence of 1.4% among all employed workers (see Table 2, page 42, and Tables 15 and 16, pages 56–57)). Among the NORA sectors, Mining sector workers reported the highest prevalence of health problems requiring the use of special equipment (1.7%), while Construction sector workers reported the lowest (1.0%).

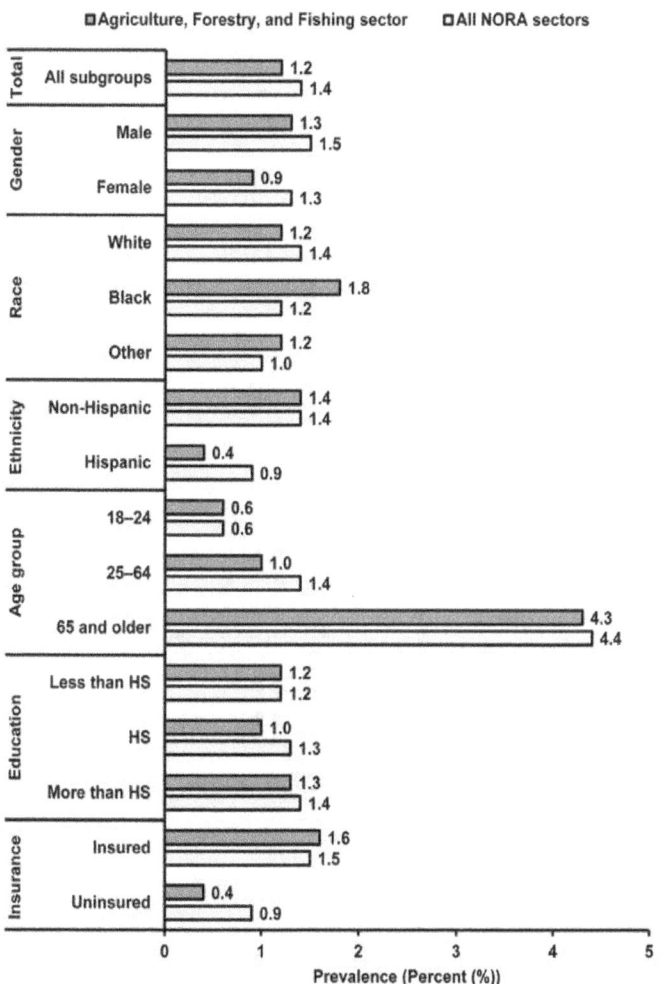

Figure 7b. Workers 18 years and older, Agriculture, Forestry, and Fishing sector and All NORA sectors, National Health Interview Survey, 1997–2007.

An estimated 1.2% of workers employed in the Agriculture, Forestry, and Fishing sector reported having a health problem that required the use of special equipment. Among the subgroups, workers 65 years of age or older reported the highest prevalence of health problems requiring the use of special equipment (4.3%), while Hispanic and uninsured workers reported the lowest (0.4%) (see Table 16, page 57). Among all U.S. workers, workers 65 years of age or older reported the highest prevalence of health problems requiring the use of special equipment (4.4%), while workers 18–24 years of age reported the lowest (0.6%) (see Table 15, page 56).

Prevalence of any functional limitations estimated for workers 18 years and older

Figure 8a. Workers 18 years and older by NORA sectors, National Health Interview Survey, 1997–2007. An estimated 21.6% of all employed U.S. workers reported experiencing any functional limitations (see Table 2, page 42, and Tables 17 and 18, pages 58–59). Among the NORA sectors, Healthcare and Social Assistance sector workers reported the highest prevalence of experiencing any functional limitations (25.1%), while Construction sector workers reported the lowest (17.8%). These functional limitations include: having difficulty walking ¼ mile without special equipment, reaching over without special equipment, attending events without special equipment, etc.

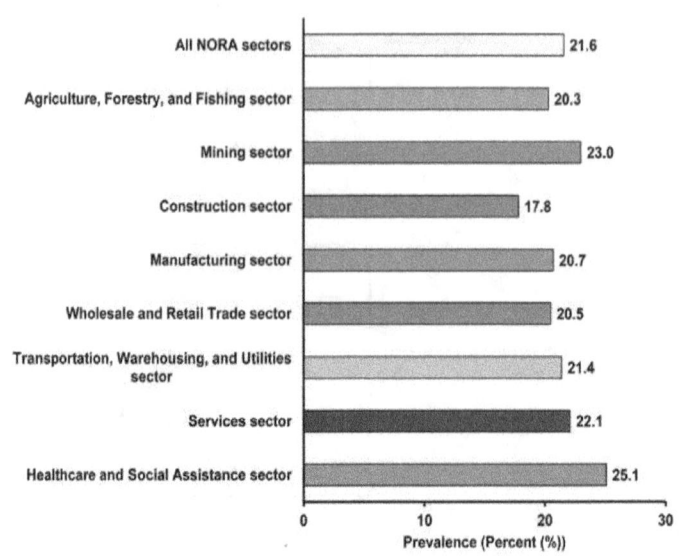

Figure 8b. Workers 18 years and older, Agriculture, Forestry, and Fishing sector and All NORA sectors, National Health Interview Survey, 1997–2007. An estimated 20.3% of workers employed in the Agriculture, Forestry, and Fishing sector reported experiencing any functional limitations. Among the subgroups, workers 65 years of age reported the highest prevalence of experiencing any functional limitations (42.8%), while Hispanic workers reported the lowest (8.4%) (see Table 18, page 59). Among all U.S. workers, those 65 years of age or older reported the highest prevalence of experiencing any functional limitations (43.7%), while workers 18–24 years of age reported the lowest (11.9%) (see Table 17, page 58).

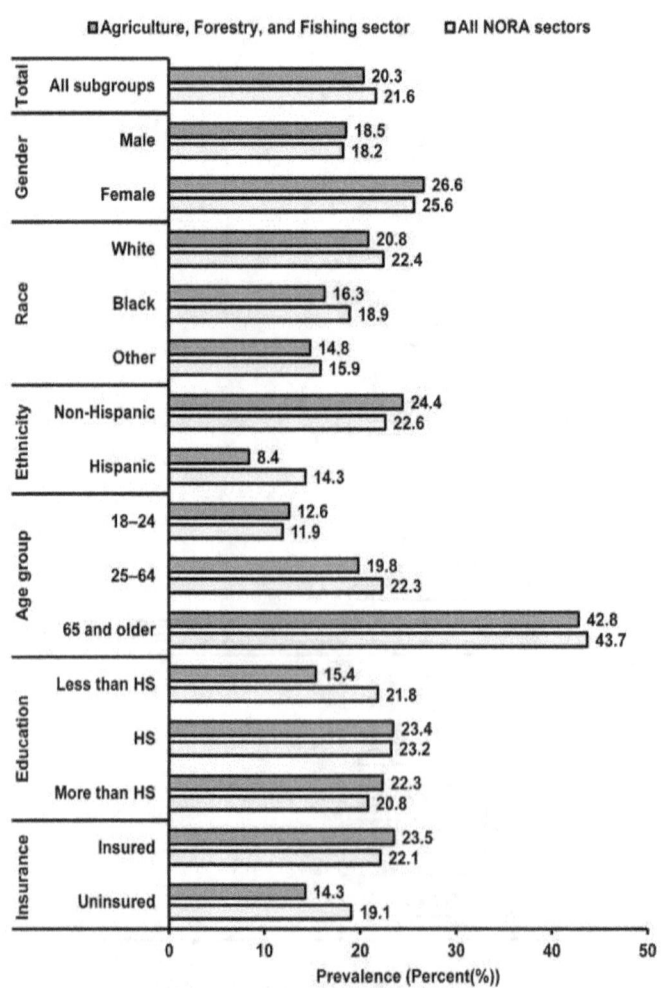

Prevalence of hearing difficulty estimated for workers 18 years and older

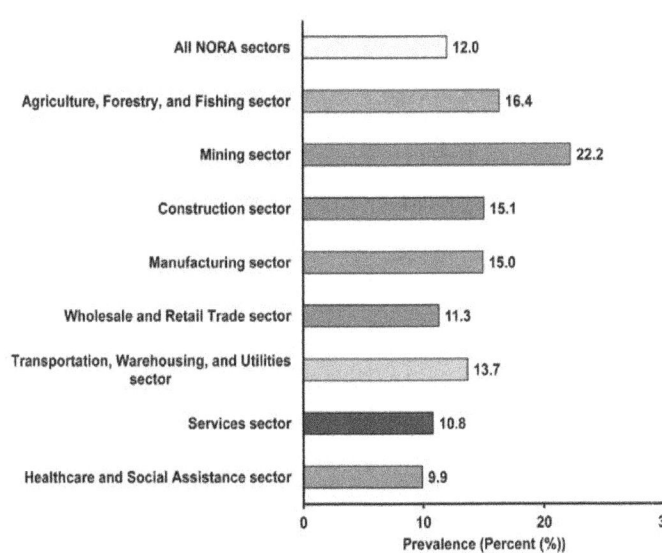

Figure 9a. Workers 18 years and older by NORA sectors, National Health Interview Survey, 1997–2007.
An estimated 12.0% of all employed U.S. workers reported any hearing difficulty (see Table 2, page 42, and Tables 19 and 20, pages 60–61). There was more than a two-fold difference in prevalence of any reported hearing difficulty (defined as a little trouble, a lot of trouble, or deaf) across the NORA sectors. Mining sector workers reported markedly higher prevalence of hearing difficulty (22.2%) relative to all other groups, while Healthcare and Social Assistance sector workers reported the lowest rate of hearing difficulty (9.9%).

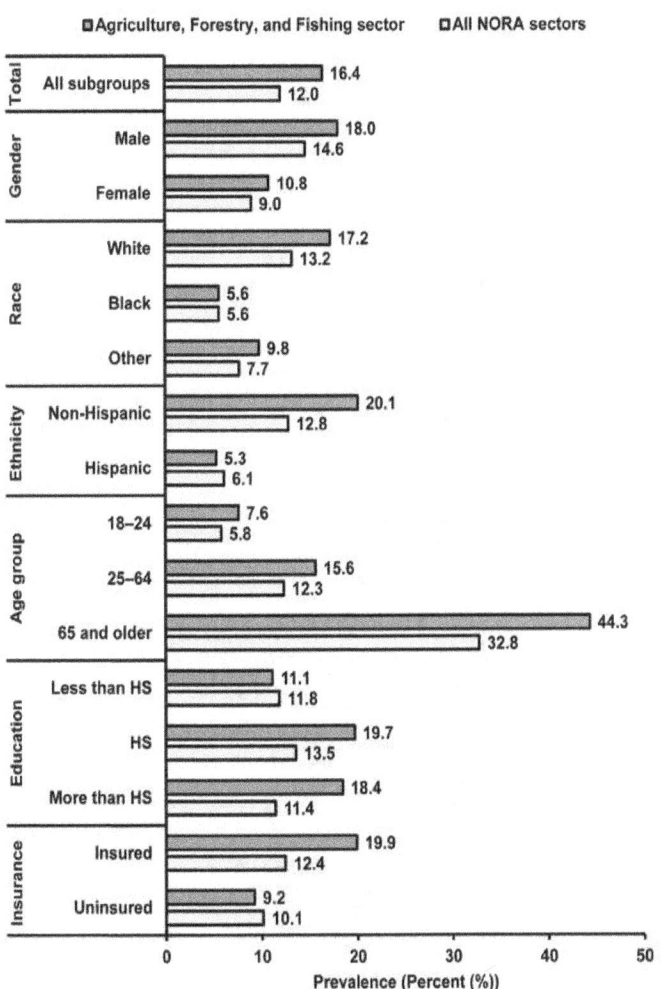

Figure 9b. Workers 18 years and older, Agriculture, Forestry, and Fishing sector and All NORA sectors, National Health Interview Survey, 1997–2007.
An estimated 16.4% of workers employed in the Agriculture, Forestry, and Fishing sector reported any hearing difficulty. Among the subgroups, workers 65 years of age or older reported the highest prevalence of any hearing difficulty (44.3%), while Hispanic workers reported the lowest (5.3%) (see Table 20, page 61). Among all U.S. workers, those 65 years of age or older reported the highest prevalence of any hearing difficulty (32.8%), while Black workers reported the lowest (5.6%) (see Table 19, page 60).

Prevalence of visual impairment estimated for workers 18 years and older

Figure 10a. Workers 18 years and older by NORA sectors, National Health Interview Survey, 1997–2007.
An estimated 6.7% of all employed U.S. workers reported current visual impairment (see Table 2, page 42, and Tables 21 and 22, pages 62–63). Among the NORA sectors, Healthcare and Social Assistance sector workers reported the highest prevalence of current visual impairment (7.7%), while Mining sector workers reported the lowest (4.7%).

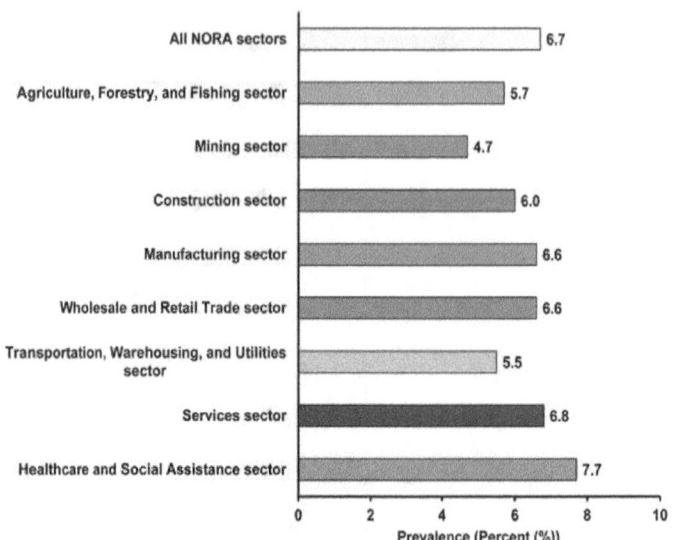

Figure 10b. Workers 18 years and older, Agriculture, Forestry, and Fishing sector and All NORA sectors, National Health Interview Survey, 1997–2007.
An estimated 5.7% of workers employed in the Agriculture, Forestry, and Fishing sector reported current visual impairment. Among the subgroups, workers 65 years of age or older reported the highest prevalence of current visual impairment (13.1%), while workers 18–24 years of age reported the lowest (3.5%) (see Table 22, page 63). Among all U.S. workers, those 65 years of age or older reported the highest prevalence of current visual impairment (10.0%), while workers 18–24 years of age reported the lowest (5.0%). Female workers also reported higher rates of current visual impairment relative to men (8.0% vs. 5.5%) (see Table 21, page 62).

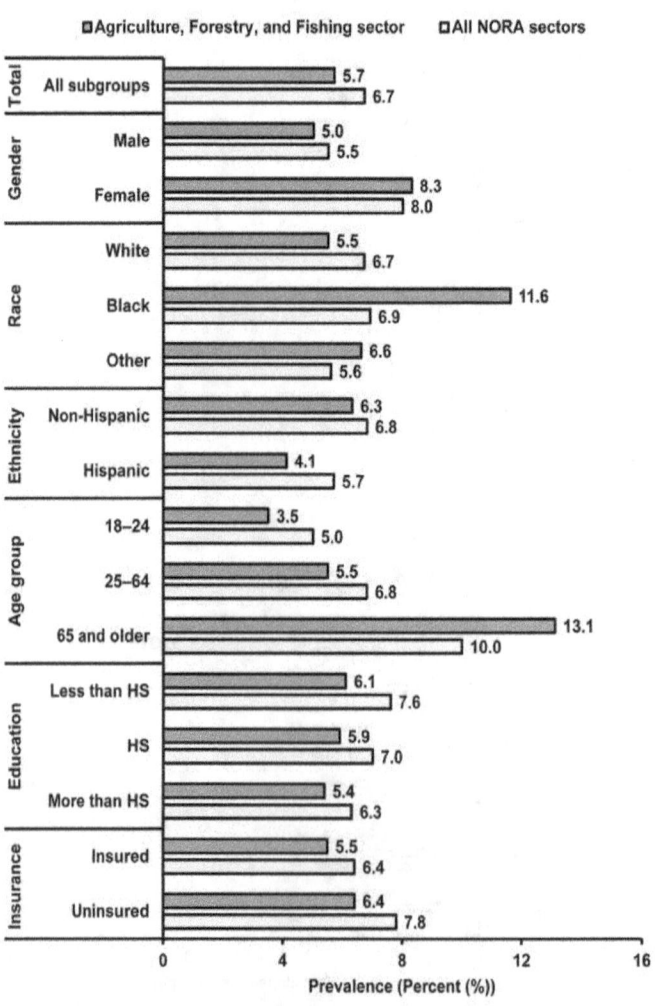

Prevalence of cancer estimated for workers 18 years and older

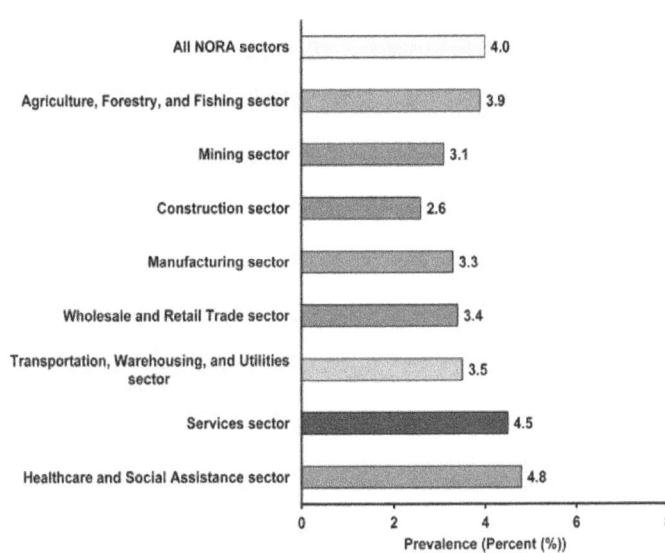

Figure 11a. Workers 18 years and older by NORA sectors, National Health Interview Survey, 1997–2007. An estimated 4.0% of all employed U.S. workers reported ever having a diagnosis of cancer (see Table 2, page 42, and Tables 23 and 24, pages 64–65). Among the NORA sectors, Healthcare and Social Assistance sector workers reported the highest prevalence of ever having a diagnosis of cancer (4.8%), while Construction sector workers reported the lowest (2.6%).

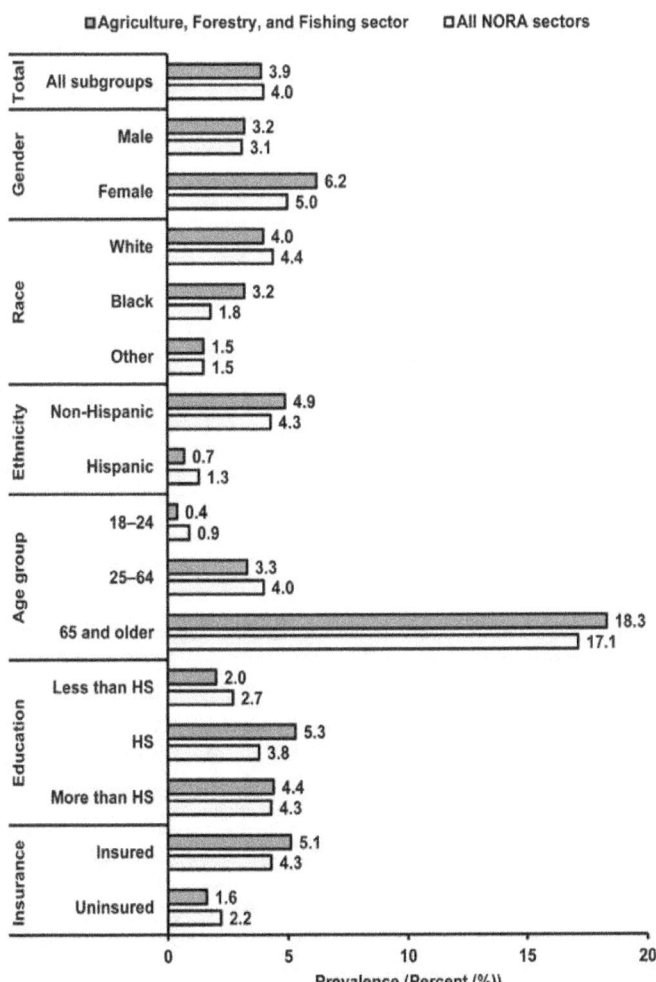

Figure 11b. Workers 18 years and older, Agriculture, Forestry, and Fishing sector and All NORA sectors, National Health Interview Survey, 1997–2007. An estimated 3.9% of workers employed in the Agriculture, Forestry, and Fishing sector reported ever having a diagnosis of cancer. Among the subgroups, workers 65 years of age or older reported the highest prevalence of ever having a diagnosis of cancer (18.3%), while workers 18–24 years of age reported the lowest (0.4%) (see Table 24, page 65). Among all U.S. workers, those 65 years of age or older reported the highest prevalence of ever having a diagnosis of cancer (17.1%), while workers 18–24 years of age reported the lowest (0.9%). Hispanics reported much lower cancer rates relative to Non-Hispanics (1.3% vs. 4.3%), while Whites reported higher rates relative to Blacks (4.4% vs. 1.8%) (see Table 23, page 64).

Prevalence of hypertension estimated for workers 18 years and older

Figure 12a. Workers 18 years and older by NORA sectors, National Health Interview Survey, 1997–2007. An estimated 17.7% of all employed U.S. workers reported ever having a diagnosis of hypertension (see Table 2, page 42, and Tables 25 and 26, pages 66–67). Among the NORA sectors, Mining sector workers reported the highest prevalence of ever having a diagnosis of hypertension (23.2%), while Construction sector workers reported the lowest (15.1%).

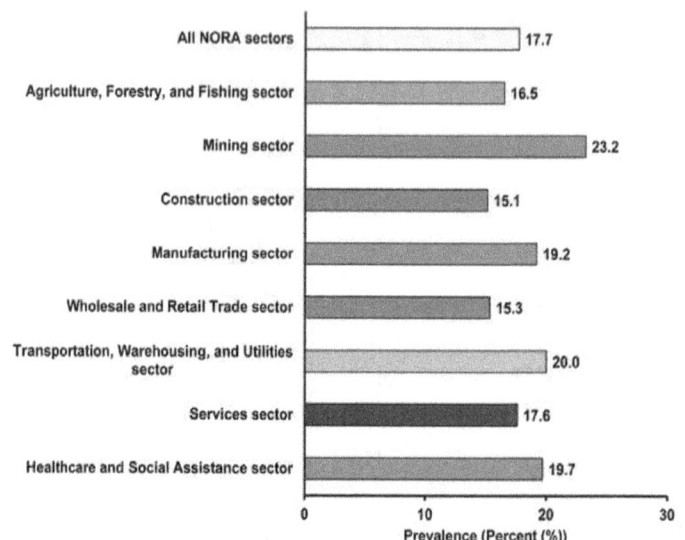

Figure 12b. Workers 18 years and older, Agriculture, Forestry, and Fishing sector and All NORA sectors, National Health Interview Survey, 1997–2007. An estimated 16.5% of workers employed in the Agriculture, Forestry, and Fishing sector reported ever having a diagnosis of hypertension. Among the subgroups, workers 65 years of age or older reported the highest prevalence of ever having a diagnosis of hypertension (45.2%), while workers 18–24 years of age reported the lowest (3.4%) (see Table 26, page 67). Among all U.S. workers, those 65 years of age or older reported the highest prevalence of ever having a diagnosis of hypertension (47.5%), while workers 18–24 years of age reported the lowest (4.6%) (see Table 25, page 66).

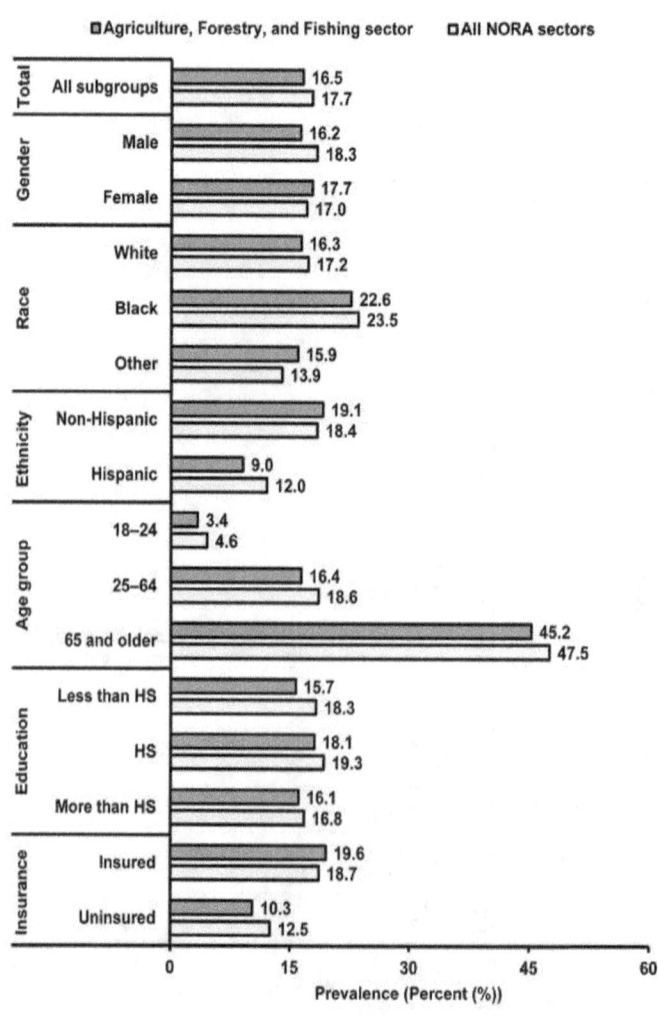

Prevalence of heart disease estimated for workers 18 years and older

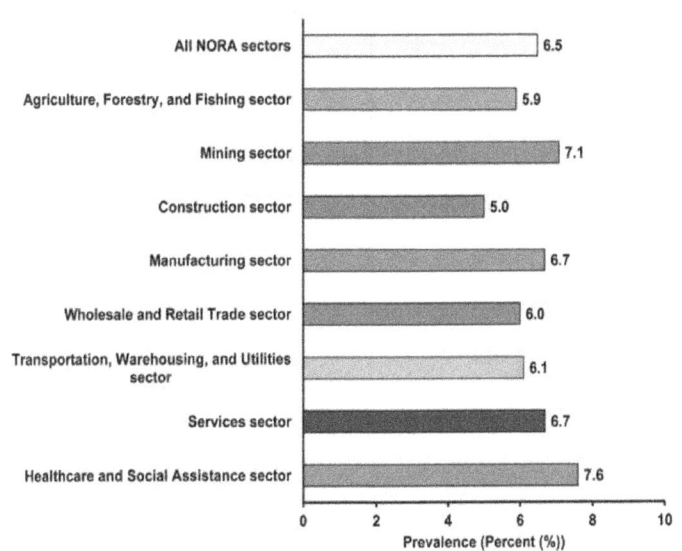

Figure 13a. Workers 18 years and older by NORA sectors, National Health Interview Survey, 1997–2007. An estimated 6.5% of all employed U.S. workers reported ever having a diagnosis of heart disease (see Table 2, page 42 and Tables 27 and 28, pages 68–69). Among the NORA sectors, Healthcare and Social Assistance sector workers reported the highest prevalence of ever having a diagnosis of heart disease (7.6%), while Construction sector workers reported the lowest (5.0%).

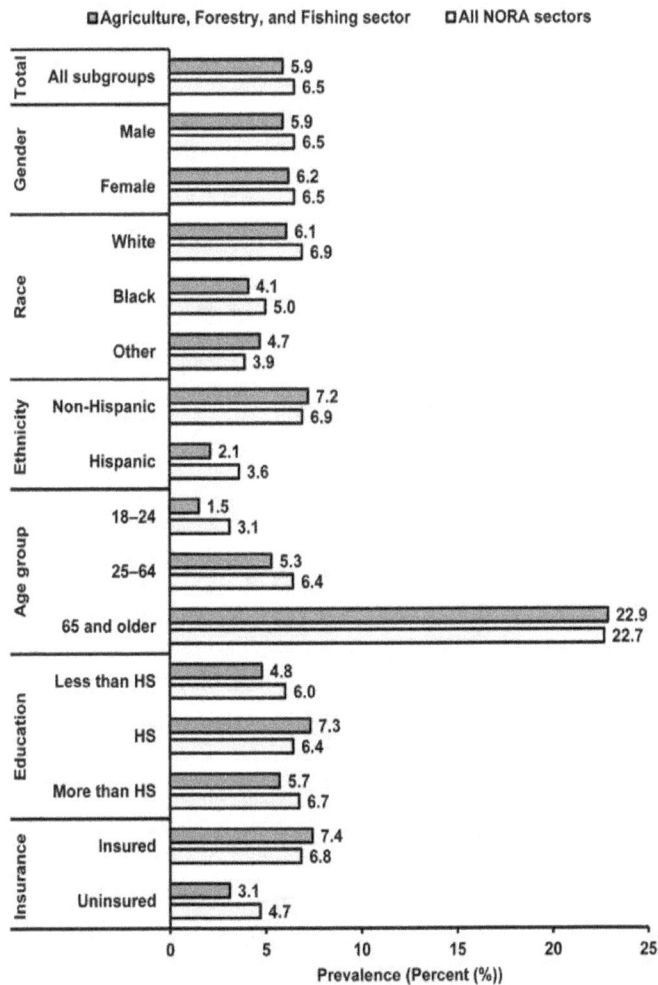

Figure 13b. Workers 18 years and older, Agriculture, Forestry, and Fishing sector and All NORA sectors, National Health Interview Survey, 1997–2007. An estimated 5.9% of workers employed in the Agriculture, Forestry, and Fishing sector reported ever having a diagnosis of heart disease. Among the subgroups, workers 65 years of age or older reported the highest prevalence of ever having a diagnosis of heart disease (22.9%), while workers 18–24 years of age reported the lowest (1.5%) (see Table 28, page 69). Among all U.S. workers, those 65 years of age or older reported the highest prevalence of ever having a diagnosis of heart disease (22.7%), while workers 18–24 years of age reported the lowest (3.1%). Men and women reported the same rates of heart disease (6.5%) (see Table 27, page 68).

Prevalence of asthma estimated for workers 18 years

Figure 14a. Workers 18 years and older by NORA sectors National Health Interview Survey, 1997–2007. An estimated 9.4% of all employed U.S. workers reported ever having a diagnosis of asthma (see Table 2, page 42, and Tables 29 and 30, pages 70–71). Among the NORA sectors, Healthcare and Social Assistance sector workers reported the highest prevalence of ever having a diagnosis of asthma (11.0%), while Agriculture, Forestry and Fishing sector workers reported the lowest (6.5%).

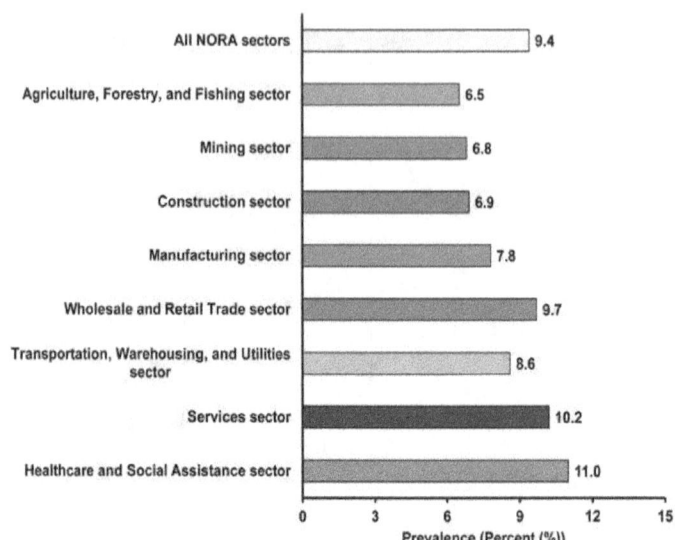

Figure 14b. Workers 18 years and older, Agriculture, Forestry, and Fishing sector and All NORA sectors National Health Interview Survey, 1997–2007. An estimated 6.5% of workers employed in the Agriculture, Forestry, and Fishing sector reported ever having a diagnosis of asthma. Among the subgroups, workers 18–24 years of age reported the highest prevalence of ever having a diagnosis of asthma (10.5%), while Hispanic workers reported the lowest (3.1%) (see Table 30, page 71). Among all U.S. workers, those 18–24 years of age reported the highest prevalence of ever having a diagnosis of asthma (13.1%), while Hispanic workers reported the lowest (6.9%) (see Table 29, page 70).

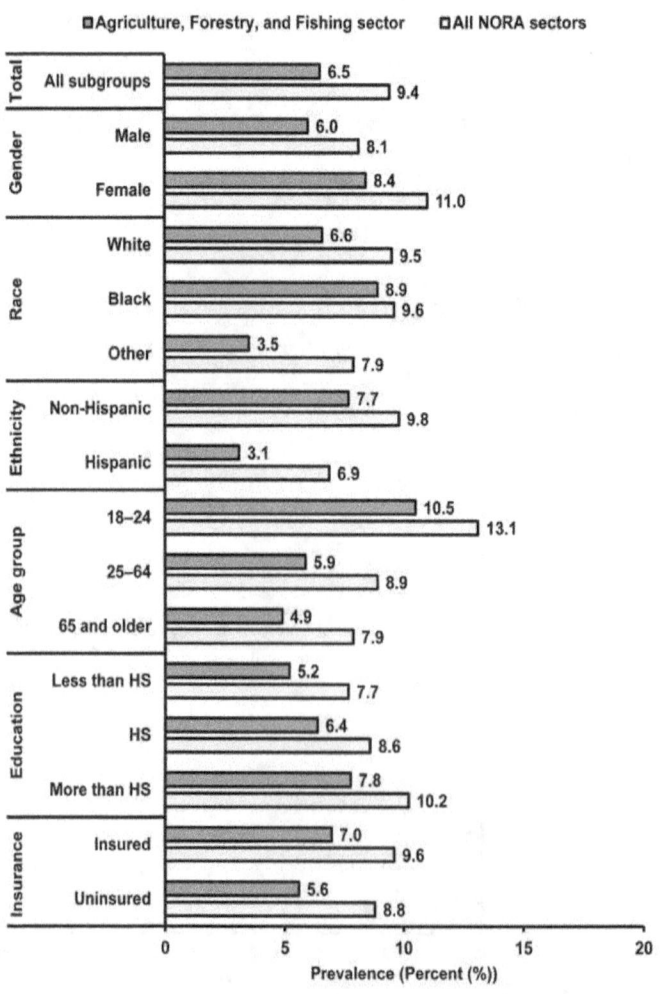

Prevalence of diabetes estimated for workers 18 years and older

Figure 15a. Workers 18 years and older by NORA sectors, National Health Interview Survey, 1997–2007.
An estimated 3.9% of all employed U.S. workers reported ever having a diagnosis of diabetes (see Table 2, page 42, and Tables 31 and 32, pages 72–73). Among the NORA sectors, Mining sector workers reported the highest prevalence of ever having a diagnosis of diabetes (5.3%), while Construction sector workers reported the lowest (2.9%).

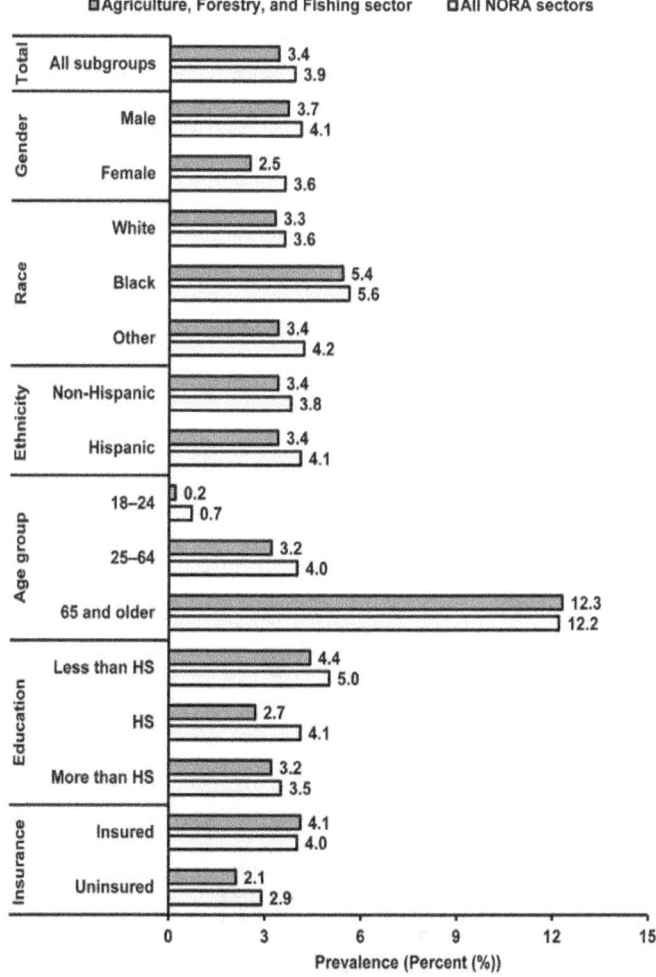

Figure 15b. Workers 18 years and older, Agriculture, Forestry, and Fishing sector and All NORA sectors, National Health Interview Survey, 1997–2007.
An estimated 3.4% of workers employed in the Agriculture, Forestry, and Fishing sector reported ever having a diagnosis of diabetes. Among the subgroups, workers 65 years of age or older reported the highest prevalence of ever having a diagnosis of diabetes (12.3%), while workers 18–24 years of age reported the lowest (0.2%) (see Table 32, page 73). Among all U.S. workers, those 65 years of age or older reported the highest prevalence of ever having a diagnosis of diabetes (12.2%), while workers 18–24 years of age reported the lowest (0.7%). Black workers reported higher rates of diabetes relative to White workers (5.6% vs. 3.6%) (see Table 31, page 72).

Prevalence of severe psychological distress estimated for workers 18 years and older

Figure 16a. Workers 18 years and older by NORA sectors, National Health Interview Survey, 1997–2007. An estimated 0.5% of all employed U.S. workers reported ever having a diagnosis of severe psychological distress (see Table 2, page 42, and Tables 33 and 34, pages 74–75). Among the NORA sectors, Wholesale and Retail Trade sector workers and Mining sector workers reported the highest prevalence of ever having a diagnosis of severe psychological distress (0.7%), while Services sector workers reported the lowest (0.4%).

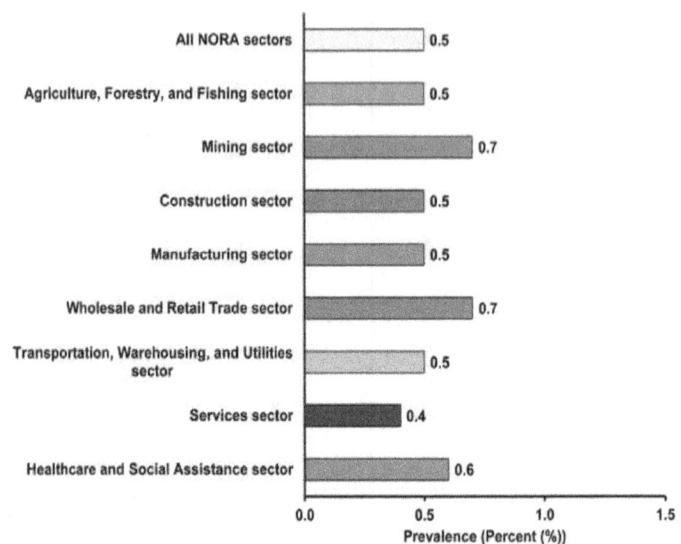

Figure 16b. Workers 18 years and older, Agriculture, Forestry, and Fishing sector and All NORA sectors, National Health Interview Survey, 1997–2007. An estimated 0.5% of workers employed in the Agriculture, Forestry, and Fishing sector reported ever having a diagnosis of severe psychological distress. Among the subgroups, workers of "Other" race reported the highest prevalence of ever having a diagnosis of severe psychological distress (0.8%), while workers 65 years of age or older and those with more than a high school education reported the lowest (0.4%) (see Table 34, page 75). Among all U.S workers, those with less than a high school education (1.2%) and uninsured workers (1.0%) reported the highest prevalence of ever having a diagnosis of severe psychological distress, with all other subgroups reporting rates below 1% (see Table 33, page 74).

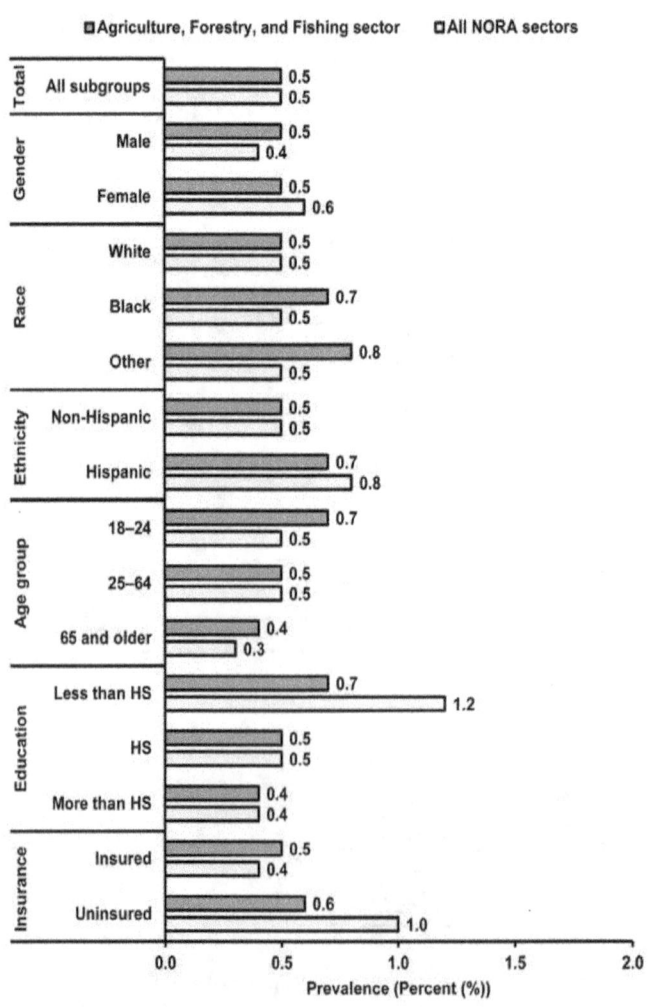

Prevalence of not having seen a primary health care provider during the past 12 months estimated for workers 18 years and older

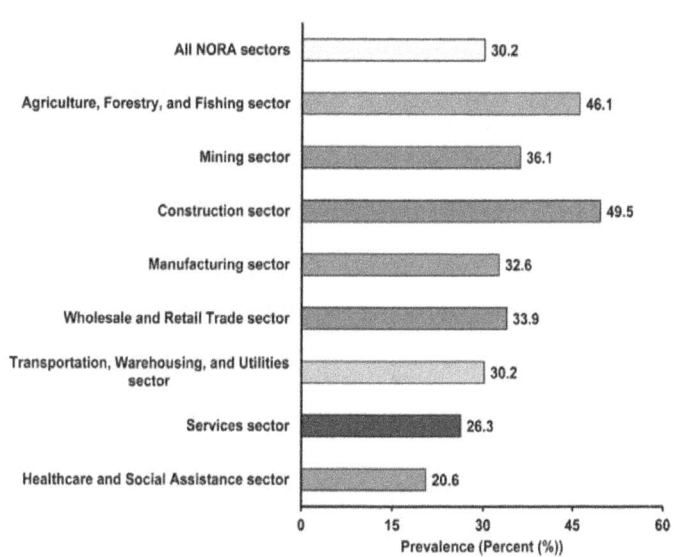

Figure 17a. Workers 18 years and older by NORA sectors, National Health Interview Survey, 1997–2007.
An estimated 30.2% of all employed U.S. workers reported not having seen a primary health care provider during the past 12 months (see Table 2, page 42, and Tables 35 and 36, pages 76–77). Among the NORA sectors, Construction sector workers reported the highest prevalence of not having seen a primary health care provider during the past 12 months (49.5%), while Healthcare and Social Assistance sector workers reported the lowest (20.6%).

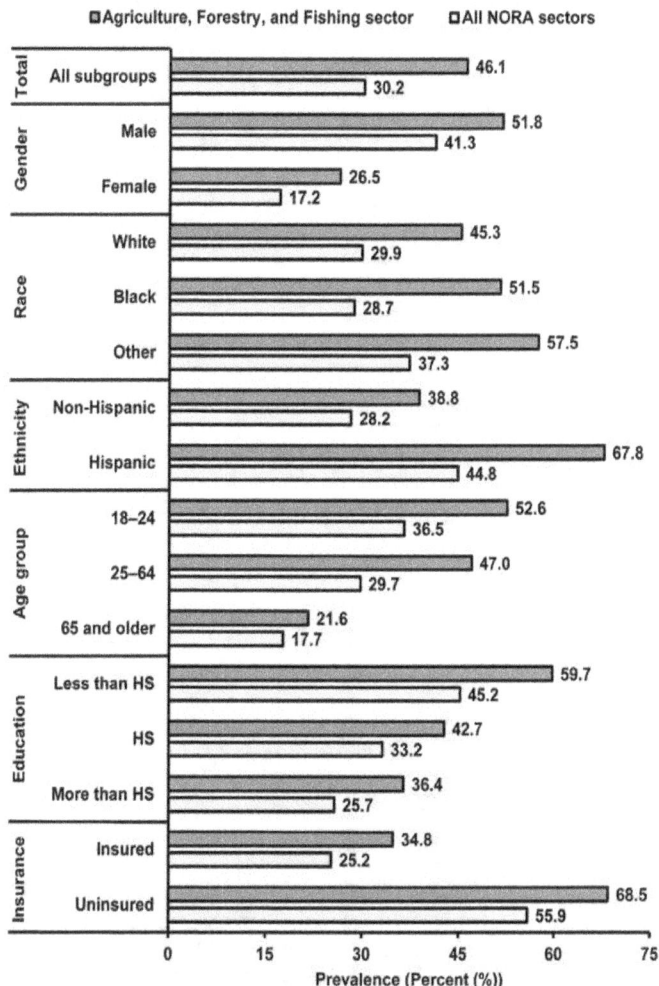

Figure 17b. Workers 18 years and older, Agriculture, Forestry, and Fishing sector and All NORA sectors, National Health Interview Survey, 1997–2007.
An estimated 46.1% of workers employed in the Agriculture, Forestry, and Fishing sector reported not having seen a primary health care provider during the past 12 months. Among the subgroups, uninsured workers reported the highest prevalence of not having seen a primary health care provider during the past 12 months (68.5%), while workers 65 years of age or older reported the lowest (21.6%) (see Table 36, page 77). Among all U.S. workers, uninsured workers reported the highest prevalence of not having seen a primary health care provider during the past 12 months (55.9%), while female workers reported the lowest (17.2%). Male workers were more than twice as likely to report not having seen a primary care provider during the past 12 months when compared to female workers (41.3% vs. 17.2%) (see Table 35, page 76).

Prevalence of dentist contact of 1 year or greater estimated for workers 18 years and older

Figure 18a. Workers 18 years and older by NORA sectors, National Health Interview Survey, 1997–2007. An estimated 34.2% of all employed U.S. workers reported not having seen a dentist during the past year (see Table 2, page 42, and Tables 37 and 38, pages 78–79). Among the NORA sectors, Agriculture, Forestry, and Fishing sector workers reported the highest prevalence of not having seen a dentist during the past year (50.3%), while Healthcare and Social Assistance sector workers reported the lowest (27.9%).

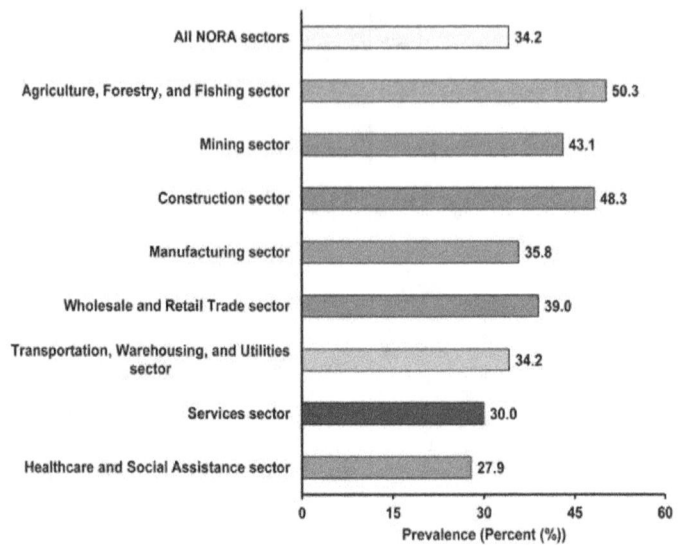

Figure 18b. Workers 18 years and older, Agriculture, Forestry, and Fishing sector and All NORA sectors, National Health Interview Survey, 1997–2007. An estimated 50.3% of workers employed in the Agriculture, Forestry, and Fishing sector reported not having seen a dentist during the past year. Among the subgroups, Hispanic workers reported the highest prevalence of not having seen a dentist during the past year (72.2%), while workers with more than high school education reported the lowest (33.7%) (see Table 38, page 79). Among all U.S. workers, uninsured workers reported the highest prevalence of not having seen a dentist during the past year (63.5%), while workers with more than a high school education reported the lowest (26.3%). Workers with less than a high school education were more than twice as likely to report not having seen a dentist during the past year when compared to workers with more than a high school education (57.1% vs. 26.3%) (see Table 37, page 78).

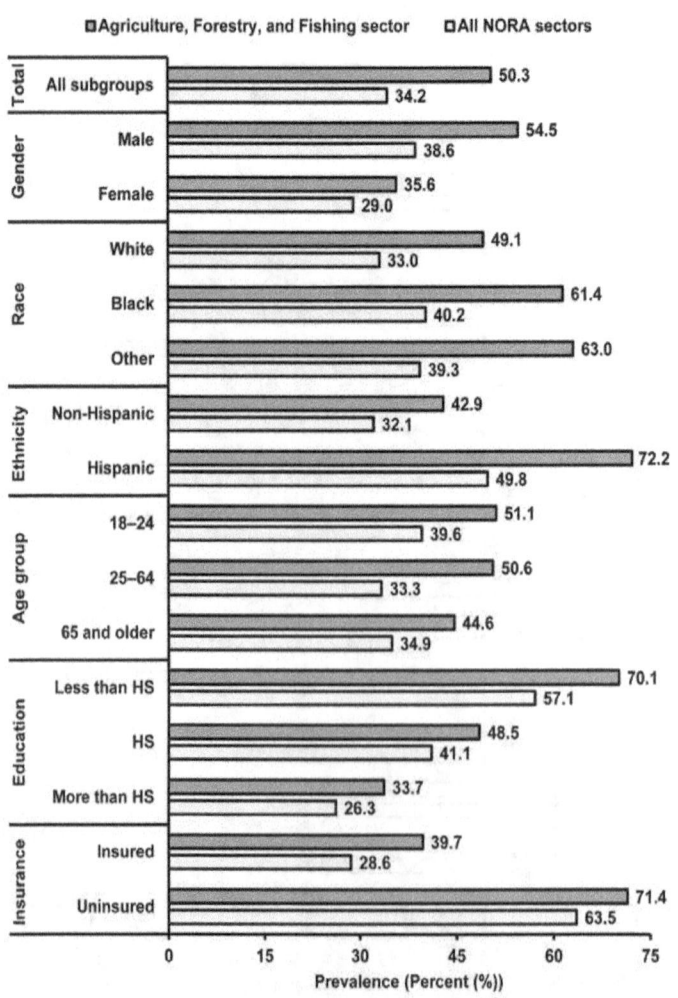

Prevalence of surgery during the past 12 months estimated for workers 18 years and older

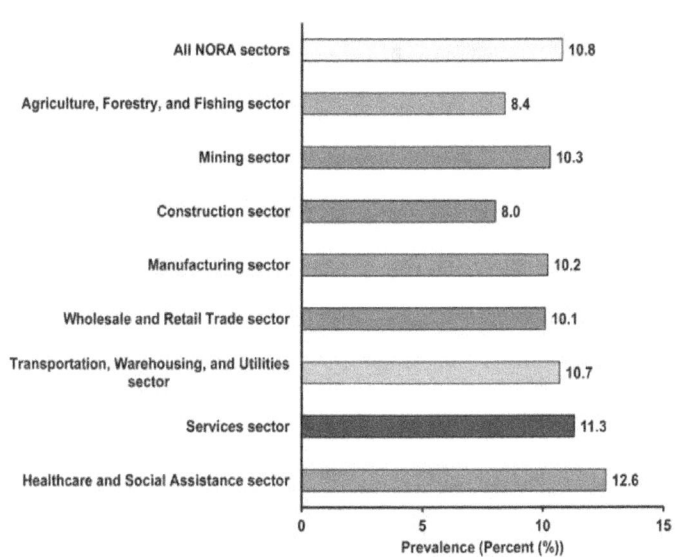

Figure 19a. Workers 18 years and older by NORA sectors, National Health Interview Survey, 19997–2007. An estimated 10.8% of all employed U.S. workers reported having surgery during the past 12 months (see Table 2, page 42, and Tables 39 and 40, pages 80–81). Among the NORA sectors, Healthcare and Social Assistance sector workers reported the highest prevalence of having surgery during the past 12 months (12.6%), while Construction sector workers reported the lowest (8.0%).

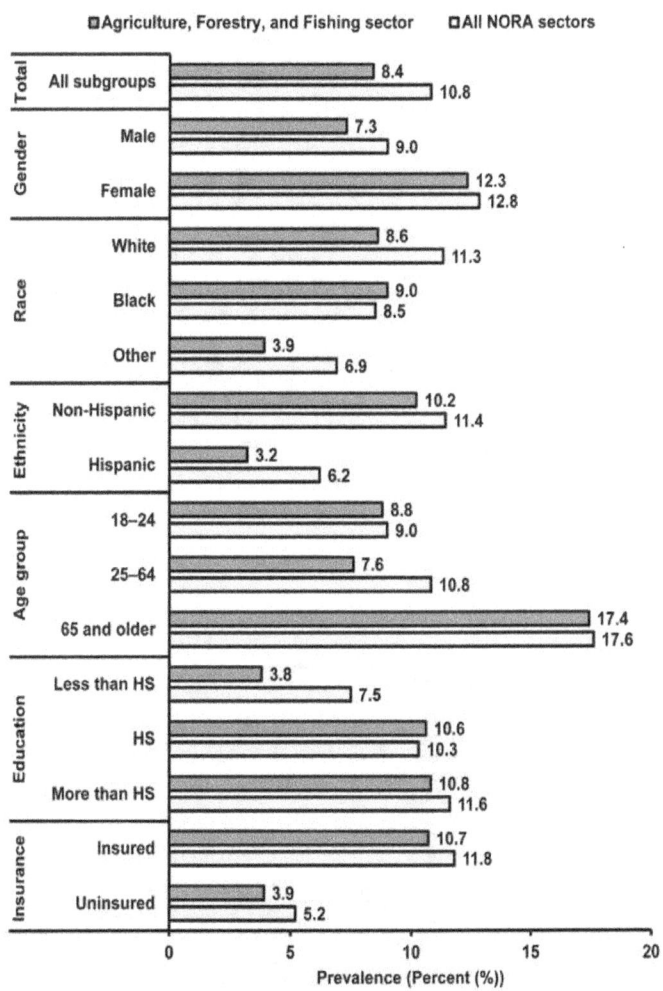

Figure 19b. Workers 18 years and older, Agriculture, Forestry, and Fishing sector and All NORA sectors, National Health Interview Survey, 19997–2007. An estimated 8.4% of workers employed in the Agriculture, Forestry, and Fishing sector reported having surgery during the past 12 months. Among the subgroups, workers 65 years of age or older reported the highest prevalence of having surgery during the past 12 months (17.4%), while Hispanic workers reported the lowest (3.2%) (see Table 40, page 81). Among all U.S. workers, those 65 years of age or older reported the highest prevalence of having surgery during the past 12 months (17.6%), while uninsured workers reported the lowest (5.2%) (see Table 39, page 80).

Prevalence of hospital emergency room visit during the past 12 months estimated for workers 18 years and older

Figure 20a. Workers 18 years and older by NORA sectors, National Health Interview Survey, 1997–2007. An estimated 17.6% of all employed U.S. workers reported at least one hospital emergency room visit during the past 12 months (see Table 2, page 42, and Tables 41 and 42, pages 82–83). Among the NORA sectors, Wholesale and Retail Trade sector workers reported the highest prevalence of at least one hospital emergency room visit during the past 12 months (19.1%), while Agriculture, Forestry, and Fishing sector workers reported the lowest (14.6%).

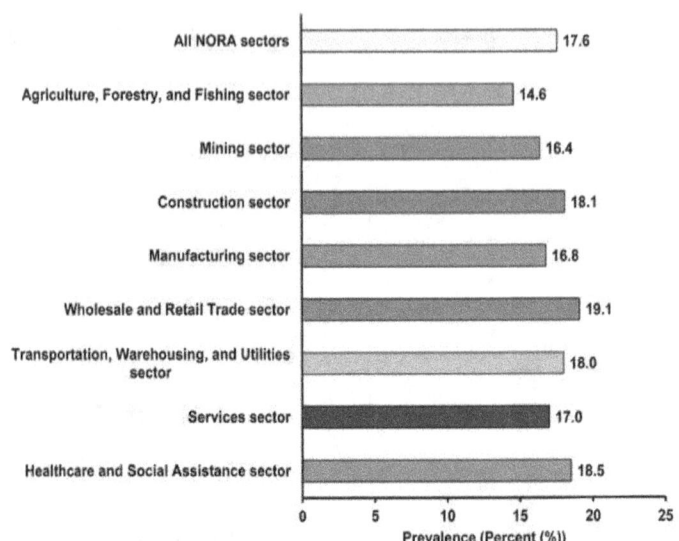

Figure 20b. Workers 18 years and older, Agriculture, Forestry, and Fishing sector and All NORA sectors, National Health Interview Survey, 1997–2007. An estimated 14.6% of workers employed in the Agriculture, Forestry, and Fishing sector reported at least one hospital emergency room visit during the past 12 months. Among the subgroups, Black workers reported the highest prevalence of at least one hospital emergency room visit during the past 12 months (26.8%), while Hispanic workers reported the lowest (10.1%) (see Table 2, page 42) (see Table 42, page 83). Among all U.S. workers, those 18–24 years of age reported the highest prevalence of at least one hospital emergency room visit during the past 12 months (24.2%), while workers of "Other" race reported the lowest (14.5%) (see Table 41, page 82).

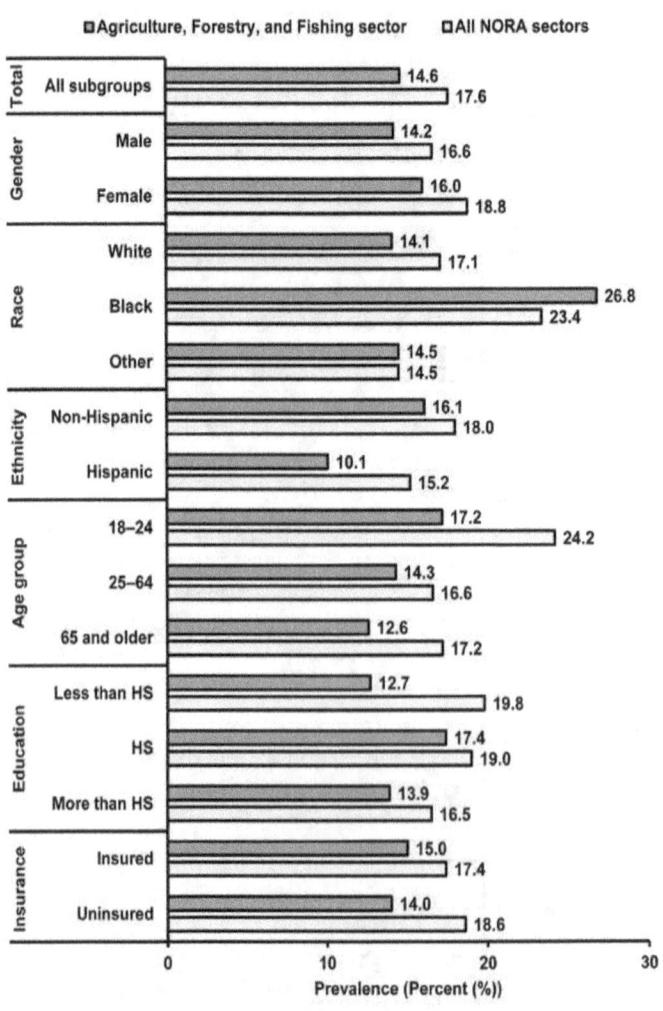

Prevalence of current smokers estimated for workers 18 years and older

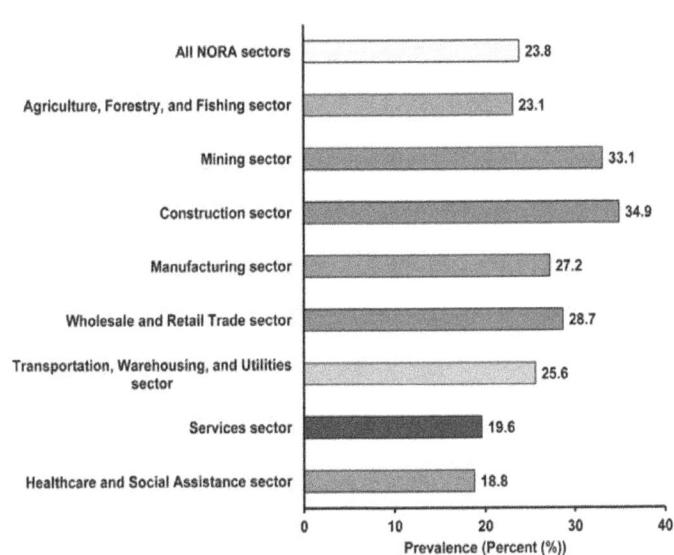

Figure 21a. Workers 18 years and older by NORA sectors, National Health Interview Survey, 1997–2007. An estimated 23.8% of employed U.S. workers reported being current smokers (see Table 2, page 42, and Tables 43 and 44, pages 84–85). Among the NORA sectors, Construction sector workers reported the highest prevalence of current smokers (34.9%), while Healthcare and Social Assistance sector workers reported the lowest (18.8%).

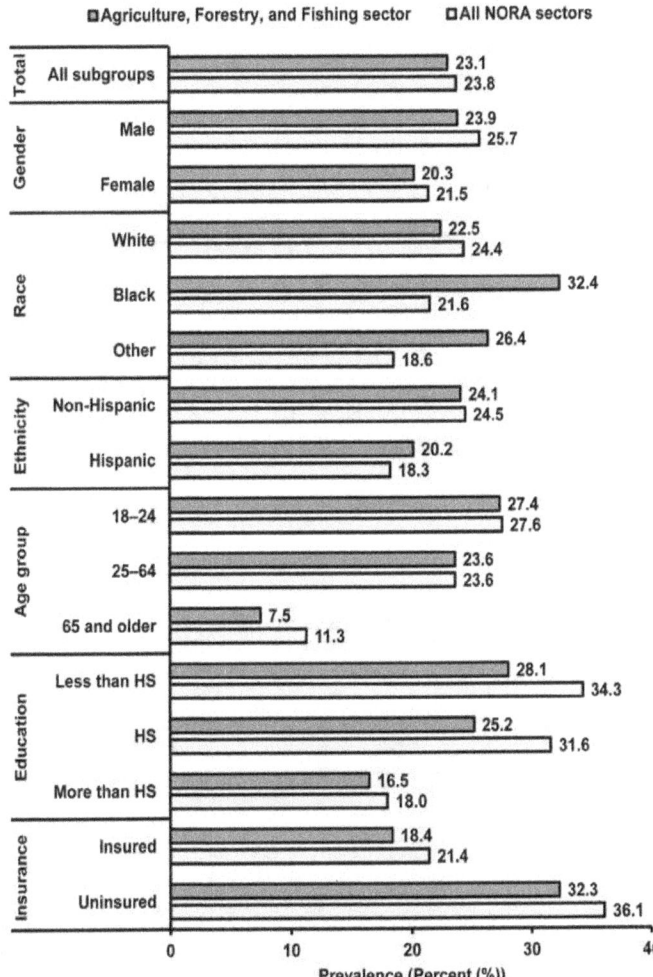

Figure 21b. Workers 18 years and older, Agriculture, Forestry, and Fishing sector and All NORA sectors, National Health Interview Survey, 1997–2007. An estimated 23.1% of workers employed in the Agriculture, Forestry, and Fishing sector reported being current smokers. Among the subgroups, Black workers reported the highest prevalence of current smokers (32.4%), while workers 65 years of age or older reported the lowest (7.5%) (see Table 44, page 85). Among all U.S. workers, uninsured workers reported the highest prevalence of current smokers (36.1%), while workers 65 years of age or older reported the lowest (11.3%). Workers with less than a high school education were more likely to report being current smokers than workers with more than a high school education (34.3% vs. 18.0%) (see Table 43, page 84).

Prevalence of current alcohol drinkers estimated for workers 18 years and older

Figure 22a. Workers 18 years and older by NORA sectors, National Health Interview Survey, 1997–2007. An estimated 70.2% of employed U.S. workers reported being current alcohol drinkers (see Table 2, page 42, and Tables 45 and 46, pages 86–87). Among the NORA sectors, Construction sector workers reported the highest prevalence of current alcohol drinkers (75.0%), while Healthcare and Social Assistance sector workers reported the lowest (64.8%).

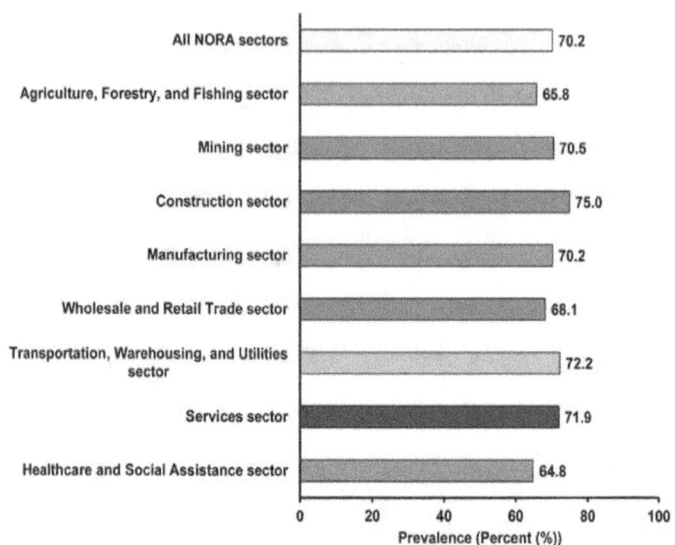

Figure 22b. Workers 18 years and older, Agriculture, Forestry, and Fishing sector and All NORA sectors, National Health Interview Survey, 1997–2007. An estimated 65.8% of workers employed in the Agriculture, Forestry, and Fishing sector reported being current alcohol drinkers. Among the subgroups, workers with more than a high school education reported the highest prevalence of current alcohol drinkers (74.5%), while workers 65 years of age or older reported the lowest (44.9%) (see Table 46, page 87). Among all U.S. workers, those with more than a high school education reported the highest prevalence of current alcohol drinkers (74.9%), while workers 65 years of age or older reported the lowest (55.8%) (see Table 45, page 86).

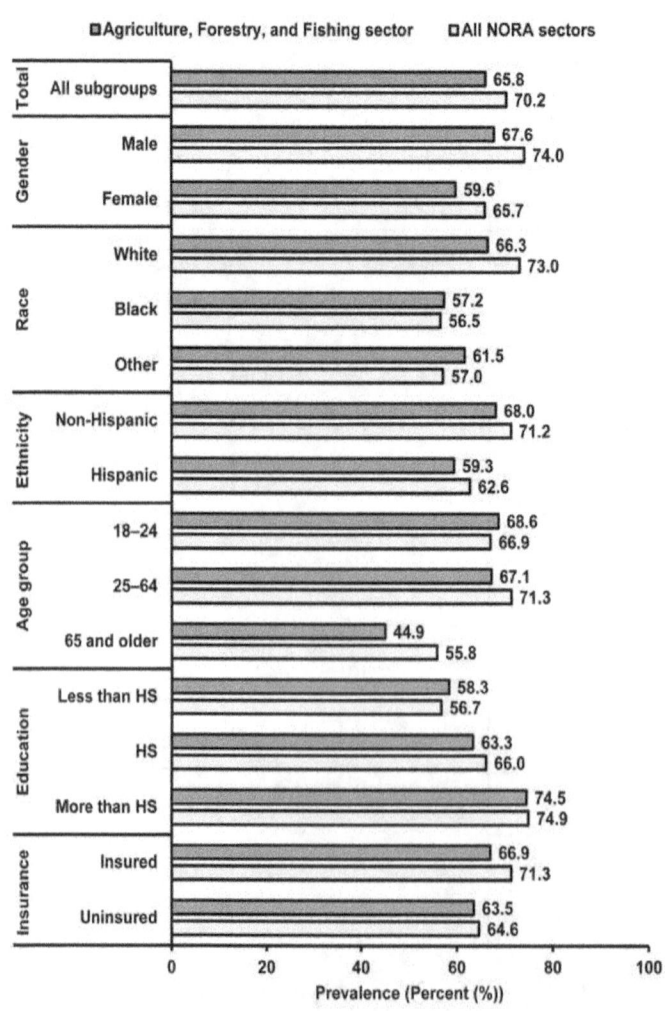

Prevalence of obesity estimated for workers 18 years and older

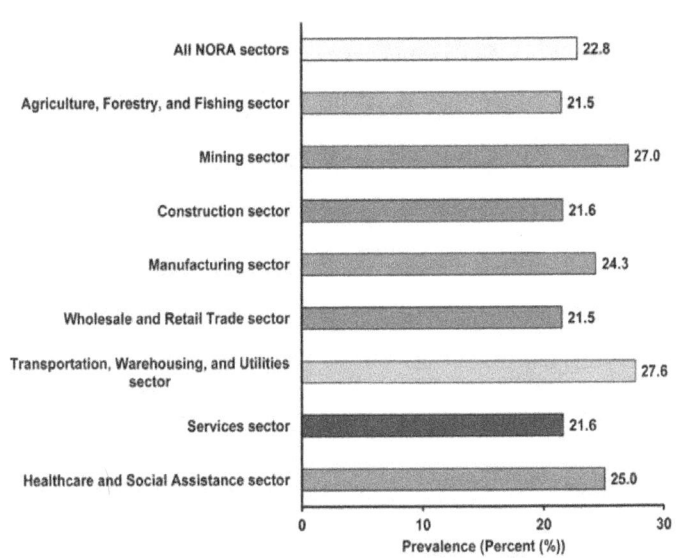

Figure 23a. Workers 18 years and older by NORA sectors, National Health Interview Survey, 1997–2007.
An estimated 22.8% of all employed U.S. workers reported being obese (having a body mass index (BMI) greater than or equal to 30) (see Table 2, page 42, and Tables 47 and 48, pages 88–89). Among the NORA sectors, Transportation, Warehousing, and Utilities sector workers reported the highest prevalence of obesity (27.6%), while Wholesale and Retail Trade sector and Agriculture, Forestry, and Fishing sector workers reported the lowest (21.5%).

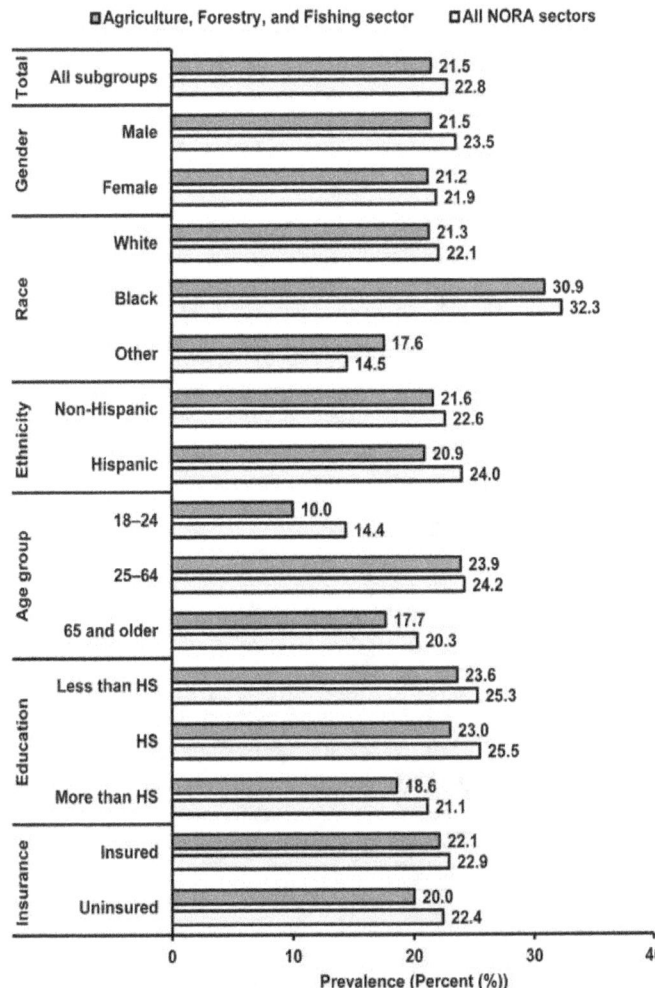

Figure 23b. Workers 18 years and older, Agriculture, Forestry, and Fishing sector and All NORA sectors, National Health Interview Survey, 1997–2007.
An estimated 21.5% of workers employed in the Agriculture, Forestry, and Fishing reported being obese (having a body mass index (BMI) greater than or equal to 30). Among the subgroups, Black workers reported the highest prevalence of obesity (30.9%), while workers 18–24 years of age reported the lowest (10.0%) (see Table 48, page 89). Among all U.S. workers, Black workers reported the highest prevalence of obesity (32.3%), while workers 18–24 years of age reported the lowest (14.4%). Obesity among Black workers was more than twice that noted for workers in the "Other" race group (32.3% vs. 14.5%) (see Table 47, page 88).

Prevalence of not meeting CDC recommended leisure time levels of physical activity estimated for workers 18 years and older

Figure 24a. Workers 18 years and older by NORA sectors, National Health Interview Survey, 1997–2007. An estimated 65.9% of all employed U.S. workers reported not meeting recommended leisure time levels of physical activity (see Table 2, page 42, and Tables 49 and 50, pages 90–91). Among the NORA sectors, Agriculture, Forestry, and Fishing sector workers reported the highest prevalence of not meeting recommended leisure time levels of physical activity (73.5%), while Services sector workers reported the lowest (62.1%).

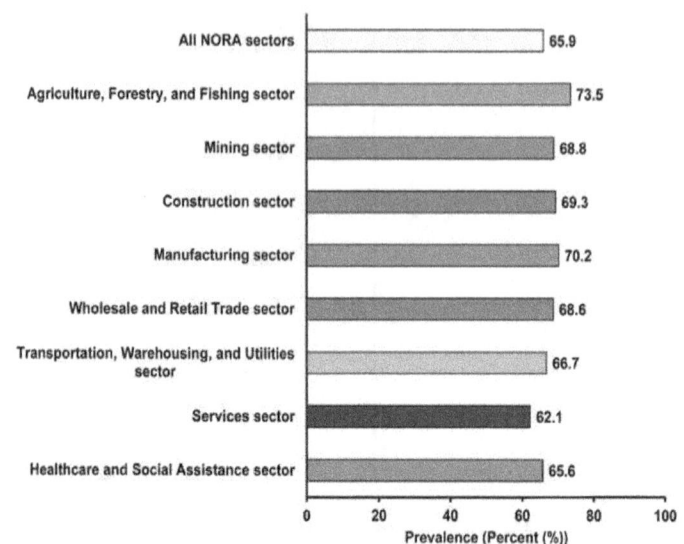

Figure 24b. Workers 18 years and older, Agriculture, Forestry, and Fishing sector and All NORA sectors, National Health Interview Survey, 1997–2007. An estimated 73.5% of workers employed in the Agriculture, Forestry, and Fishing sector reported not meeting recommended leisure time levels of physical activity. Among the subgroups, Hispanic workers reported the highest prevalence of not meeting recommended leisure time levels of physical activity (84.0%), while workers with more than a high school education reported the lowest (64.2%) (see Table 50, page 91). Among all U.S. workers, those with less than a high school education reported the highest prevalence of not meeting recommended leisure time levels of physical activity (78.9%), while workers with more than a high school education reported the lowest (60.0%) (see Table 49 page 90).

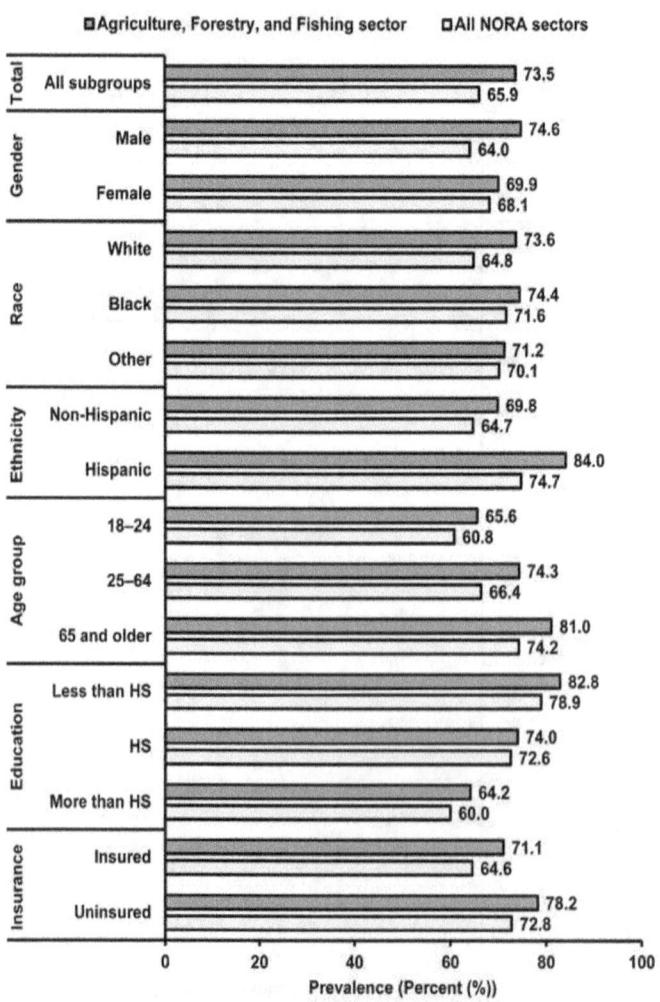

Prevalence of lifetime HIV test estimated for workers 18 years and older

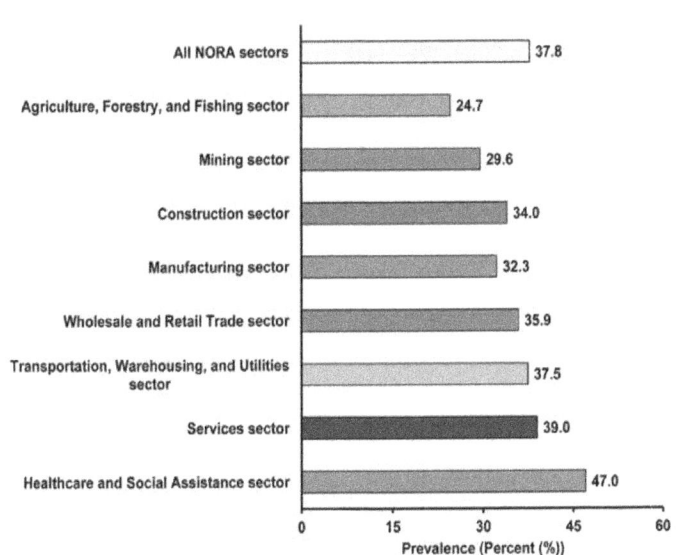

Figure 25a. Workers 18 years and older by NORA sectors, National Health Interview Survey, 1997–2007. An estimated 37.8% of all employed U.S. workers reported ever being tested for HIV (see Table 2, page 42, and Tables 51 and 52, pages 92–93). Among the NORA sectors, Healthcare and Social Assistance sector workers reported the highest prevalence of ever being tested for HIV (47.0%), while Agriculture, Forestry, and Fishing sector workers reported the lowest (24.7%).

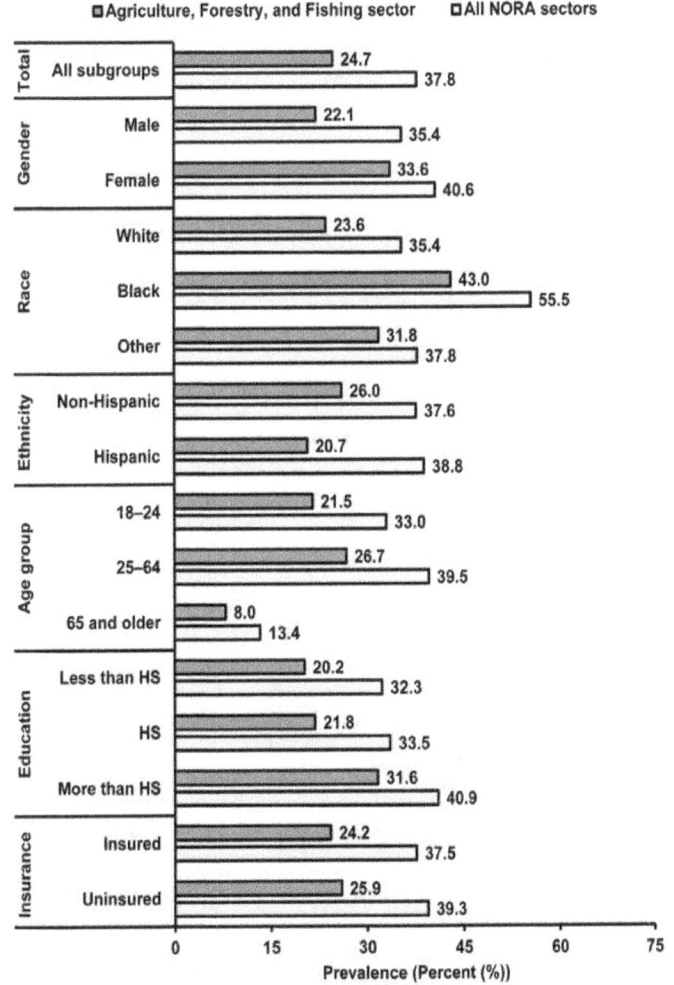

Figure 25b. Workers 18 years and older, Agriculture, Forestry, and Fishing sector and All NORA sectors, National Health Interview Survey, 1997–2007. An estimated 24.7% of workers employed in the Agriculture, Forestry, and Fishing sector reported ever being tested for HIV. Among the subgroups, Black workers reported the highest prevalence of ever being tested for HIV (43.0%), while workers 65 years of age or older reported the lowest (8.0%) (see Table 52, page 93). Among all U.S. workers, Black workers reported the highest prevalence of ever being tested for HIV (55.5%), while workers 65 years of age or older reported the lowest prevalence (13.4%) (see Table 51, page 92).

Prevalence of not receiving an influenza vaccination during the past 12 months estimated for workers 18 years and older

Figure 26a. Workers 18 years and older by NORA sectors, National Health Interview Survey, 1997–2007. An estimated 79.1% of all employed U.S. workers reported not receiving an influenza vaccination during the past 12 months (see Table 2, page 42, and Tables 53 and 54, pages 94–95). Among the NORA sectors, Construction sector workers reported the highest prevalence of not receiving an influenza vaccination during the past 12 months (89.3%), while Healthcare and Social Assistance sector workers reported the lowest (64.5%).

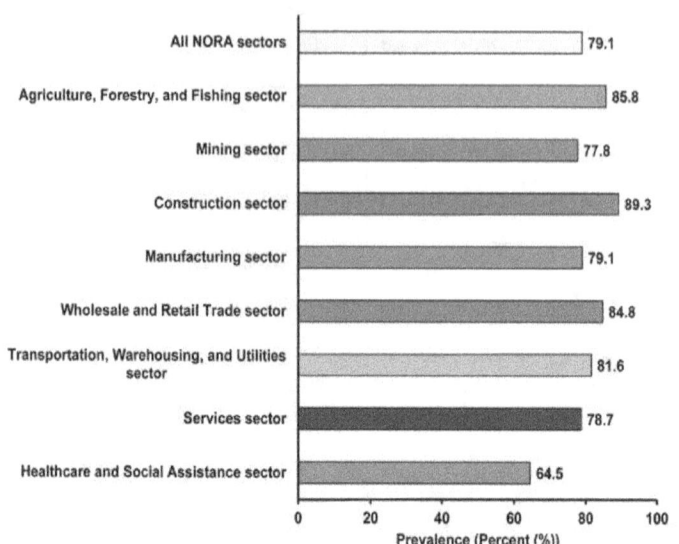

Figure 26b. Workers 18 years and older, Agriculture, Forestry, and Fishing sector and All NORA sectors, National Health Interview Survey, 1997–2007. An estimated 85.8% of workers employed in the Agriculture, Forestry, and Fishing sector reported not receiving an influenza vaccination during the past 12 months. Among the subgroups, uninsured workers reported the highest prevalence of not receiving an influenza vaccination during the past 12 months (93.7%), while workers 65 years of age or older reported the lowest (47.0%) (see Table 54, page 95). Among all U.S. workers, uninsured workers reported the highest prevalence of not receiving an influenza vaccination during the past 12 months (90.8%), while workers 65 years of age or older reported the lowest (42.9%). A large proportion of workers 18–24 years of age also reported not receiving an influenza vaccination during the past 12 months (87.1%) (see Table 53, page 94).

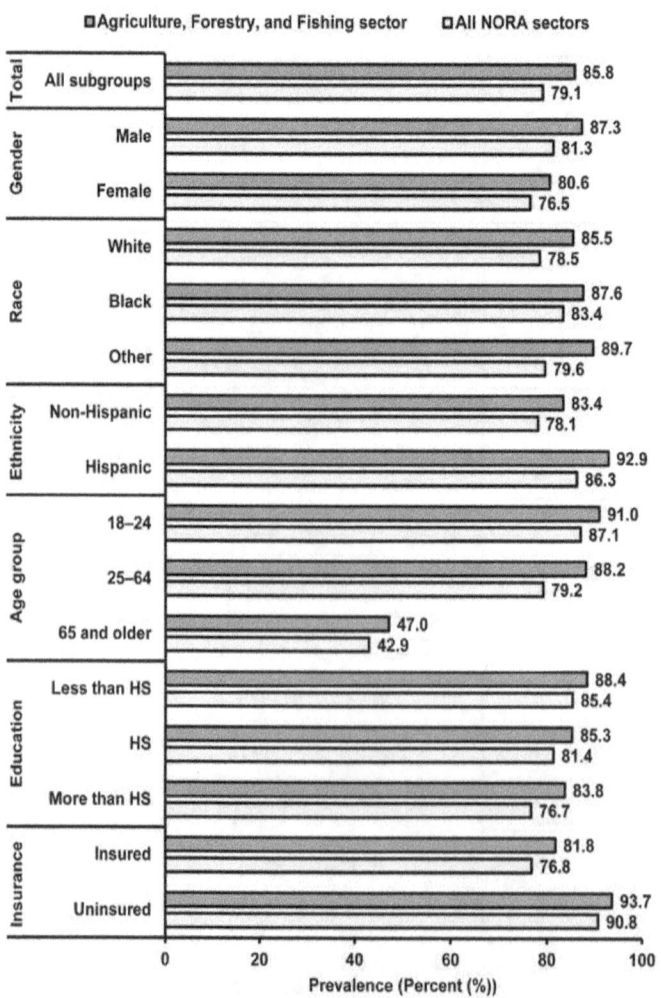

Prevalence of never receiving a pneumococcal vaccination estimated for workers 60 years and older

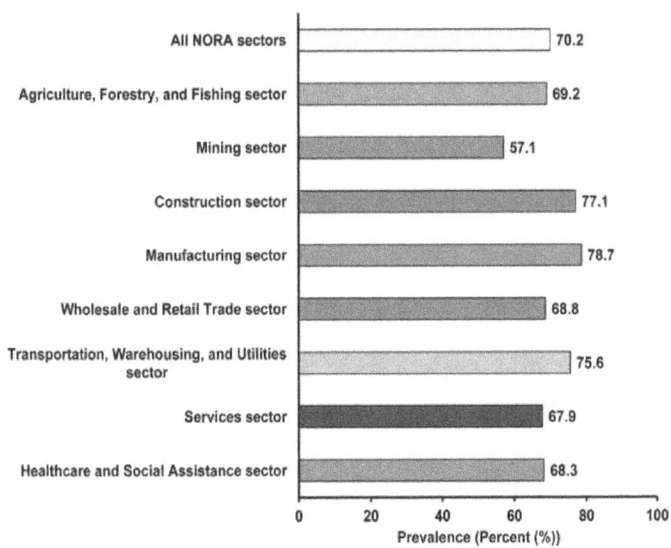

Figure 27a. Workers 60 years and older by NORA sectors, National Health Interview Survey, 1997–2007.
An estimated 70.2% of all employed U.S. workers 60 years and older reported never receiving a pneumococcal vaccination (see Table 2, page 42, and Tables 55 and 56, pages 96–97). Among the NORA sectors, Manufacturing sector workers reported the highest prevalence of never receiving a pneumococcal vaccination (78.7%), while Mining sector workers reported the lowest (57.1%).

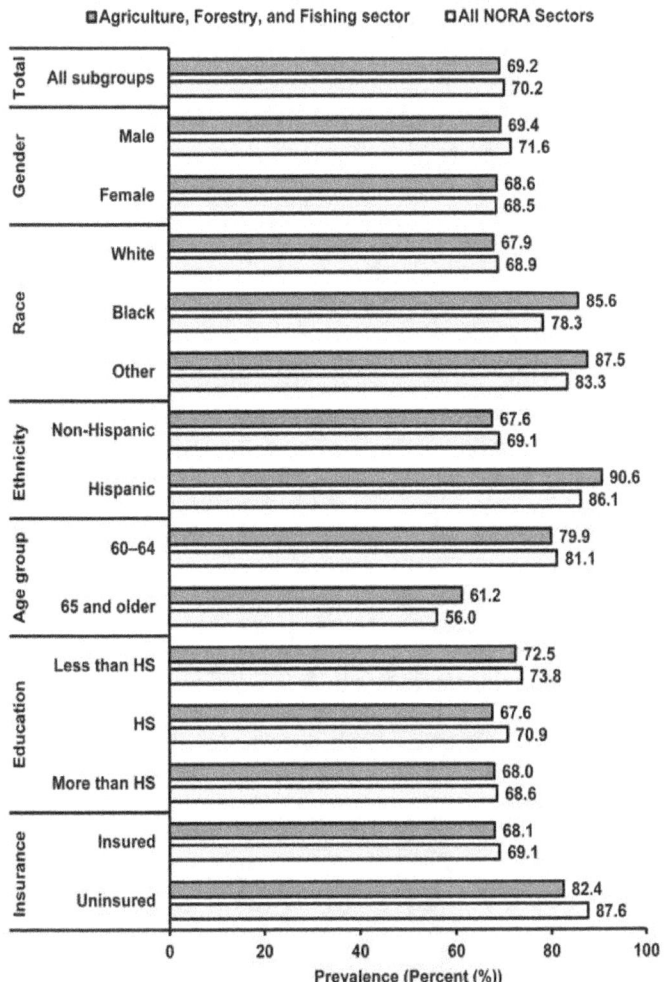

Figure 27b. Workers 60 years and older, Agriculture, Forestry, and Fishing sector and All NORA sectors, National Health Interview Survey, 1997–2007.
An estimated 69.2% of workers 60 years and older employed in the Agriculture, Forestry, and Fishing sector reported never receiving a pneumococcal vaccination. Among the subgroups, Hispanic workers reported the highest prevalence of never receiving a pneumococcal vaccination (90.6%), while workers 65 years of age or older reported the lowest (61.2%) (see Table 56, page 97). Among all U.S. workers, uninsured workers reported the highest prevalence of never receiving a pneumococcal vaccination (87.6%), while workers 65 years of age or older reported the lowest (56.0%). Hispanic workers reported lower pneumococcal vaccination rates relative to Non-Hispanics workers (13.9% vs. 30.9%) (see Table 55, page 96).

Tables

Table 1. Estimated U.S. worker population and sample size for workers 18 years and older, All NORA sectors and Agriculture, Forestry, and Fishing sector[1], National Health Interview Survey, 1997–2007

Subgroup	All NORA sectors			Agriculture, Forestry, and Fishing sector		
	U.S. Worker Population Estimates		NHIS N[1]	U.S. Worker Population Estimates		NHIS N[1]
	Number	Percent (%)		Number	Percent (%)	
Overall Total	126,898,030	100.0%	196,924	2,694,267	100.0%	4,378
Gender						
Male	68,530,792	54.0%	97,768	2,088,446	77.5%	3,367
Female	58,367,238	46.0%	99,156	605,820	22.5%	1,011
Race						
White	105,313,053	83.0%	157,040	2,462,020	91.4%	3,908
Black	14,056,560	11.1%	27,262	95,149	3.5%	184
Other	7,528,417	5.9%	12,622	137,098	5.1%	286
Ethnicity						
Non-Hispanic	111,862,532	88.2%	163,004	2,014,159	74.8%	2,839
Hispanic	15,035,498	11.8%	33,920	680,108	25.2%	1,539
Age group						
18–24	16,959,193	13.4%	21,858	389,835	14.5%	544
25–64	105,946,456	83.5%	167,739	2,120,076	78.7%	3,508
65 and older	3,992,381	3.1%	7,327	184,356	6.8%	326
Education[2]						
Less than high school graduate	14,798,890	11.7%	26,367	865,745	32.1%	1,669
High school graduate or GED	36,048,733	28.4%	54,264	843,218	31.3%	1,254
Some college or higher	75,434,176	59.4%	115,325	962,165	35.7%	1,407
Insurance						
Insured	106,279,655	83.8%	161,665	1,787,027	66.3%	2,692
Uninsured	20,282,002	16.0%	34,830	894,314	33.2%	1,671

[1] Sample size (N) from the National Health Interview Survey (NHIS) for the years 1997–2007.
[2] Response categoroes include (1) less than High School graduate, (2) High School graduate or GED, and (3) Some college or higher education.
Note: Subgroup percentages may not total 100% due to missing covariate values. Sample weights are also used to estimate the number of workers in the U.S. with various health conditions. In some cases these values will be underestimates due to either (1) the presence of missing data for the condition of interest (e.g., respondent did not respond to a chronic disease condition), or (2) in the case of stratified analyses, there are missing values for the stratification variable (e.g., educational attainment).

Table 2. U.S. Health status, Disability and Morbidity Prevalence (percent) estimates for workers 18 years and older, NORA sectors[1], National Health Interview Survey, 1997–2007

Health status, Disability and Morbidity domains	All NORA sectors	Agriculture	Mining	Construction	Manufacturing	Wholesale and Retail trades	Transportation, Warehousing, Utilities	Services	Healthcare and Social Assistance
Health status									
Health worse than last year	5.4	4.4	5.7	4.8	5.4	5.5	5.2	5.4	6.0
Self-rated health (fair to poor)	5.3	6.2	6.5	5.3	5.7	5.5	5.1	4.9	5.8
Bed Days from illness in past year									
Mean bed disability days	1.9	1.4	1.7	1.7	1.7	1.9	1.9	2.0	2.2
2 or more bed disability days	25.3	18.1	22.8	20.6	22.6	24.7	23.8	26.9	28.5
Work loss days									
Mean number of work loss days	3.9	3.6	5.1	3.8	4.1	3.6	4.9	3.6	4.2
Work loss ≥ 6 days in last 12 months	11.1	8.8	11.2	10.1	10.8	9.9	13.1	11.0	12.9
Disability									
Needs special equipment	1.4	1.2	1.7	1.0	1.3	1.3	1.5	1.5	1.4
Experiences any functional activity limitation	21.6	20.3	23.0	17.8	20.7	20.5	21.4	22.1	25.1
Any hearing impairment	12.0	16.4	22.2	15.1	15.0	11.3	13.7	10.8	9.9
Visual impairment	6.7	5.7	4.7	6.0	6.6	6.6	5.5	6.8	7.7
Health conditions (ever diagnosed)									
Cancer	4.0	3.9	3.1	2.6	3.3	3.4	3.5	4.5	4.8
Hypertension	17.7	16.5	23.2	15.1	19.2	15.3	20.0	17.6	19.7
Heart disease	6.5	5.9	7.1	5.0	6.7	6.0	6.1	6.7	7.6
Asthma	9.4	6.5	6.8	6.9	7.8	9.7	8.6	10.2	11.0
Diabetes	3.9	3.4	5.3	2.9	4.0	3.4	4.4	3.8	4.6
Severe psychological distress	0.5	0.5	0.7	0.5	0.5	0.7	0.5	0.4	0.6

Table 2. Continued

Health status, Disability and Morbidity domains	All NORA sectors	Agriculture	Mining	Construction	Manufacturing	Wholesale and Retail trades	Transportation, Warehousing, Utilities	Services	Healthcare and Social Assistance
Health care utilization									
Primary health care provider (not seen health care provider in past 12 months)	30.2	46.1	36.1	49.5	32.6	33.9	30.2	26.3	20.6
Dental (not seen dentist in past 12 months)	34.2	50.3	43.1	48.3	35.8	39.0	34.2	30.0	27.9
Surgery during past 12 months	10.8	8.4	10.3	8.0	10.2	10.1	10.7	11.3	12.6
Emergency room visit in past 12 months	17.6	14.6	16.4	18.1	16.8	19.1	18.0	17.0	18.5
Health behaviors									
Smoking status – current smoker	23.8	23.1	33.1	34.9	27.2	28.7	25.6	19.6	18.8
Drinking status – current drinker	70.2	65.8	70.5	75.0	70.2	68.1	72.2	71.9	64.8
Obesity – Body mass index ≥ 30	22.8	21.5	27.0	21.6	24.3	21.5	27.6	21.6	25.0
Does not meet CDC guidelines for leisure time levels of physical activity	65.9	73.5	68.8	69.3	70.2	68.6	66.7	62.1	65.6
HIV/AIDS test (ever tested)	37.8	24.7	29.6	34.0	32.3	35.9	37.5	39.0	47.0
No Influenza vaccination in past 12 months	79.1	85.8	77.8	89.3	79.1	84.8	81.6	78.7	64.5
No Pneumococcal vaccination (ages 60 years and older, only)	70.2	69.2	57.1	77.1	78.7	68.8	75.6	67.9	68.3

[1] Source: Contract Report (March 2010). NORA Morbidity and Disability: The National Health Interview Survey (NHIS) 1997–2007. Department of Epidemiology and Public Health, University of Miami School of Medicine

Note: The Contract Report includes extensive tables with prevalence estimates for worker characteristics such as gender (male, female), race (white, black, other), ethnicity (Hispanic, non-Hispanic), age group (18–24, 25–64, 65 and older), education (Less than high school (HS) graduate; HS graduate or GED; and >HS= Some college or higher); and insurance coverage (insured, uninsured).

Table 3. Prevalence of a reported decline in health when compared to health status 12 months prior estimated for workers 18 years and older, All NORA sectors, National Health Interview Survey, 1997–2007

Subgroup	US Estimated Worker Population	NHIS sample size[1]	Better			About the same			Worse		
			Number	Percent[2]	Standard error	Number	Percent[2]	Standard error	Number	Percent[2]	Standard error
All subgroups	126,898,030	196,924	36,706	18.2	0.12	148,682	76.4	0.13	11,187	5.4	0.07
Gender											
Male	68,530,792	97,768	17,228	17.4	0.15	75,534	77.9	0.17	4,829	4.8	0.09
Female	58,367,238	99,156	19,478	19.2	0.17	73,148	74.7	0.18	6,358	6.1	0.10
Race											
White	105,313,053	157,040	28,729	17.9	0.13	119,115	76.7	0.14	8,923	5.4	0.08
Black	14,056,560	27,262	5,409	19.8	0.34	20,281	75.0	0.36	1,517	5.2	0.15
Other	7,528,417	12,622	2,568	20.0	0.45	9,286	74.4	0.48	747	5.6	0.27
Ethnicity											
Non-Hispanic	111,862,532	163,004	29,600	17.9	0.13	123,769	76.7	0.14	9,343	5.4	0.07
Hispanic	15,035,498	33,920	7,106	20.7	0.32	24,913	74.3	0.32	1,844	5.0	0.15
Age group											
18–24	16,959,193	21,858	4,517	20.6	0.35	16,286	75.1	0.38	1,023	4.3	0.16
25–64	105,946,456	167,739	31,138	18.0	0.13	126,575	76.5	0.14	9,729	5.5	0.08
65 and older	3,992,381	7,327	1,051	14.6	0.52	5,821	79.3	0.56	435	6.1	0.33
Education[3]											
Less than HS	14,798,890	26,367	4,636	17.1	0.29	20,015	77.0	0.32	1,667	5.9	0.18
High school	36,048,733	54,264	9,416	17.1	0.22	41,650	77.4	0.23	3,096	5.6	0.13
More than HS	75,434,176	115,325	22,519	19.0	0.15	86,280	75.8	0.16	6,369	5.2	0.08
Insurance											
Insured	106,279,655	161,665	30,361	18.3	0.13	122,217	76.5	0.14	8,810	5.2	0.07
Uninsured	20,282,002	34,830	6,265	17.8	0.26	26,131	75.6	0.29	2,364	6.6	0.16

Source: Contract Report (March 2010). NORA Morbidity and Disability: The National Health Interview Survey (NHIS) 1997–2007. Department of Epidemiology and Public Health, University of Miami School of Medicine
The estimates from this table are based on a question from the National Health Interview Survey that asked respondents "Compared with 12 MONTHS AGO, would you say your health is (better, worse, or about the same)?
[1] Sample size from the National Health Interview Survey for the years 1997–2007
[2] Percent (prevalence) estimated from the National Health Interview Survey for the years 1997–2007
[3] Response categories include (1) less than High School graduate, (2) High School graduate or GED, and (3) Some college or higher education.

Table 4. Prevalence of a reported decline in health when compared to health status 12 months prior estimated for workers 18 years and older, Agriculture, Forestry, and Fishing sector, National Health Interview Survey, 1997–2007

Subgroup	US Estimated Worker Population	NHIS sample size[1]	Better			About the same			Worse		
			Number	Percent[2]	Standard error	Number	Percent[2]	Standard error	Number	Percent[2]	Standard error
All subgroups	2,694,267	4,378	703	15.3	0.66	3,466	80.3	0.73	202	4.4	0.33
Gender											
Male	2,088,446	3,367	520	14.8	0.75	2,693	81.1	0.85	150	4.1	0.38
Female	605,820	1,011	183	17.2	1.41	773	77.6	1.62	52	5.1	0.81
Race											
White	2,462,020	3,908	611	14.9	0.68	3,118	80.9	0.75	172	4.1	0.33
Black	95,149	184	29	17.8	3.41	139	74.7	3.67	16	7.5	2.14
Other	137,098	286	63	21.1	3.24	209	72.8	3.45	14	6.1	2.28
Ethnicity											
Non-Hispanic	2,014,159	2,839	421	14.7	0.75	2,266	80.6	0.85	147	4.7	0.40
Hispanic	680,108	1,539	282	17.2	1.23	1,200	79.3	1.37	55	3.5	0.59
Age group											
18–24	389,835	544	99	17.8	2.18	426	78.8	2.30	18	3.4	0.94
25–64	2,120,076	3,508	556	15.0	0.72	2,787	80.6	0.80	160	4.3	0.37
65 and older	184,356	326	48	13.5	2.00	253	79.7	2.42	24	6.8	1.63
Education[3]											
Less than HS	865,745	1,669	281	16.0	1.16	1,315	79.8	1.27	72	4.1	0.57
High school	843,218	1,254	171	13.4	1.18	1,014	81.7	1.36	65	4.9	0.70
More than HS	962,165	1,407	242	16.3	1.06	1,100	79.6	1.18	64	4.1	0.55
Insurance											
Insured	1,787,027	2,692	432	14.9	0.75	2,135	81.0	0.85	121	4.1	0.41
Uninsured	894,314	1,671	269	16.2	1.19	1,318	78.8	1.33	81	5.0	0.60

Source: Contract Report (March 2010). NORA Morbidity and Disability: The National Health Interview Survey (NHIS) 1997–2007. Department of Epidemiology and Public Health, University of Miami School of Medicine
The estimates from this table are based on a question from the National Health Interview Survey that asked respondents "Compared with 12 MONTHS AGO, would you say your health is (better, worse, or about the same)?
[1] Sample size from the National Health Interview Survey for the years 1997–2007
[2] Percent (prevalence) estimated from the National Health Interview Survey for the years 1997–2007
[3] Response categories include (1) less than High School graduate, (2) High School graduate or GED, and (3) Some college or higher education.

Table 5. Prevalence of fair or poor self-rated health status estimated for workers 18 years and older, All NORA sectors, National Health Interview Survey, 1997–2007

Subgroup	US Estimated Worker Population	NHIS sample size[1]	Excellent or Good			Fair or Poor		
			Number	Percent[2]	Standard error	Number	Percent[2]	Standard error
All subgroups	126,898,030	196,924	185,203	94.7	0.07	11,637	5.3	0.07
Gender								
Male	68,530,792	97,768	92,409	95.0	0.09	5,315	5.0	0.09
Female	58,367,238	99,156	92,794	94.3	0.09	6,322	5.7	0.09
Race								
White	105,313,053	157,040	148,561	95.1	0.07	8,419	4.9	0.07
Black	14,056,560	27,262	24,873	92.1	0.20	2,372	7.9	0.20
Other	7,528,417	12,622	11,769	93.9	0.28	846	6.1	0.28
Ethnicity								
Non-Hispanic	111,862,532	163,004	153,950	95.0	0.07	8,983	5.0	0.07
Hispanic	15,035,498	33,920	31,253	92.7	0.18	2,654	7.3	0.18
Age group								
18–24	16,959,193	21,858	21,162	97.3	0.12	693	2.7	0.12
25–64	105,946,456	167,739	157,494	94.5	0.07	10,171	5.5	0.07
65 and older	3,992,381	7,327	6,547	89.6	0.42	773	10.4	0.42
Education[3]								
Less than HS	14,798,890	26,367	23,175	88.8	0.24	3,177	11.2	0.24
High school	36,048,733	54,264	50,532	93.7	0.12	3,715	6.3	0.12
More than HS	75,434,176	115,325	110,627	96.4	0.07	4,658	3.6	0.07
Insurance								
Insured	106,279,655	161,665	153,036	95.2	0.07	8,564	4.8	0.07
Uninsured	20,282,002	34,830	31,762	91.9	0.18	3,052	8.1	0.18

Source: Contract Report (March 2010). NORA Morbidity and Disability: The National Health Interview Survey (NHIS) 1997–2007. Department of Epidemiology and Public Health, University of Miami School of Medicine
The estimates from this table are based on a question from the National Health Interview Survey that asked respondents "Would you say your health in general is excellent, very good, good, fair, or poor?"
[1] Sample size from the National Health Interview Survey for the years 1997–2007
[2] Percent (prevalence) estimated from the National Health Interview Survey for the years 1997–2007
[3] Response categories include (1) less than High School graduate, (2) High School graduate or GED, and (3) Some college or higher education.

Table 6. Prevalence of fair or poor self-rated health status estimated for workers 18 years and older, Agriculture, Forestry, and Fishing sector, National Health Interview Survey, 1997–2007

Subgroup	US Estimated Worker Population	NHIS sample size[1]	Excellent or Good			Fair or Poor		
			Number	Percent[2]	Standard error	Number	Percent[2]	Standard error
All subgroups	2,694,267	4,378	4,073	93.8	0.43	303	6.2	0.43
Gender								
Male	2,088,446	3,367	3,128	93.8	0.51	237	6.2	0.51
Female	605,820	1,011	945	93.8	0.86	66	6.2	0.86
Race								
White	2,462,020	3,908	3,666	94.3	0.44	240	5.7	0.44
Black	95,149	184	156	86.3	2.41	28	13.7	2.41
Other	137,098	286	251	89.8	2.08	35	10.2	2.08
Ethnicity								
Non-Hispanic	2,014,159	2,839	2,653	94.2	0.51	184	5.8	0.51
Hispanic	680,108	1,539	1,420	92.5	0.78	119	7.5	0.78
Age group								
18–24	389,835	544	523	97.0	0.76	21	3.0	0.76
25–64	2,120,076	3,508	3,257	93.5	0.49	249	6.5	0.49
65 and older	184,356	326	293	90.1	1.53	33	9.9	1.53
Education[3]								
Less than HS	865,745	1,669	1,483	89.0	0.92	185	11.0	0.92
High school	843,218	1,254	1,185	95.3	0.63	69	4.7	0.63
More than HS	962,165	1,407	1,361	96.9	0.48	45	3.1	0.48
Insurance								
Insured	1,787,027	2,692	2,533	94.9	0.49	158	5.1	0.49
Uninsured	894,314	1,671	1,525	91.5	0.88	145	8.5	0.88

Source: Contract Report (March 2010). NORA Morbidity and Disability: The National Health Interview Survey (NHIS) 1997–2007 Department of Epidemiology and Public Health, University of Miami School of Medicine
The estimates from this table are based on a question from the National Health Interview Survey that asked respondents "Would you say your health in general is excellent, very good, good, fair, or poor? "
[1] Sample size from the National Health Interview Survey for the years 1997–2007
[2] Percent (prevalence) estimated from the National Health Interview Survey for the years 1997–2007
[3] Response categories include (1) less than High School graduate, (2) High School graduate or GED, and (3) Some college or higher education.

Table 7. Mean number of bed disability days during the past 12 months estimated for workers 18 years and older, All NORA sectors, National Health Interview Survey, 1997–2007

Subgroup	US Estimated Worker Population	NHIS sample size[1]	Mean	95% confidence interval	Standard error
All subgroups	126,898,030	195,418	1.9	1.9--1.9	0.02
Gender					
Male	68,530,792	97,078	1.5	1.4--1.6	0.03
Female	58,367,238	98,340	2.4	2.3--2.5	0.04
Race					
White	105,313,053	155,967	1.9	1.9--1.9	0.03
Black	14,056,560	26,948	2.1	2.0--2.2	0.06
Other	7,528,417	12,503	1.6	1.4--1.8	0.09
Ethnicity					
Non-Hispanic	111,862,532	161,751	2.0	2.0--2.0	0.02
Hispanic	15,035,498	33,667	1.4	1.3--1.5	0.05
Age group					
18–24	16,959,193	21,700	1.9	1.8--2.0	0.07
25–64	105,946,456	166,457	1.9	1.9--1.9	0.03
65 and older	3,992,381	7,261	1.9	1.6--2.2	0.18
Education[2]					
Less than HS	14,798,890	26,119	1.9	1.7--2.1	0.08
High school	36,048,733	53,809	2.0	1.9--2.1	0.04
More than HS	75,434,176	114,659	1.9	1.9--1.9	0.02
Insurance					
Insured	106,279,655	160,491	1.9	1.9--1.9	0.02
Uninsured	20,282,002	34,516	2.0	1.9--2.1	0.06

Source: Contract Report (March 2010). NORA Morbidity and Disability: The National Health Interview Survey (NHIS) 1997–2007. Department of Epidemiology and Public Health, University of Miami School of Medicine

The estimates from this table are based on a question from the National Health Interview Survey that asked respondents "During the PAST 12 MONTHS ABOUT how many days did illness or injury keep you in bed for more than half the day? (include days while an overnight patient in a hospital)."

[1] Sample size from the National Health Interview Survey for the years 1997–2007

[2] Response categories include (1) less than High School graduate, (2) High School graduate or GED, and (3) Some college or higher education.

Table 8. Mean number of bed disability days during the past 12 months estimated for workers 18 years and older, Agriculture, Forestry, and Fishing sector, National Health Interview Survey, 1997–2007

Subgroup	US Estimated Worker Population	NHIS sample size[1]	Mean	95% confidence interval	Standard error
All subgroups	2,694,267	4,336	1.4	1.1–1.7	0.18
Gender					
Male	2,088,446	3,334	1.2	0.9–1.5	0.14
Female	605,820	1,002	2.3	1.1–3.5	0.61
Race					
White	2,462,020	3,876	1.4	1.0–1.8	0.19
Black	95,149	181	2.8	0.7–4.9	1.07
Other	137,098	279	0.9	0.5–1.3	0.18
Ethnicity					
Non-Hispanic	2,014,159	2,820	1.6	1.2–2.0	0.22
Hispanic	680,108	1,516	1.0	0.6–1.4	0.20
Age group					
18–24	389,835	536	1.7	0.8–2.6	0.46
25–64	2,120,076	3,475	1.4	1.0–1.8	0.20
65 and older	184,356	325	0.9	0.6–1.2	0.16
Education[2]					
Less than HS	865,745	1,649	1.1	0.7–1.5	0.20
High school	843,218	1,244	1.4	1.0–1.8	0.22
More than HS	962,165	1,402	1.8	1.0–2.6	0.40
Insurance					
Insured	1,787,027	2,676	1.6	1.1–2.1	0.25
Uninsured	894,314	1,645	1.1	0.7–1.5	0.18

Source: Contract Report (March 2010). NORA Morbidity and Disability: The National Health Interview Survey (NHIS) 1997–2007. Department of Epidemiology and Public Health, University of Miami School of Medicine

The estimates from this table are based on a question from the National Health Interview Survey that asked respondents "During the PAST 12 MONTHS ABOUT how many days did illness or injury keep you in bed for more than half the day? (include days while an overnight patient in a hospital)."

[1] Sample size from the National Health Interview Survey for the years 1997–2007
[2] Response categories include (1) less than High School graduate, (2) High School graduate or GED, and (3) Some college or higher education.

Table 9. Prevalence of having 2 or more bed disability days during the past 12 months estimated for workers 18 years and older, All NORA sectors, National Health Interview Survey, 1997–2007

Subgroup	US Estimated Worker Population	NHIS sample size[1]	0 Days			1 Day			2 or More Days		
			Number	Percent[2]	Standard error	Number	Percent[2]	Standard error	Number	Percent[2]	Standard error
All subgroups	126,898,030	196,924	123,857	63.5	0.18	21,082	11.2	0.10	50,479	25.3	0.15
Gender											
Male	68,530,792	97,768	67,050	68.5	0.23	9,911	10.7	0.14	20,117	20.8	0.19
Female	58,367,238	99,156	56,807	57.7	0.23	11,171	11.8	0.13	30,362	30.5	0.20
Race											
White	105,313,053	157,040	97,826	62.8	0.20	17,524	11.7	0.11	40,617	25.6	0.16
Black	14,056,560	27,262	17,546	66.3	0.40	2,365	8.9	0.22	7,037	24.8	0.33
Other	7,528,417	12,622	8,485	69.0	0.53	1,193	9.4	0.31	2,825	21.7	0.46
Ethnicity											
Non-Hispanic	111,862,532	163,004	99,786	62.3	0.19	18,266	11.6	0.11	43,699	26.1	0.16
Hispanic	15,035,498	33,920	24,071	72.6	0.36	2,816	8.5	0.20	6,780	19.0	0.29
Age group											
18–24	16,959,193	21,858	13,059	60.6	0.48	2,579	12.2	0.28	6,062	27.2	0.40
25–64	105,946,456	167,739	105,173	63.4	0.18	18,172	11.3	0.11	43,112	25.2	0.15
65 and older	3,992,381	7,327	5,625	77.6	0.57	331	4.8	0.31	1,305	17.5	0.52
Education[3]											
Less than HS	14,798,890	26,367	19,151	72.6	0.37	1,651	6.7	0.20	5,317	20.6	0.33
High school	36,048,733	54,264	35,467	65.7	0.29	5,167	10.0	0.16	13,175	24.3	0.25
More than HS	75,434,176	115,325	68,601	60.6	0.21	14,218	12.7	0.13	31,840	26.7	0.17
Insurance											
Insured	106,279,655	161,665	99,742	62.6	0.19	18,260	11.7	0.11	42,489	25.7	0.15
Uninsured	20,282,002	34,830	23,829	68.4	0.37	2,788	8.6	0.20	7,899	23.0	0.31

Source: Contract Report (March 2010). NORA Morbidity and Disability: The National Health Interview Survey (NHIS) 1997–2007. Department of Epidemiology and Public Health, University of Miami School of Medicine

The estimates from this table are based on a question from the National Health Interview Survey that asked respondents "During the PAST 12 MONTHS ABOUT how many days did illness or injury keep you in bed for more than half the day? (include days while an overnight patient in a hospital)."

[1] Sample size from the National Health Interview Survey for the years 1997–2007
[2] Percent (prevalence) estimated from the National Health Interview Survey for the years 1997–2007
[3] Response categories include (1) less than High School graduate, (2) High School graduate or GED, and (3) Some college or higher education.

Table 10. Prevalence of having 2 or more bed disability days during the past 12 months estimated for workers 18 years and older, Agriculture, Forestry, and Fishing sector, National Health Interview Survey, 1997–2007

Subgroup	US Estimated Worker Population	NHIS sample size[1]	0 Days			1 Day			2 or More Days		
			Number	Percent[2]	Standard error	Number	Percent[2]	Standard error	Number	Percent[2]	Standard error
All subgroups	2,694,267	4,378	3,309	75.2	0.83	268	6.7	0.44	759	18.1	0.76
Gender											
Male	2,088,446	3,367	2,625	77.8	0.90	189	6.2	0.48	520	16.1	0.81
Female	605,820	1,011	684	66.3	1.78	79	8.6	1.13	239	25.1	1.63
Race											
White	2,462,020	3,908	2,941	74.7	0.88	255	7.1	0.47	680	18.3	0.81
Black	95,149	184	139	77.9	3.82	6	3.5	1.43	36	18.6	3.74
Other	137,098	286	229	83.0	2.81	7	2.6	1.14	43	14.4	2.64
Ethnicity											
Non-Hispanic	2,014,159	2,839	2,032	72.2	1.02	212	7.7	0.56	576	20.1	0.94
Hispanic	680,108	1,539	1,277	84.2	1.19	56	3.8	0.57	183	12.0	1.10
Age group											
18–24	389,835	544	392	69.7	2.52	34	7.5	1.54	110	22.8	2.48
25–64	2,120,076	3,508	2,646	75.4	0.90	227	7.0	0.49	602	17.6	0.80
65 and older	184,356	326	271	84.4	1.88	7	1.9	0.73	47	13.7	1.76
Education[3]											
Less than HS	865,745	1,669	1,368	82.4	1.21	49	3.3	0.57	232	14.3	1.15
High school	843,218	1,254	939	74.2	1.44	84	7.5	0.85	221	18.3	1.27
More than HS	962,165	1,407	965	69.4	1.46	135	9.2	0.91	302	21.4	1.29
Insurance											
Insured	1,787,027	2,692	1,979	73.7	0.97	194	7.5	0.57	503	18.8	0.86
Uninsured	894,314	1,671	1,319	78.1	1.40	72	5.0	0.68	254	16.9	1.36

Source: Contract Report (March 2010). NORA Morbidity and Disability: The National Health Interview Survey (NHIS) 1997–2007. Department of Epidemiology and Public Health, University of Miami School of Medicine
The estimates from this table are based on a question from the National Health Interview Survey that asked respondents "During the PAST 12 MONTHS ABOUT how many days did illness or injury keep you in bed for more than half the day? (include days while an overnight patient in a hospital)."
[1] Sample size from the National Health Interview Survey for the years 1997–2007
[2] Percent (prevalence) estimated from the National Health Interview Survey for the years 1997–2007
[3] Response categories include (1) less than High School graduate, (2) High School graduate or GED, and (3) Some college or higher education.

Table 11. Mean number of work loss days during the past 12 months estimated for workers 18 years and older, All NORA sectors, National Health Interview Survey, 1997–2007

Subgroup	US Estimated Worker Population	NHIS sample size[1]	Mean	95% confidence interval	Standard error
All subgroups	126,898,030	194,982	3.9	3.8–4.0	0.04
Gender					
Male	68,530,792	96,875	3.5	3.4–3.6	0.06
Female	58,367,238	98,107	4.3	4.2–4.4	0.06
Race					
White	105,313,053	155,651	3.8	3.7–3.9	0.05
Black	14,056,560	26,852	4.5	4.3–4.7	0.12
Other	7,528,417	12,479	3.4	3.1–3.7	0.17
Ethnicity					
Non-Hispanic	111,862,532	161,408	3.9	3.8–4.0	0.04
Hispanic	15,035,498	33,574	3.3	3.1–3.5	0.10
Age group					
18–24	16,959,193	21,664	3.1	2.9–3.3	0.10
25–64	105,946,456	166,104	4.0	3.9–4.1	0.05
65 and older	3,992,381	7,214	3.6	3.2–4.0	0.21
Education[2]					
Less than HS	14,798,890	26,034	4.3	4.0–4.6	0.14
High school	36,048,733	53,655	4.4	4.2–4.6	0.09
More than HS	75,434,176	114,480	3.5	3.4–3.6	0.05
Insurance					
Insured	106,279,655	160,161	3.9	3.8–4.0	0.05
Uninsured	20,282,002	34,410	3.6	3.4–3.8	0.11

Source: Contract Report (March 2010). NORA Morbidity and Disability: The National Health Interview Survey (NHIS) 1997–2007. Department of Epidemiology and Public Health, University of Miami School of Medicine
The estimates from this table are based on a question from the National Health Interview Survey that asked respondents "During the PAST 12 MONTHS ABOUT how many days did you miss work at a job or business because of illness or injury (do not include matenity leave)?"
[1] Sample size from the National Health Interview Survey for the years 1997–2007
[2] Response categories include (1) less than High School graduate, (2) High School graduate or GED, and (3) Some college or higher education.

Table 12. Mean number of work loss days during the past 12 months estimated for workers 18 years and older, Agriculture, Forestry, and Fishing sector, National Health Interview Survey, 1997–2007

Subgroup	US Estimated Worker Population	NHIS sample size[1]	Mean	95% confidence interval	Standard error
All subgroups	2,694,267	4,321	3.6	2.9–4.3	0.34
Gender					
Male	2,088,446	3,326	3.2	2.6–3.8	0.33
Female	605,820	995	4.8	2.8–6.8	1.04
Race					
White	2,462,020	3,866	3.5	2.8–4.2	0.33
Black	95,149	177	3.5	1.4–5.6	1.09
Other	137,098	278	5.9	0–12.1	3.13
Ethnicity					
Non-Hispanic	2,014,159	2,808	4.1	3.2–5.0	0.45
Hispanic	680,108	1,513	2.0	1.4–2.6	0.31
Age group					
18–24	389,835	534	2.6	1.5–3.7	0.55
25–64	2,120,076	3,466	3.8	3.0–4.6	0.42
65 and older	184,356	321	3.5	2.1–4.9	0.71
Education[2]					
Less than HS	865,745	1,641	3.4	2.3–4.6	0.58
High school	843,218	1,239	3.5	2.5–4.5	0.51
More than HS	962,165	1,400	3.9	2.6–5.2	0.66
Insurance					
Insured	1,787,027	2,669	3.7	2.8–4.6	0.45
Uninsured	894,314	1,637	3.4	2.3–4.5	0.54

Source: Contract Report (March 2010). NORA Morbidity and Disability: The National Health Interview Survey (NHIS) 1997–2007.
Department of Epidemiology and Public Health, University of Miami School of Medicine
The estimates from this table are based on a question from the National Health Interview Survey that asked respondents "During the PAST 12 MONTHS ABOUT how many days did you miss work at a job or business because of illness or injury (do not include matenity leave)?"
[1] Sample size from the National Health Interview Survey for the years 1997–2007
[2] Response categories include (1) less than High School graduate, (2) High School graduate or GED, and (3) Some college or higher education.

Table 13. Prevalence of 6 or more work loss days during the past 12 months estimated for workers 18 years and older, All NORA sectors, National Health Interview Survey, 1997–2007

Subgroup	US Estimated Worker Population	NHIS sample size[1]	0 Days			1 Day			2–5 Days			6 or more Days		
			Number	Percent[2]	Standard error	Number	Percent[2]	Standard error	Number	Percent[2]	Standard error	Number	Percent[2]	Standard error
All subgroups	126,898,030	196,924	104,332	53.4	0.17	16,632	9.0	0.09	51,311	26.5	0.14	22,707	11.1	0.09
Gender														
Male	68,530,792	97,768	57,192	58.1	0.23	7,965	8.7	0.12	22,325	23.8	0.19	9,393	9.4	0.12
Female	58,367,238	99,156	47,140	48.0	0.23	8,667	9.3	0.12	28,986	29.8	0.19	13,314	13.0	0.13
Race														
White	105,313,053	157,040	82,562	52.8	0.19	14,038	9.4	0.09	41,315	26.8	0.15	17,736	10.9	0.10
Black	14,056,560	27,262	14,406	54.6	0.40	1,680	6.6	0.21	7,061	25.9	0.35	3,705	12.9	0.26
Other	7,528,417	12,622	7,364	59.9	0.57	914	7.2	0.26	2,935	23.5	0.49	1,266	9.4	0.32
Ethnicity														
Non-Hispanic	111,862,532	163,004	83,388	52.2	0.18	14,362	9.2	0.09	44,263	27.3	0.15	19,395	11.3	0.09
Hispanic	15,035,498	33,920	20,944	63.1	0.38	2,270	6.9	0.18	7,048	20.9	0.30	3,312	9.2	0.21
Age group														
18–24	16,959,193	21,858	11,158	51.2	0.43	2,146	10.3	0.27	6,138	28.6	0.38	2,222	9.9	0.25
25–64	105,946,456	167,739	88,002	53.1	0.18	14,205	8.9	0.09	44,184	26.7	0.15	19,713	11.3	0.10
65 and older	3,992,381	7,327	5,172	71.9	0.62	281	3.9	0.25	989	13.7	0.46	772	10.6	0.42
Education[3]														
Less than HS	14,798,890	26,367	16,642	62.7	0.40	1,419	5.8	0.19	4,907	19.8	0.30	3,066	11.7	0.25
High school	36,048,733	54,264	29,378	54.3	0.29	4,128	8.0	0.15	13,492	25.6	0.24	6,657	12.2	0.16
More than HS	75,434,176	115,325	57,769	51.2	0.20	11,047	10.1	0.11	32,757	28.3	0.17	12,907	10.4	0.11
Insurance														
Insured	106,279,655	161,665	82,525	51.9	0.18	14,439	9.4	0.09	44,063	27.4	0.15	19,134	11.3	0.10
Uninsured	20,282,002	34,830	21,555	61.6	0.35	2,163	6.5	0.17	7,148	21.8	0.28	3,544	10.1	0.22

Source: Contract Report (March 2010). NORA Morbidity and Disability: The National Health Interview Survey (NHIS) 1997–2007. Department of Epidemiology and Public Health, University of Miami School of Medicine
The estimates from this table are based on a question from the National Health Interview Survey that asked respondents "During the PAST 12 MONTHS ABOUT how many days did you miss work at a job or business because of illness or injury (do not include maternity leave)?"
[1] Sample size from the National Health Interview Survey for the years 1997–2007
[2] Percent (prevalence) estimated from the National Health Interview Survey for the years 1997–2007
[3] Response categories include (1) less than High School graduate, (2) High School graduate or GED, and (3) Some college or higher education.

Table 14. Prevalence of 6 or more work loss days during the past 12 months estimated for workers 18 years and older, Agriculture, Forestry, and Fishing sector, National Health Interview Survey, 1997–2007

Subgroup	US Estimated Worker Population	NHIS sample size[1]	0 Days			1 Day			2–5 Days			6 or more Days		
			Number	Percent[2]	Standard error	Number	Percent[2]	Standard error	Number	Percent[2]	Standard error	Number	Percent[2]	Standard error
All subgroups	2,694,267	4,378	3,070	69.6	0.88	211	5.2	0.40	656	16.3	0.72	384	8.8	0.53
Gender														
Male	2,088,446	3,367	2,419	71.2	1.02	165	5.2	0.44	457	15.1	0.79	285	8.5	0.63
Female	605,820	1,011	651	64.2	1.77	46	5.2	0.93	199	20.7	1.56	99	9.9	1.07
Race														
White	2,462,020	3,908	2,736	69.1	0.93	190	5.3	0.42	605	16.9	0.76	335	8.7	0.53
Black	95,149	184	125	70.8	4.35	9	5.6	2.05	22	12.7	2.95	21	11.0	2.80
Other	137,098	286	209	77.6	3.44	12	3.2	1.23	29	8.8	2.12	28	10.4	2.61
Ethnicity														
Non-Hispanic	2,014,159	2,839	1,887	66.6	1.12	156	5.8	0.52	477	17.6	0.86	288	10.0	0.67
Hispanic	680,108	1,539	1,183	78.6	1.15	55	3.4	0.58	179	12.4	1.03	96	5.5	0.69
Age group														
18–24	389,835	544	355	62.4	2.82	35	6.4	1.26	99	23.3	2.60	45	8.0	1.63
25–64	2,120,076	3,508	2,462	70.1	0.93	170	5.3	0.45	527	15.7	0.76	307	8.9	0.57
65 and older	184,356	326	253	79.1	2.65	6	2.1	0.89	30	8.9	1.83	32	9.9	1.78
Education[3]														
Less than HS	865,745	1,669	1,263	76.3	1.17	49	3.1	0.55	187	11.9	0.94	142	8.8	0.83
High school	843,218	1,254	880	68.6	1.67	58	5.2	0.70	187	16.7	1.40	114	9.5	1.00
More than HS	962,165	1,407	892	64.3	1.53	104	7.3	0.79	277	19.9	1.21	127	8.4	0.81
Insurance														
Insured	1,787,027	2,692	1,841	67.9	1.16	152	6.1	0.53	435	17.4	0.98	241	8.6	0.62
Uninsured	894,314	1,671	1,218	72.9	1.38	58	3.6	0.57	218	14.1	1.16	143	9.4	0.96

Source: Contract Report (March 2010). NORA Morbidity and Disability: The National Health Interview Survey (NHIS) 1997–2007. Department of Epidemiology and Public Health, University of Miami School of Medicine
The estimates from this table are based on a question from the National Health Interview Survey that asked respondents "During the PAST 12 MONTHS ABOUT how many days did you miss work at a job or business because of illness or injury (do not include maternity leave)?"
[1] Sample size from the National Health Interview Survey for the years 1997–2007
[2] Percent (prevalence) estimated from the National Health Interview Survey for the years 1997–2007
[3] Response categories include (1) less than High School graduate, (2) High School graduate or GED, and (3) Some college or higher education.

Table 15. Prevalence of health problems requiring the use of special equipment estimated for workers 18 years and older, All NORA sectors, National Health Interview Survey, 1997–2007

Subgroup	US Estimated Worker Population	NHIS sample size[1]	No			Yes		
			Number	Percent[2]	Standard error	Number	Percent[2]	Standard error
All subgroups	126,898,030	196,924	193,976	98.6	0.03	2,796	1.4	0.03
Gender								
Male	68,530,792	97,768	96,261	98.5	0.05	1,420	1.5	0.05
Female	58,367,238	99,156	97,715	98.7	0.04	1,376	1.3	0.04
Race								
White	105,313,053	157,040	154,619	98.6	0.04	2,302	1.4	0.04
Black	14,056,560	27,262	26,873	98.8	0.08	367	1.2	0.08
Other	7,528,417	12,622	12,484	99.0	0.10	127	1.0	0.10
Ethnicity								
Non-Hispanic	111,862,532	163,004	160,366	98.6	0.04	2,516	1.4	0.04
Hispanic	15,035,498	33,920	33,610	99.1	0.07	280	0.9	0.07
Age group								
18–24	16,959,193	21,858	21,713	99.4	0.07	132	0.6	0.07
25–64	105,946,456	167,739	165,273	98.6	0.04	2,343	1.4	0.04
65 and older	3,992,381	7,327	6,990	95.6	0.27	321	4.4	0.27
Education[3]								
Less than HS	14,798,890	26,367	26,039	98.8	0.09	302	1.2	0.09
High school	36,048,733	54,264	53,504	98.7	0.06	710	1.3	0.06
More than HS	75,434,176	115,325	113,492	98.6	0.04	1,765	1.4	0.04
Insurance								
Insured	106,279,655	161,665	159,074	98.5	0.04	2,470	1.5	0.04
Uninsured	20,282,002	34,830	34,478	99.1	0.07	321	0.9	0.07

Source: Contract Report (March 2010). NORA Morbidity and Disability: The National Health Interview Survey (NHIS) 1997–2007. Department of Epidemiology and Public Health, University of Miami School of Medicine
The estimates from this table are based on a question from the National Health Interview Survey that asked respondents "Do you now have any health problem that requires you to use special equipment, such as a cane, a wheelchair, a special bed, or a special telephone?"
[1] Sample size from the National Health Interview Survey for the years 1997–2007
[2] Percent (prevalence) estimated from the National Health Interview Survey for the years 1997–2007
[3] Respondents are asked the question "What is the higest level of education that you have completed. Analysis categories summarize the responses by (1) less than High School graduate, (2) High School graduate or GED, and (3) Some college or higher education.

Table 16. Prevalence of health problems requiring the use of special equipment estimated for workers 18 years and older, Agriculture, Forestry, and Fishing sector, National Health Interview Survey, 1997–2007

Subgroup	US Estimated Worker Population	NHIS sample size[1]	No			Yes		
			Number	Percent[2]	Standard error	Number	Percent[2]	Standard error
All subgroups	2,694,267	4,378	4,326	98.8	0.19	49	1.2	0.19
Gender								
Male	2,088,446	3,367	3,325	98.7	0.23	40	1.3	0.23
Female	605,820	1,011	1,001	99.1	0.30	9	0.9	0.30
Race								
White	2,462,020	3,908	3,862	98.8	0.20	43	1.2	0.20
Black	95,149	184	180	98.2	0.98	4	1.8	0.98
Other	137,098	286	284	98.8	0.88	2	1.2	0.88
Ethnicity								
Non-Hispanic	2,014,159	2,839	2,794	98.6	0.25	43	1.4	0.25
Hispanic	680,108	1,539	1,532	99.6	0.19	6	0.4	0.19
Age group								
18–24	389,835	544	539	99.4	0.32	4	0.6	0.32
25–64	2,120,076	3,508	3,474	99.0	0.20	33	1.0	0.20
65 and older	184,356	326	313	95.7	1.54	12	4.3	1.54
Education[3]								
Less than HS	865,745	1,669	1,653	98.8	0.38	15	1.2	0.38
High school	843,218	1,254	1,237	99.0	0.28	15	1.0	0.28
More than HS	962,165	1,407	1,388	98.7	0.31	19	1.3	0.31
Insurance								
Insured	1,787,027	2,692	2,649	98.4	0.28	42	1.6	0.28
Uninsured	894,314	1,671	1,662	99.6	0.17	7	0.4	0.17

Source: Contract Report (March 2010). NORA Morbidity and Disability: The National Health Interview Survey (NHIS) 1997–2007. Department of Epidemiology and Public Health, University of Miami School of Medicine
The estimates from this table are based on a question from the National Health Interview Survey that asked respondents "Do you now have any health problem that requires you to use special equipment, such as a cane, a wheelchair, a special bed, or a special telephone?"
[1] Sample size from the National Health Interview Survey for the years 1997–2007
[2] Percent (prevalence) estimated from the National Health Interview Survey for the years 1997–2007
[3] Respondents are asked the question "What is the higest level of education that you have completed. Analysis categories summarize the responses by (1) less than High School graduate, (2) High School graduate or GED, and (3) Some college or higher education.

Table 17. Prevalence of any functional limitations estimated for workers 18 years and older, All NORA sectors, National Health Interview Survey, 1997–2007

Subgroup	US Estimated Worker Population	NHIS sample size[1]	No			Yes		
			Number	Percent[2]	Standard error	Number	Percent[2]	Standard error
All subgroups	126,898,030	196,924	153,444	78.4	0.18	43,097	21.6	0.18
Gender								
Male	68,530,792	97,768	80,077	81.8	0.20	17,486	18.2	0.20
Female	58,367,238	99,156	73,367	74.4	0.23	25,611	25.6	0.23
Race								
White	105,313,053	157,040	121,278	77.6	0.20	35,476	22.4	0.20
Black	14,056,560	27,262	21,703	81.1	0.31	5,496	18.9	0.31
Other	7,528,417	12,622	10,463	84.1	0.45	2,125	15.9	0.45
Ethnicity								
Non-Hispanic	111,862,532	163,004	124,654	77.4	0.19	38,024	22.6	0.19
Hispanic	15,035,498	33,920	28,790	85.7	0.28	5,073	14.3	0.28
Age group								
18–24	16,959,193	21,858	19,261	88.1	0.31	2,570	11.9	0.31
25–64	105,946,456	167,739	130,063	77.7	0.19	37,362	22.3	0.19
65 and older	3,992,381	7,327	4,120	56.3	0.70	3,165	43.7	0.70
Education[3]								
Less than HS	14,798,890	26,367	20,694	78.2	0.39	5,616	21.8	0.39
High school	36,048,733	54,264	41,449	76.8	0.25	12,698	23.2	0.25
More than HS	75,434,176	115,325	90,523	79.2	0.20	24,613	20.8	0.20
Insurance								
Insured	106,279,655	161,665	124,931	77.9	0.18	36,414	22.1	0.18
Uninsured	20,282,002	34,830	28,153	80.9	0.34	6,614	19.1	0.34

Source: Contract Report (March 2010). NORA Morbidity and Disability: The National Health Interview Survey (NHIS) 1997-2007. Department of Epidemiology and Public Health, University of Miami School of Medicine

The estimates from this table are based on a question from the National Health Interview Survey that asked respondents Information on activity limitations. "How difficult it is for you to walk ¼ mile w/out special equipment; climb 10 steps w/o special equipment; stand 2 hours w/o special equipment; Sit 2 hours w/o special equipmentstoop, bend or kneel w/o special equipment; reach over w/o special equipment; grasp small objects w/o special equipment; lift/carry 10 lbs w/o special equipment; push large objects w/o special equipment; go out to events w/o special equipment; participate in social activities w/o special equipment; or relax at home w/o special equipment?"

[1] Sample size from the National Health Interview Survey for the years 1997–2007
[2] Percent (prevalence) estimated from the National Health Interview Survey for the years 1997–2007
[3] Respondents are asked the question "What is the higest level of education that you have completed. Analysis categories summarize the responses by (1) less than High School graduate, (2) High School graduate or GED, and (3) Some college or higher education.

Table 18. Prevalence of any functional limitations estimated for workers 18 years and older, Agriculture, Forestry, and Fishing sector, National Health Interview Survey, 1997–2007

Subgroup	US Estimated Worker Population	NHIS sample size[1]	No			Yes		
			Number	Percent[2]	Standard error	Number	Percent[2]	Standard error
All subgroups	2,694,267	4,378	3,533	79.7	0.90	840	20.3	0.90
Gender								
Male	2,088,446	3,367	2,778	81.5	1.01	584	18.5	1.01
Female	605,820	1,011	755	73.4	1.73	256	26.6	1.73
Race								
White	2,462,020	3,908	3,143	79.2	0.96	762	20.8	0.96
Black	95,149	184	149	83.7	3.55	34	16.3	3.55
Other	137,098	286	241	85.2	2.71	44	14.8	2.71
Ethnicity								
Non-Hispanic	2,014,159	2,839	2,124	75.6	1.09	712	24.4	1.09
Hispanic	680,108	1,539	1,409	91.6	0.79	128	8.4	0.79
Age group								
18–24	389,835	544	491	87.4	2.03	52	12.6	2.03
25–64	2,120,076	3,508	2,852	80.2	0.92	654	19.8	0.92
65 and older	184,356	326	190	57.2	2.96	134	42.8	2.96
Education[3]								
Less than HS	865,745	1,669	1,435	84.6	1.11	231	15.4	1.11
High school	843,218	1,254	962	76.6	1.65	290	23.4	1.65
More than HS	962,165	1,407	1,093	77.7	1.39	314	22.3	1.39
Insurance								
Insured	1,787,027	2,692	2,056	76.5	1.18	633	23.5	1.18
Uninsured	894,314	1,671	1,463	85.7	1.22	206	14.3	1.22

Source: Contract Report (March 2010). NORA Morbidity and Disability: The National Health Interview Survey (NHIS) 1997-2007. Department of Epidemiology and Public Health, University of Miami School of Medicine

The estimates from this table are based on a question from the National Health Interview Survey that asked respondents Information on activity limitations. "How difficult it is for you to walk ¼ mile w/out special equipment; climb 10 steps w/o special equipment; stand 2 hours w/o special equipment; Sit 2 hours w/o special equipmentstoop, bend or kneel w/o special equipment; reach over w/o special equipment; grasp small objects w/o special equipment; lift/carry 10 lbs w/o special equipment; push large objects w/o special equipment; go out to events w/o special equipment; participate in social activities w/o special equipment; or relax at home w/o special equipment?"

[1] Sample size from the National Health Interview Survey for the years 1997–2007
[2] Percent (prevalence) estimated from the National Health Interview Survey for the years 1997–2007
[3] Respondents are asked the question "What is the higest level of education that you have completed. Analysis categories summarize the responses by (1) less than High School graduate, (2) High School graduate or GED, and (3) Some college or higher education.

Table 19. Prevalence of hearing difficulty estimated for workers 18 years and older, All NORA sectors, National Health Interview Survey, 1997–2007

Subgroup	US Estimated Worker Population	NHIS sample size[1]	No			Yes		
			Number	Percent[2]	Standard error	Number	Percent[2]	Standard error
All subgroups	126,898,030	196,924	174,139	88.0	0.12	22,726	12.0	0.12
Gender								
Male	68,530,792	97,768	83,911	85.4	0.17	13,833	14.6	0.17
Female	58,367,238	99,156	90,228	91.0	0.13	8,893	9.0	0.13
Race								
White	105,313,053	157,040	136,854	86.8	0.14	20,136	13.2	0.14
Black	14,056,560	27,262	25,647	94.4	0.17	1,609	5.6	0.17
Other	7,528,417	12,622	11,638	92.3	0.32	981	7.7	0.32
Ethnicity								
Non-Hispanic	111,862,532	163,004	142,305	87.2	0.14	20,646	12.8	0.14
Hispanic	15,035,498	33,920	31,834	93.9	0.17	2,080	6.1	0.17
Age group								
18–24	16,959,193	21,858	20,603	94.2	0.20	1,250	5.8	0.20
25–64	105,946,456	167,739	148,440	87.7	0.13	19,250	12.3	0.13
65 and older	3,992,381	7,327	5,096	67.2	0.66	2,226	32.8	0.66
Education[3]								
Less than HS	14,798,890	26,367	23,552	88.2	0.27	2,809	11.8	0.27
High school	36,048,733	54,264	47,221	86.5	0.20	7,028	13.5	0.20
More than HS	75,434,176	115,325	102,518	88.6	0.14	12,776	11.4	0.14
Insurance								
Insured	106,279,655	161,665	142,257	87.6	0.13	19,357	12.4	0.13
Uninsured	20,282,002	34,830	31,504	89.9	0.23	3,319	10.1	0.23

Source: Contract Report (March 2010). NORA Morbidity and Disability: The National Health Interview Survey (NHIS) 1997–2007. Department of Epidemiology and Public Health, University of Miami School of Medicine

The estimates from this table are based on questions from the National Health Interview Survey that asked respondents "Which statement best describes your hearing (without a hearing aid): good, a little trouble, a lot of trouble, deaf?"

[1] Sample size from the National Health Interview Survey for the years 1997–2007
[2] Percent (prevalence) estimated from the National Health Interview Survey for the years 1997–2007
[3] Response categories include (1) less than High School graduate, (2) High School graduate or GED, and (3) Some college or higher education.

Table 20. Prevalence of hearing difficulty estimated for workers 18 years and older, Agriculture, Forestry, and Fishing sector, National Health Interview Survey, 1997–2007

Subgroup	US Estimated Worker Population	NHIS sample size[1]	No			Yes		
			Number	Percent[2]	Standard error	Number	Percent[2]	Standard error
All subgroups	2,694,267	4,378	3,713	83.6	0.78	665	16.4	0.78
Gender								
Male	2,088,446	3,367	2,809	82.0	0.95	558	18.0	0.95
Female	605,820	1,011	904	89.2	1.11	107	10.8	1.11
Race								
White	2,462,020	3,908	3,283	82.8	0.83	625	17.2	0.83
Black	95,149	184	171	94.4	1.51	13	5.6	1.51
Other	137,098	286	259	90.2	2.53	27	9.8	2.53
Ethnicity								
Non-Hispanic	2,014,159	2,839	2,257	79.9	0.90	582	20.1	0.90
Hispanic	680,108	1,539	1,456	94.7	0.78	83	5.3	0.78
Age group								
18–24	389,835	544	507	92.4	1.65	37	7.6	1.65
25–64	2,120,076	3,508	3,015	84.4	0.79	493	15.6	0.79
65 and older	184,356	326	191	55.7	2.85	135	44.3	2.85
Education[3]								
Less than HS	865,745	1,669	1,508	88.9	1.11	161	11.1	1.11
High school	843,218	1,254	1,005	80.3	1.22	249	19.7	1.22
More than HS	962,165	1,407	1,155	81.6	1.26	252	18.4	1.26
Insurance								
Insured	1,787,027	2,692	2,174	80.1	0.97	518	19.9	0.97
Uninsured	894,314	1,671	1,526	90.8	0.94	145	9.2	0.94

Source: Contract Report (March 2010). NORA Morbidity and Disability: The National Health Interview Survey (NHIS) 1997–2007. Department of Epidemiology and Public Health, University of Miami School of Medicine

The estimates from this table are based on questions from the National Health Interview Survey that asked respondents "Which statement best describes your hearing (without a hearing aid): good, a little trouble, a lot of trouble, deaf?"

[1] Sample size from the National Health Interview Survey for the years 1997–2007
[2] Percent (prevalence) estimated from the National Health Interview Survey for the years 1997–2007
[3] Response categories include (1) less than High School graduate, (2) High School graduate or GED, and (3) Some college or higher education.

Table 21. Prevalence of visual impairment estimated for workers 18 years and older, All NORA sectors, National Health Interview Survey, 1997–2007

Subgroup	US Estimated Worker Population	NHIS sample size[1]	No			Yes		
			Number	Percent[2]	Standard error	Number	Percent[2]	Standard error
All subgroups	126,898,030	196,924	183,289	93.3	0.09	13,537	6.7	0.09
Gender								
Male	68,530,792	97,768	92,232	94.5	0.10	5,496	5.5	0.10
Female	58,367,238	99,156	91,057	92.0	0.12	8,041	8.0	0.12
Race								
White	105,313,053	157,040	146,208	93.3	0.09	10,754	6.7	0.09
Black	14,056,560	27,262	25,255	93.1	0.19	1,990	6.9	0.19
Other	7,528,417	12,622	11,826	94.4	0.27	793	5.6	0.27
Ethnicity								
Non-Hispanic	111,862,532	163,004	151,389	93.2	0.09	11,530	6.8	0.09
Hispanic	15,035,498	33,920	31,900	94.3	0.18	2,007	5.7	0.18
Age group								
18–24	16,959,193	21,858	20,698	95.0	0.19	1,150	5.0	0.19
25–64	105,946,456	167,739	156,005	93.2	0.09	11,654	6.8	0.09
65 and older	3,992,381	7,327	6,586	90.0	0.42	733	10.0	0.42
Education[3]								
Less than HS	14,798,890	26,367	24,367	92.4	0.22	1,986	7.6	0.22
High school	36,048,733	54,264	50,331	93.0	0.14	3,904	7.0	0.14
More than HS	75,434,176	115,325	107,692	93.7	0.10	7,589	6.3	0.10
Insurance								
Insured	106,279,655	161,665	150,810	93.6	0.09	10,776	6.4	0.09
Uninsured	20,282,002	34,830	32,082	92.2	0.20	2,730	7.8	0.20

Source: Contract Report (March 2010). NORA Morbidity and Disability: The National Health Interview Survey (NHIS) 1997–2007. Department of Epidemiology and Public Health, University of Miami School of Medicine
The estimates from this table are based on questions from the National Health Interview Survey that asked respondents "Do you have trouble seeing, even when wearing glasses or contact lenses?; and, Are you blind or unable to see at all?"
[1] Sample size from the National Health Interview Survey for the years 1997–2007
[2] Percent (prevalence) estimated from the National Health Interview Survey for the years 1997–2007
[3] Response categories include (1) less than High School graduate, (2) High School graduate or GED, and (3) Some college or higher education.

Table 22. Prevalence of visual impairment estimated for workers 18 years and older, Agriculture, Forestry, and Fishing sector, National Health Interview Survey, 1997–2007

Subgroup	US Estimated Worker Population	NHIS sample size[1]	No			Yes		
			Number	Percent[2]	Standard error	Number	Percent[2]	Standard error
All subgroups	2,694,267	4,378	4,123	94.3	0.47	253	5.7	0.47
Gender								
Male	2,088,446	3,367	3,186	95.0	0.49	179	5.0	0.49
Female	605,820	1,011	937	91.7	1.13	74	8.3	1.13
Race								
White	2,462,020	3,908	3,695	94.5	0.46	211	5.5	0.46
Black	95,149	184	161	88.4	2.90	23	11.6	2.90
Other	137,098	286	267	93.4	2.68	19	6.6	2.68
Ethnicity								
Non-Hispanic	2,014,159	2,839	2,651	93.7	0.54	187	6.3	0.54
Hispanic	680,108	1,539	1,472	95.9	0.85	66	4.1	0.85
Age group								
18–24	389,835	544	523	96.5	0.91	21	3.5	0.91
25–64	2,120,076	3,508	3,314	94.5	0.49	192	5.5	0.49
65 and older	184,356	326	286	86.9	2.22	40	13.1	2.22
Education[3]								
Less than HS	865,745	1,669	1,570	93.9	0.86	98	6.1	0.86
High school	843,218	1,254	1,179	94.1	0.75	74	5.9	0.75
More than HS	962,165	1,407	1,327	94.6	0.67	80	5.4	0.67
Insurance								
Insured	1,787,027	2,692	2,539	94.5	0.52	152	5.5	0.52
Uninsured	894,314	1,671	1,569	93.6	0.84	101	6.4	0.84

Source: Contract Report (March 2010). NORA Morbidity and Disability: The National Health Interview Survey (NHIS) 1997–2007. Department of Epidemiology and Public Health, University of Miami School of Medicine
The estimates from this table are based on questions from the National Health Interview Survey that asked respondents "Do you have trouble seeing, even when wearing glasses or contact lenses?; and, Are you blind or unable to see at all?"
[1] Sample size from the National Health Interview Survey for the years 1997–2007
[2] Percent (prevalence) estimated from the National Health Interview Survey for the years 1997–2007
[3] Response categories include (1) less than High School graduate, (2) High School graduate or GED, and (3) Some college or higher education.

Table 23. Prevalence of cancer estimated for workers 18 years and older, All NORA sectors, National Health Interview Survey, 1997–2007

Subgroup	US Estimated Worker Population	NHIS sample size[1]	No			Yes		
			Number	Percent[2]	Standard error	Number	Percent[2]	Standard error
All subgroups	126,898,030	196,924	188,905	96.0	0.05	7,897	4.0	0.05
Gender								
Male	68,530,792	97,768	94,776	96.9	0.07	2,937	3.1	0.07
Female	58,367,238	99,156	94,129	95.0	0.09	4,960	5.0	0.09
Race								
White	105,313,053	157,040	149,793	95.6	0.06	7,152	4.4	0.06
Black	14,056,560	27,262	26,707	98.2	0.10	539	1.8	0.10
Other	7,528,417	12,622	12,405	98.5	0.13	206	1.5	0.13
Ethnicity								
Non-Hispanic	111,862,532	163,004	155,476	95.7	0.06	7,418	4.3	0.06
Hispanic	15,035,498	33,920	33,429	98.7	0.07	479	1.3	0.07
Age group								
18–24	16,959,193	21,858	21,640	99.1	0.07	210	0.9	0.07
25–64	105,946,456	167,739	161,134	96.0	0.06	6,501	4.0	0.06
65 and older	3,992,381	7,327	6,131	82.9	0.53	1,186	17.1	0.53
Education[3]								
Less than HS	14,798,890	26,367	25,636	97.3	0.12	714	2.7	0.12
High school	36,048,733	54,264	52,115	96.2	0.10	2,118	3.8	0.10
More than HS	75,434,176	115,325	110,215	95.7	0.07	5,041	4.3	0.07
Insurance								
Insured	106,279,655	161,665	154,453	95.7	0.06	7,112	4.3	0.06
Uninsured	20,282,002	34,830	34,028	97.8	0.09	780	2.2	0.09

Source: Contract Report (March 2010). NORA Morbidity and Disability: The National Health Interview Survey (NHIS) 1997–2007. Department of Epidemiology and Public Health, University of Miami School of Medicine

The estimates from this table are based on a question from the National Health Interview Survey that asked respondents "Have you EVER been told by a doctor or other health professional that you had cancer or a malignancy of any kind?"

[1] Sample size from the National Health Interview Survey for the years 1997–2007
[2] Percent (prevalence) estimated from the National Health Interview Survey for the years 1997–2007
[3] Response categories include (1) less than High School graduate, (2) High School graduate or GED, and (3) Some college or higher education.

Table 24. Prevalence of cancer estimated for workers 18 years and older, Agriculture, Forestry, and Fishing sector, National Health Interview Survey, 1997–2007

Subgroup	US Estimated Worker Population	NHIS sample size[1]	No			Yes		
			Number	Percent[2]	Standard error	Number	Percent[2]	Standard error
All subgroups	2,694,267	4,378	4,209	96.1	0.32	162	3.9	0.32
Gender								
Male	2,088,446	3,367	3,260	96.8	0.33	102	3.2	0.33
Female	605,820	1,011	949	93.8	0.86	60	6.2	0.86
Race								
White	2,462,020	3,908	3,749	96.0	0.35	154	4.0	0.35
Black	95,149	184	179	96.8	1.51	5	3.2	1.51
Other	137,098	286	281	98.5	1.10	3	1.5	1.10
Ethnicity								
Non-Hispanic	2,014,159	2,839	2,685	95.1	0.42	150	4.9	0.42
Hispanic	680,108	1,539	1,524	99.3	0.24	12	0.7	0.24
Age group								
18–24	389,835	544	543	99.6	0.41	1	0.4	0.41
25–64	2,120,076	3,508	3,395	96.7	0.34	106	3.3	0.34
65 and older	184,356	326	271	81.7	2.63	55	18.3	2.63
Education[3]								
Less than HS	865,745	1,669	1,636	98.0	0.39	30	2.0	0.39
High school	843,218	1,254	1,191	94.7	0.65	61	5.3	0.65
More than HS	962,165	1,407	1,336	95.6	0.56	70	4.4	0.56
Insurance								
Insured	1,787,027	2,692	2,549	94.9	0.45	139	5.1	0.45
Uninsured	894,314	1,671	1,645	98.4	0.37	23	1.6	0.37

Source: Contract Report (March 2010). NORA Morbidity and Disability: The National Health Interview Survey (NHIS) 1997–2007. Department of Epidemiology and Public Health, University of Miami School of Medicine
The estimates from this table are based on a question from the National Health Interview Survey that asked respondents "Have you EVER been told by a doctor or other health professional that you had cancer or a malignancy of any kind? "
[1] Sample size from the National Health Interview Survey for the years 1997–2007
[2] Percent (prevalence) estimated from the National Health Interview Survey for the years 1997–2007
[3] Response categories include (1) less than High School graduate, (2) High School graduate or GED, and (3) Some college or higher education.

Table 25. Prevalence of hypertension estimated for workers 18 years and older, All NORA sectors, National Health Interview Survey, 1997–2007

Subgroup	US Estimated Worker Population	NHIS sample size[1]	No			Yes		
			Number	Percent[2]	Standard error	Number	Percent[2]	Standard error
All subgroups	126,898,030	196,924	161,325	82.3	0.13	35,522	17.7	0.13
Gender								
Male	68,530,792	97,768	79,864	81.7	0.17	17,859	18.3	0.17
Female	58,367,238	99,156	81,461	83.0	0.16	17,663	17.0	0.16
Race								
White	105,313,053	157,040	130,025	82.8	0.14	26,956	17.2	0.14
Black	14,056,560	27,262	20,423	76.5	0.33	6,828	23.5	0.33
Other	7,528,417	12,622	10,877	86.1	0.41	1,738	13.9	0.41
Ethnicity								
Non-Hispanic	111,862,532	163,004	131,564	81.6	0.14	31,374	18.4	0.14
Hispanic	15,035,498	33,920	29,761	88.0	0.25	4,148	12.0	0.25
Age group								
18–24	16,959,193	21,858	20,803	95.4	0.18	1,046	4.6	0.18
25–64	105,946,456	167,739	136,687	81.4	0.14	30,987	18.6	0.14
65 and older	3,992,381	7,327	3,835	52.5	0.71	3,489	47.5	0.71
Education[3]								
Less than HS	14,798,890	26,367	21,495	81.7	0.32	4,859	18.3	0.32
High school	36,048,733	54,264	43,489	80.7	0.22	10,752	19.3	0.22
More than HS	75,434,176	115,325	95,554	83.2	0.15	19,733	16.8	0.15
Insurance								
Insured	106,279,655	161,665	130,659	81.3	0.14	30,947	18.7	0.14
Uninsured	20,282,002	34,830	30,291	87.5	0.25	4,522	12.5	0.25

Source: Contract Report (March 2010). NORA Morbidity and Disability: The National Health Interview Survey (NHIS) 1997–2007. Department of Epidemiology and Public Health, University of Miami School of Medicine
The estimates from this table are based on a question from the National Health Interview Survey that asked respondents "Have you EVER been told by a doctor or other health professional that you had hypertension, also called high blood pressure?"
[1] Sample size from the National Health Interview Survey for the years 1997–2007
[2] Percent (prevalence) estimated from the National Health Interview Survey for the years 1997–2007
[3] Response categories include (1) less than High School graduate, (2) High School graduate or GED, and (3) Some college or higher education.

Table 26. Prevalence of hypertension estimated for workers 18 years and older, Agriculture, Forestry, and Fishing sector, National Health Interview Survey, 1997–2007

Subgroup	US Estimated Worker Population	NHIS sample size[1]	No			Yes		
			Number	Percent[2]	Standard error	Number	Percent[2]	Standard error
All subgroups	2,694,267	4,378	3,662	83.5	0.75	709	16.5	0.75
Gender								
Male	2,088,446	3,367	2,820	83.8	0.85	540	16.2	0.85
Female	605,820	1,011	842	82.3	1.35	169	17.7	1.35
Race								
White	2,462,020	3,908	3,284	83.7	0.81	619	16.3	0.81
Black	95,149	184	136	77.4	2.69	47	22.6	2.69
Other	137,098	286	242	84.1	2.86	43	15.9	2.86
Ethnicity								
Non-Hispanic	2,014,159	2,839	2,262	80.9	0.94	571	19.1	0.94
Hispanic	680,108	1,539	1,400	91.0	1.01	138	9.0	1.01
Age group								
18–24	389,835	544	523	96.6	0.86	20	3.4	0.86
25–64	2,120,076	3,508	2,946	83.6	0.80	556	16.4	0.80
65 and older	184,356	326	193	54.8	3.19	133	45.2	3.19
Education[3]								
Less than HS	865,745	1,669	1,426	84.3	1.18	240	15.7	1.18
High school	843,218	1,254	1,023	81.9	1.36	228	18.1	1.36
More than HS	962,165	1,407	1,169	83.9	1.25	237	16.1	1.25
Insurance								
Insured	1,787,027	2,692	2,158	80.4	0.97	530	19.6	0.97
Uninsured	894,314	1,671	1,490	89.7	0.96	178	10.3	0.96

Source: Contract Report (March 2010). NORA Morbidity and Disability: The National Health Interview Survey (NHIS) 1997–2007. Department of Epidemiology and Public Health, University of Miami School of Medicine
The estimates from this table are based on a question from the National Health Interview Survey that asked respondents "Have you EVER been told by a doctor or other health professional that you had hypertension, also called high blood pressure?"
[1] Sample size from the National Health Interview Survey for the years 1997–2007
[2] Percent (prevalence) estimated from the National Health Interview Survey for the years 1997–2007
[3] Response categories include (1) less than High School graduate, (2) High School graduate or GED, and (3) Some college or higher education.

Table 27. Prevalence of heart disease estimated for workers 18 years and older, All NORA sectors, National Health Interview Survey, 1997–2007

Subgroup	US Estimated Worker Population	NHIS sample size[1]	No			Yes		
			Number	Percent[2]	Standard error	Number	Percent[2]	Standard error
All subgroups	126,898,030	196,924	184,045	93.5	0.07	12,815	6.5	0.07
Gender								
Male	68,530,792	97,768	91,420	93.5	0.10	6,314	6.5	0.10
Female	58,367,238	99,156	92,625	93.5	0.10	6,501	6.5	0.10
Race								
White	105,313,053	157,040	146,143	93.1	0.08	10,848	6.9	0.08
Black	14,056,560	27,262	25,774	95.0	0.17	1,477	5.0	0.17
Other	7,528,417	12,622	12,128	96.1	0.23	490	3.9	0.23
Ethnicity								
Non-Hispanic	111,862,532	163,004	151,396	93.1	0.08	11,554	6.9	0.08
Hispanic	15,035,498	33,920	32,649	96.4	0.13	1,261	3.6	0.13
Age group								
18–24	16,959,193	21,858	21,157	96.9	0.15	698	3.1	0.15
25–64	105,946,456	167,739	157,135	93.6	0.08	10,549	6.4	0.08
65 and older	3,992,381	7,327	5,753	77.3	0.57	1,568	22.7	0.57
Education[3]								
Less than HS	14,798,890	26,367	24,798	94.0	0.20	1,558	6.0	0.20
High school	36,048,733	54,264	50,797	93.6	0.13	3,450	6.4	0.13
More than HS	75,434,176	115,325	107,535	93.3	0.09	7,758	6.7	0.09
Insurance								
Insured	106,279,655	161,665	150,477	93.2	0.08	11,137	6.8	0.08
Uninsured	20,282,002	34,830	33,153	95.3	0.14	1,664	4.7	0.14

Source: Contract Report (March 2010). NORA Morbidity and Disability: The National Health Interview Survey (NHIS) 1997–2007. Department of Epidemiology and Public Health, University of Miami School of Medicine

The estimates from this table are based on a question from the National Health Interview Survey that asked respondents "Have you EVER been told by a doctor or other health professional that you had heart disease?. Based on NHIS questions of specific diseases: Coronary heart disease, Angina, Heart attack, or Any kind of heart condition or heart disease?

[1] Sample size from the National Health Interview Survey for the years 1997–2007
[2] Percent (prevalence) estimated from the National Health Interview Survey for the years 1997–2007
[3] Response categories include (1) less than High School graduate, (2) High School graduate or GED, and (3) Some college or higher education.

Table 28. Prevalence of heart disease estimated for workers 18 years and older, Agriculture, Forestry, and Fishing sector, National Health Interview Survey, 1997–2007

Subgroup	US Estimated Worker Population	NHIS sample size[1]	No			Yes		
			Number	Percent[2]	Standard error	Number	Percent[2]	Standard error
All subgroups	2,694,267	4,378	4,127	94.1	0.41	249	5.9	0.41
Gender								
Male	2,088,446	3,367	3,174	94.1	0.47	191	5.9	0.47
Female	605,820	1,011	953	93.8	0.89	58	6.2	0.89
Race								
White	2,462,020	3,908	3,679	93.9	0.43	228	6.1	0.43
Black	95,149	184	177	95.9	1.84	7	4.1	1.84
Other	137,098	286	271	95.3	1.90	14	4.7	1.90
Ethnicity								
Non-Hispanic	2,014,159	2,839	2,624	92.8	0.51	214	7.2	0.51
Hispanic	680,108	1,539	1,503	97.9	0.42	35	2.1	0.42
Age group								
18–24	389,835	544	535	98.5	0.57	9	1.5	0.57
25–64	2,120,076	3,508	3,332	94.7	0.44	174	5.3	0.44
65 and older	184,356	326	260	77.1	2.59	66	22.9	2.59
Education[3]								
Less than HS	865,745	1,669	1,596	95.2	0.69	72	4.8	0.69
High school	843,218	1,254	1,160	92.7	0.79	94	7.3	0.79
More than HS	962,165	1,407	1,326	94.3	0.65	81	5.7	0.65
Insurance								
Insured	1,787,027	2,692	2,499	92.6	0.55	192	7.4	0.55
Uninsured	894,314	1,671	1,613	96.9	0.47	57	3.1	0.47

Source: Contract Report (March 2010). NORA Morbidity and Disability: The National Health Interview Survey (NHIS) 1997–2007. Department of Epidemiology and Public Health, University of Miami School of Medicine
The estimates from this table are based on a question from the National Health Interview Survey that asked respondents "Have you EVER been told by a doctor or other health professional that you had heart disease?. Based on NHIS questions of specific diseases: Coronary heart disease, Angina, Heart attack, or Any kind of heart condition or heart disease?
[1] Sample size from the National Health Interview Survey for the years 1997–2007
[2] Percent (prevalence) estimated from the National Health Interview Survey for the years 1997–2007
[3] Response categories include (1) less than High School graduate, (2) High School graduate or GED, and (3) Some college or higher education.

Table 29. Prevalence of asthma estimated for workers 18 years and older, All NORA sectors, National Health Interview Survey, 1997–2007

Subgroup	US Estimated Worker Population	NHIS sample size[1]	No			Yes		
			Number	Percent[2]	Standard error	Number	Percent[2]	Standard error
All subgroups	126,898,030	196,924	178,336	90.6	0.09	18,462	9.4	0.09
Gender								
Male	68,530,792	97,768	90,054	91.9	0.11	7,653	8.1	0.11
Female	58,367,238	99,156	88,282	89.0	0.13	10,809	11.0	0.13
Race								
White	105,313,053	157,040	142,231	90.5	0.10	14,708	9.5	0.10
Black	14,056,560	27,262	24,540	90.4	0.24	2,705	9.6	0.24
Other	7,528,417	12,622	11,565	92.1	0.32	1,049	7.9	0.32
Ethnicity								
Non-Hispanic	111,862,532	163,004	146,836	90.2	0.10	16,056	9.8	0.10
Hispanic	15,035,498	33,920	31,500	93.1	0.21	2,406	6.9	0.21
Age group								
18–24	16,959,193	21,858	19,070	86.9	0.28	2,776	13.1	0.28
25–64	105,946,456	167,739	152,519	91.1	0.10	15,119	8.9	0.10
65 and older	3,992,381	7,327	6,747	92.1	0.37	567	7.9	0.37
Education[3]								
Less than HS	14,798,890	26,367	24,435	92.3	0.22	1,912	7.7	0.22
High school	36,048,733	54,264	49,653	91.4	0.15	4,581	8.6	0.15
More than HS	75,434,176	115,325	103,344	89.8	0.12	11,913	10.2	0.12
Insurance								
Insured	106,279,655	161,665	145,999	90.4	0.10	15,562	9.6	0.10
Uninsured	20,282,002	34,830	31,949	91.2	0.21	2,860	8.8	0.21

Source: Contract Report (March 2010). NORA Morbidity and Disability: The National Health Interview Survey (NHIS) 1997–2007. Department of Epidemiology and Public Health, University of Miami School of Medicine

The estimates from this table are based on a question from the National Health Interview Survey that asked respondents "Have you EVER been told by a doctor or other health professional that you had asthma?

[1] Sample size from the National Health Interview Survey for the years 1997–2007
[2] Percent (prevalence) estimated from the National Health Interview Survey for the years 1997–2007
[3] Response categories include (1) less than High School graduate, (2) High School graduate or GED, and (3) Some college or higher education.

Table 30. Prevalence of asthma estimated for workers 18 years and older, Agriculture, Forestry, and Fishing sector, National Health Interview Survey, 1997–2007

Subgroup	US Estimated Worker Population	NHIS sample size[1]	No			Yes		
			Number	Percent[2]	Standard error	Number	Percent[2]	Standard error
All subgroups	2,694,267	4,378	4,118	93.5	0.46	254	6.5	0.46
Gender								
Male	2,088,446	3,367	3,191	94.0	0.52	171	6.0	0.52
Female	605,820	1,011	927	91.6	0.96	83	8.4	0.96
Race								
White	2,462,020	3,908	3,678	93.4	0.49	227	6.6	0.49
Black	95,149	184	169	91.1	2.55	15	8.9	2.55
Other	137,098	286	271	96.5	1.26	12	3.5	1.26
Ethnicity								
Non-Hispanic	2,014,159	2,839	2,626	92.3	0.57	210	7.7	0.57
Hispanic	680,108	1,539	1,492	96.9	0.69	44	3.1	0.69
Age group								
18–24	389,835	544	498	89.5	1.85	45	10.5	1.85
25–64	2,120,076	3,508	3,311	94.1	0.47	193	5.9	0.47
65 and older	184,356	326	309	95.1	1.29	16	4.9	1.29
Education[3]								
Less than HS	865,745	1,669	1,599	94.8	0.81	67	5.2	0.81
High school	843,218	1,254	1,175	93.6	0.82	78	6.4	0.82
More than HS	962,165	1,407	1,299	92.2	0.84	108	7.8	0.84
Insurance								
Insured	1,787,027	2,692	2,511	93.0	0.58	179	7.0	0.58
Uninsured	894,314	1,671	1,592	94.4	0.83	75	5.6	0.83

Source: Contract Report (March 2010). NORA Morbidity and Disability: The National Health Interview Survey (NHIS) 1997–2007. Department of Epidemiology and Public Health, University of Miami School of Medicine
The estimates from this table are based on a question from the National Health Interview Survey that asked respondents "Have you EVER been told by a doctor or other health professional that you had asthma?
[1] Sample size from the National Health Interview Survey for the years 1997–2007
[2] Percent (prevalence) estimated from the National Health Interview Survey for the years 1997–2007
[3] Response categories include (1) less than High School graduate, (2) High School graduate or GED, and (3) Some college or higher education.

Table 31. Prevalence of diabetes estimated for workers 18 years and older, All NORA sectors, National Health Interview Survey, 1997–2007

Subgroup	US Estimated Worker Population	NHIS sample size[1]	No			Yes		
			Number	Percent[2]	Standard error	Number	Percent[2]	Standard error
All subgroups	126,898,030	196,924	187,575	96.1	0.05	7,783	3.9	0.05
Gender								
Male	68,530,792	97,768	92,999	95.9	0.08	4,032	4.1	0.08
Female	58,367,238	99,156	94,576	96.4	0.07	3,751	3.6	0.07
Race								
White	105,313,053	157,040	150,173	96.4	0.06	5,676	3.6	0.06
Black	14,056,560	27,262	25,401	94.4	0.17	1,591	5.6	0.17
Other	7,528,417	12,622	12,001	95.8	0.24	516	4.2	0.24
Ethnicity								
Non-Hispanic	111,862,532	163,004	155,300	96.2	0.06	6,384	3.8	0.06
Hispanic	15,035,498	33,920	32,275	95.9	0.13	1,399	4.1	0.13
Age group								
18–24	16,959,193	21,858	21,637	99.3	0.07	163	0.7	0.07
25–64	105,946,456	167,739	159,636	96.0	0.06	6,743	4.0	0.06
65 and older	3,992,381	7,327	6,302	87.8	0.46	877	12.2	0.46
Education[3]								
Less than HS	14,798,890	26,367	24,742	95.0	0.16	1,367	5.0	0.16
High school	36,048,733	54,264	51,490	95.9	0.10	2,297	4.1	0.10
More than HS	75,434,176	115,325	110,431	96.5	0.07	4,076	3.5	0.07
Insurance								
Insured	106,279,655	161,665	153,649	96.0	0.06	6,701	4.0	0.06
Uninsured	20,282,002	34,830	33,513	97.1	0.11	1,070	2.9	0.11

Source: Contract Report (March 2010). NORA Morbidity and Disability: The National Health Interview Survey (NHIS) 1997–2007. Department of Epidemiology and Public Health, University of Miami School of Medicine
The estimates from this table are based on a question from the National Health Interview Survey that asked respondents "Have you EVER been told by a doctor or other health professional that you have diabetes or sugar diabetes?
[1] Sample size from the National Health Interview Survey for the years 1997–2007
[2] Percent (prevalence) estimated from the National Health Interview Survey for the years 1997–2007
[3] Response categories include (1) less than High School graduate, (2) High School graduate or GED, and (3) Some college or higher education.

Table 32. Prevalence of diabetes estimated for workers 18 years and older, Agriculture, Forestry, and Fishing sector, National Health Interview Survey, 1997–2007

Subgroup	US Estimated Worker Population	NHIS sample size[1]	No			Yes		
			Number	Percent[2]	Standard error	Number	Percent[2]	Standard error
All subgroups	2,694,267	4,378	4,193	96.6	0.32	151	3.4	0.32
Gender								
Male	2,088,446	3,367	3,221	96.3	0.40	121	3.7	0.40
Female	605,820	1,011	972	97.5	0.49	30	2.5	0.49
Race								
White	2,462,020	3,908	3,749	96.7	0.33	129	3.3	0.33
Black	95,149	184	171	94.6	1.72	12	5.4	1.72
Other	137,098	286	273	96.6	1.33	10	3.4	1.33
Ethnicity								
Non-Hispanic	2,014,159	2,839	2,713	96.6	0.38	104	3.4	0.38
Hispanic	680,108	1,539	1,480	96.6	0.59	47	3.4	0.59
Age group								
18–24	389,835	544	541	99.8	0.14	3	0.2	0.14
25–64	2,120,076	3,508	3,370	96.8	0.36	110	3.2	0.36
65 and older	184,356	326	282	87.7	2.10	38	12.3	2.10
Education[3]								
Less than HS	865,745	1,669	1,588	95.6	0.58	68	4.4	0.58
High school	843,218	1,254	1,204	97.3	0.47	36	2.7	0.47
More than HS	962,165	1,407	1,355	96.8	0.57	46	3.2	0.57
Insurance								
Insured	1,787,027	2,692	2,557	95.9	0.46	111	4.1	0.46
Uninsured	894,314	1,671	1,621	97.9	0.40	40	2.1	0.40

Source: Contract Report (March 2010). NORA Morbidity and Disability: The National Health Interview Survey (NHIS) 1997–2007. Department of Epidemiology and Public Health, University of Miami School of Medicine
The estimates from this table are based on a question from the National Health Interview Survey that asked respondents "Have you EVER been told by a doctor or other health professional that you have diabetes or sugar diabetes?
[1] Sample size from the National Health Interview Survey for the years 1997–2007
[2] Percent (prevalence) estimated from the National Health Interview Survey for the years 1997–2007
[3] Response categories include (1) less than High School graduate, (2) High School graduate or GED, and (3) Some college or higher education.

Table 33. Prevalence of severe psychological distress estimated for workers 18 years and older, All NORA sectors, National Health Interview Survey, 1997–2007

Subgroup	US Estimated Worker Population	NHIS sample size[1]	No			Yes		
			Number	Percent[2]	Standard error	Number	Percent[2]	Standard error
All subgroups	126,898,030	196,924	194,031	99.5	0.02	1,200	0.5	0.02
Gender								
Male	68,530,792	97,768	96,329	99.6	0.02	449	0.4	0.02
Female	58,367,238	99,156	97,702	99.4	0.03	751	0.6	0.03
Race								
White	105,313,053	157,040	154,782	99.5	0.02	938	0.5	0.02
Black	14,056,560	27,262	26,877	99.5	0.05	173	0.5	0.05
Other	7,528,417	12,622	12,372	99.5	0.08	89	0.5	0.08
Ethnicity								
Non-Hispanic	111,862,532	163,004	160,715	99.5	0.02	875	0.5	0.02
Hispanic	15,035,498	33,920	33,316	99.2	0.06	325	0.8	0.06
Age group								
18–24	16,959,193	21,858	21,568	99.5	0.06	130	0.5	0.06
25–64	105,946,456	167,739	165,244	99.5	0.02	1,048	0.5	0.02
65 and older	3,992,381	7,327	7,219	99.7	0.08	22	0.3	0.08
Education[3]								
Less than HS	14,798,890	26,367	25,731	98.8	0.08	359	1.2	0.08
High school	36,048,733	54,264	53,394	99.5	0.03	356	0.5	0.03
More than HS	75,434,176	115,325	114,089	99.6	0.02	472	0.4	0.02
Insurance								
Insured	106,279,655	161,665	159,562	99.6	0.02	790	0.4	0.02
Uninsured	20,282,002	34,830	34,055	99.0	0.06	409	1.0	0.06

Source: Contract Report (March 2010). NORA Morbidity and Disability: The National Health Interview Survey (NHIS) 1997–2007. Department of Epidemiology and Public Health, University of Miami School of Medicine

The estimates from this table are based on a question from the National Health Interview Survey that asked how often respondents experienced certain symptoms of psychological distress during the past 30 days: "How oftern did you feel (1) so sad that nothing could cheer you up?; (2) nervous?; (3) restless or fidgety?; (4) hopeless?; (5) that everything was an effort ?; and worthless?" See Pratt LA, Dey AN, Cohen AJ. Characteristics of adults with serious psychological distress as measured by the K6 scale. United States, 2001–04. Advance data from vital and health statistics; No. 382. Hyattsville, MD: National Center for Health Statistics, 2007. DHHS Publication No. (PHS) 2007-1250.

[1] Sample size from the National Health Interview Survey for the years 1997–2007
[2] Percent (prevalence) estimated from the National Health Interview Survey for the years 1997–2007
[3] Response categories include (1) less than High School graduate, (2) High School graduate or GED, and (3) Some college or higher education.

Table 34. Prevalence of severe psychological distress estimated for workers 18 years and older, Agriculture, Forestry, and Fishing sector, National Health Interview Survey, 1997–2007

Subgroup	US Estimated Worker Population	NHIS sample size[1]	No			Yes		
			Number	Percent[2]	Standard error	Number	Percent[2]	Standard error
All subgroups	2,694,267	4,378	4,289	99.5	0.12	25	0.5	0.12
Gender								
Male	2,088,446	3,367	3,295	99.5	0.13	21	0.5	0.13
Female	605,820	1,011	994	99.5	0.26	4	0.5	0.26
Race								
White	2,462,020	3,908	3,833	99.5	0.12	20	0.5	0.12
Black	95,149	184	181	99.3	0.49	2	0.7	0.49
Other	137,098	286	275	99.2	0.48	3	0.8	0.48
Ethnicity								
Non-Hispanic	2,014,159	2,839	2,794	99.5	0.14	13	0.5	0.14
Hispanic	680,108	1,539	1,495	99.3	0.22	12	0.7	0.22
Age group								
18–24	389,835	544	532	99.3	0.46	3	0.7	0.46
25–64	2,120,076	3,508	3,434	99.5	0.12	21	0.5	0.12
65 and older	184,356	326	323	99.6	0.35	1	0.4	0.35
Education[3]								
Less than HS	865,745	1,669	1,631	99.3	0.19	13	0.7	0.19
High school	843,218	1,254	1,228	99.5	0.20	6	0.5	0.20
More than HS	962,165	1,407	1,389	99.6	0.22	5	0.4	0.22
Insurance								
Insured	1,787,027	2,692	2,645	99.5	0.15	14	0.5	0.15
Uninsured	894,314	1,671	1,630	99.4	0.19	11	0.6	0.19

Source: Contract Report (March 2010). NORA Morbidity and Disability: The National Health Interview Survey (NHIS) 1997–2007. Department of Epidemiology and Public Health, University of Miami School of Medicine
The estimates from this table are based on a question from the National Health Interview Survey that asked how often respondents experienced certain symptoms of psychological distress during the past 30 days: "How oftern did you feel (1) so sad that nothing could cheer you up?; (2) nervous?; (3) restless or fidgety?; (4) hopeless?; (5) that everything was an effort ?; and worthless?" See Pratt LA, Dey AN, Cohen AJ. Characteristics of adults with serious psychological distress as measured by the K6 scale. United States, 2001–04. Advance data from vital and health statistics; No. 382. Hyattsville, MD: National Center for Health Statistics, 2007. DHHS Publication No. (PHS) 2007-1250.
[1] Sample size from the National Health Interview Survey for the years 1997–2007
[2] Percent (prevalence) estimated from the National Health Interview Survey for the years 1997–2007
[3] Response categories include (1) less than High School graduate, (2) High School graduate or GED, and (3) Some college or higher education.

Table 35. Prevalence of not having seen a primary health care provider during the past 12 months estimated for workers 18 years and older, All NORA sectors, National Health Interview Survey, 1997–2007

Subgroup	US Estimated Worker Population	NHIS sample size[1]	Past 12 months			1 year or greater		
			Number	Percent[2]	Standard error	Number	Percent[2]	Standard error
All subgroups	126,898,030	196,924	136,250	69.8	0.18	59,536	30.2	0.18
Gender								
Male	68,530,792	97,768	55,443	58.7	0.24	41,710	41.3	0.24
Female	58,367,238	99,156	80,807	82.8	0.18	17,826	17.2	0.18
Race								
White	105,313,053	157,040	108,698	70.1	0.19	47,471	29.9	0.19
Black	14,056,560	27,262	19,731	71.3	0.37	7,353	28.7	0.37
Other	7,528,417	12,622	7,821	62.7	0.61	4,712	37.3	0.61
Ethnicity								
Non-Hispanic	111,862,532	163,004	117,104	71.8	0.17	44,965	28.2	0.17
Hispanic	15,035,498	33,920	19,146	55.2	0.45	14,571	44.8	0.45
Age group								
18–24	16,959,193	21,858	13,739	63.5	0.45	7,995	36.5	0.45
25–64	105,946,456	167,739	116,570	70.3	0.18	50,204	29.7	0.18
65 and older	3,992,381	7,327	5,941	82.3	0.53	1,337	17.7	0.53
Education[3]								
Less than HS	14,798,890	26,367	14,262	54.8	0.44	11,948	45.2	0.44
High school	36,048,733	54,264	36,098	66.8	0.29	17,854	33.2	0.29
More than HS	75,434,176	115,325	85,401	74.3	0.19	29,316	25.7	0.19
Insurance								
Insured	106,279,655	161,665	120,791	74.8	0.16	39,982	25.2	0.16
Uninsured	20,282,002	34,830	15,238	44.1	0.36	19,361	55.9	0.36

Source: Contract Report (March 2010). NORA Morbidity and Disability: The National Health Interview Survey (NHIS) 1997–2007. Department of Epidemiology and Public Health, University of Miami School of Medicine

The estimates from this table are based on a question from the National Health Interview Survey that asked respondents "During the past 12 months, have you seen a primary health care provider (any of the following): Ob/GYN , general doctor?"

[1] Sample size from the National Health Interview Survey for the years 1997–2007
[2] Percent (prevalence) estimated from the National Health Interview Survey for the years 1997–2007
[3] Response categories include (1) less than High School graduate, (2) High School graduate or GED, and (3) Some college or higher education.

Table 36. Prevalence of not having seen a primary health care provider during the past 12 months estimated for workers 18 years and older, Agriculture, Forestry, and Fishing sector, National Health Interview Survey, 1997–2007

Subgroup	US Estimated Worker Population	NHIS sample size[1]	Past 12 months			1 year or greater		
			Number	Percent[2]	Standard error	Number	Percent[2]	Standard error
All subgroups	2,694,267	4,378	2,219	53.9	1.05	2,135	46.1	1.05
Gender								
Male	2,088,446	3,367	1,497	48.2	1.19	1,851	51.8	1.19
Female	605,820	1,011	722	73.5	1.69	284	26.5	1.69
Race								
White	2,462,020	3,908	2,023	54.7	1.10	1,862	45.3	1.10
Black	95,149	184	87	48.5	4.03	97	51.5	4.03
Other	137,098	286	109	42.5	3.62	176	57.5	3.62
Ethnicity								
Non-Hispanic	2,014,159	2,839	1,710	61.2	1.18	1,118	38.8	1.18
Hispanic	680,108	1,539	509	32.2	1.46	1,017	67.8	1.46
Age group								
18–24	389,835	544	217	47.4	2.76	324	52.6	2.76
25–64	2,120,076	3,508	1,758	53.0	1.15	1,731	47.0	1.15
65 and older	184,356	326	244	78.4	2.47	80	21.6	2.47
Education[3]								
Less than HS	865,745	1,669	633	40.3	1.64	1,027	59.7	1.64
High school	843,218	1,254	694	57.3	1.65	549	42.7	1.65
More than HS	962,165	1,407	876	63.6	1.70	529	36.4	1.70
Insurance								
Insured	1,787,027	2,692	1,717	65.2	1.17	965	34.8	1.17
Uninsured	894,314	1,671	496	31.5	1.48	1,161	68.5	1.48

Source: Contract Report (March 2010). NORA Morbidity and Disability: The National Health Interview Survey (NHIS) 1997–2007. Department of Epidemiology and Public Health, University of Miami School of Medicine
The estimates from this table are based on a question from the National Health Interview Survey that asked respondents "During the past 12 months, have you seen a primary health care provider (any of the following): Ob/GYN , general doctor?"
[1] Sample size from the National Health Interview Survey for the years 1997–2007
[2] Percent (prevalence) estimated from the National Health Interview Survey for the years 1997–2007
[3] Response categories include (1) less than High School graduate, (2) High School graduate or GED, and (3) Some college or higher education.

Table 37. Prevalence of no dentist contact during the past year estimated for workers 18 years and older, All NORA sectors, National Health Interview Survey, 1997–2007

Subgroup	US Estimated Worker Population	NHIS sample size[1]	Past year			1 year or greater		
			Number	Percent[2]	Standard error	Number	Percent[2]	Standard error
All subgroups	126,898,030	196,924	125,540	65.8	0.20	69,530	34.2	0.20
Gender								
Male	68,530,792	97,768	57,405	61.4	0.26	39,340	38.6	0.26
Female	58,367,238	99,156	68,135	71.0	0.22	30,190	29.0	0.22
Race								
White	105,313,053	157,040	102,144	67.0	0.22	53,528	33.0	0.22
Black	14,056,560	27,262	16,025	59.8	0.47	10,892	40.2	0.47
Other	7,528,417	12,622	7,371	60.7	0.62	5,110	39.3	0.62
Ethnicity								
Non-Hispanic	111,862,532	163,004	108,733	67.9	0.20	52,768	32.1	0.20
Hispanic	15,035,498	33,920	16,807	50.2	0.49	16,762	49.8	0.49
Age group								
18–24	16,959,193	21,858	12,653	60.4	0.47	8,982	39.6	0.47
25–64	105,946,456	167,739	108,270	66.7	0.20	57,933	33.3	0.20
65 and older	3,992,381	7,327	4,617	65.1	0.71	2,615	34.9	0.71
Education[3]								
Less than HS	14,798,890	26,367	10,743	42.9	0.43	15,321	57.1	0.43
High school	36,048,733	54,264	31,151	58.9	0.30	22,524	41.1	0.30
More than HS	75,434,176	115,325	83,235	73.7	0.19	31,259	26.3	0.19
Insurance								
Insured	106,279,655	161,665	112,993	71.4	0.19	47,278	28.6	0.19
Uninsured	20,282,002	34,830	12,331	36.5	0.35	22,064	63.5	0.35

Source: Contract Report (March 2010). NORA Morbidity and Disability: The National Health Interview Survey (NHIS) 1997–2007. Department of Epidemiology and Public Health, University of Miami School of Medicine

The estimates from this table are based on a question from the National Health Interview Survey that asked respondents "About how long has it been since you last saw or talked to a dentist? Include all types of dentists, such as orthodontists, oral surgeons, and all other dental specialists, as well as dental hygienists."

[1] Sample size from the National Health Interview Survey for the years 1997–2007
[2] Percent (prevalence) estimated from the National Health Interview Survey for the years 1997–2007
[3] Response categories include (1) less than High School graduate, (2) High School graduate or GED, and (3) Some college or higher education.

Table 38. Prevalence of no dentist contact during the past year estimated for workers 18 years and older, Agriculture, Forestry, and Fishing sector, National Health Interview Survey, 1997–2007

Subgroup	US Estimated Worker Population	NHIS sample size[1]	Past year			1 year or greater		
			Number	Percent[2]	Standard error	Number	Percent[2]	Standard error
All subgroups	2,694,267	4,378	1,967	49.7	1.03	2,351	50.3	1.03
Gender								
Male	2,088,446	3,367	1,366	45.5	1.17	1,950	54.5	1.17
Female	605,820	1,011	601	64.4	1.80	401	35.6	1.80
Race								
White	2,462,020	3,908	1,805	50.9	1.07	2,050	49.1	1.07
Black	95,149	184	60	38.6	4.29	122	61.4	4.29
Other	137,098	286	102	37.0	3.78	179	63.0	3.78
Ethnicity								
Non-Hispanic	2,014,159	2,839	1,558	57.1	1.12	1,247	42.9	1.12
Hispanic	680,108	1,539	409	27.8	1.61	1,104	72.2	1.61
Age group								
18–24	389,835	544	215	48.9	2.82	320	51.1	2.82
25–64	2,120,076	3,508	1,585	49.4	1.09	1,876	50.6	1.09
65 and older	184,356	326	167	55.4	3.06	155	44.6	3.06
Education[3]								
Less than HS	865,745	1,669	441	29.9	1.58	1,208	70.1	1.58
High school	843,218	1,254	604	51.5	1.71	626	48.5	1.71
More than HS	962,165	1,407	912	66.3	1.48	486	33.7	1.48
Insurance								
Insured	1,787,027	2,692	1,537	60.3	1.17	1,124	39.7	1.17
Uninsured	894,314	1,671	424	28.6	1.54	1,219	71.4	1.54

Source: Contract Report (March 2010). NORA Morbidity and Disability: The National Health Interview Survey (NHIS) 1997–2007. Department of Epidemiology and Public Health, University of Miami School of Medicine
The estimates from this table are based on a question from the National Health Interview Survey that asked respondents "About how long has it been since you last saw or talked to a dentist? Include all types of dentists, such as orthodontists, oral surgeons, and all other dental specialists, as well as dental hygienists."
[1] Sample size from the National Health Interview Survey for the years 1997–2007
[2] Percent (prevalence) estimated from the National Health Interview Survey for the years 1997–2007
[3] Response categories include (1) less than High School graduate, (2) High School graduate or GED, and (3) Some college or higher education.

Table 39. Prevalence of surgery during the past 12 months estimated for workers 18 years and older, All NORA sectors, National Health Interview Survey, 1997–2007

Subgroup	US Estimated Worker Population	NHIS sample size[1]	1 year or greater			Past 12 months		
			Number	Percent[2]	Standard error	Number	Percent[2]	Standard error
All subgroups	126,898,030	196,924	175,240	89.2	0.10	20,586	10.8	0.10
Gender								
Male	68,530,792	97,768	88,896	91.0	0.12	8,305	9.0	0.12
Female	58,367,238	99,156	86,344	87.2	0.13	12,281	12.8	0.13
Race								
White	105,313,053	157,040	138,866	88.7	0.10	17,340	11.3	0.10
Black	14,056,560	27,262	24,718	91.5	0.22	2,360	8.5	0.22
Other	7,528,417	12,622	11,656	93.1	0.30	886	6.9	0.30
Ethnicity								
Non-Hispanic	111,862,532	163,004	143,682	88.6	0.10	18,419	11.4	0.10
Hispanic	15,035,498	33,920	31,558	93.8	0.17	2,167	6.2	0.17
Age group								
18–24	16,959,193	21,858	19,811	91.0	0.24	1,931	9.0	0.24
25–64	105,946,456	167,739	149,354	89.2	0.10	17,454	10.8	0.10
65 and older	3,992,381	7,327	6,075	82.4	0.53	1,201	17.6	0.53
Education[3]								
Less than HS	14,798,890	26,367	24,349	92.5	0.22	1,869	7.5	0.22
High school	36,048,733	54,264	48,552	89.7	0.16	5,417	10.3	0.16
More than HS	75,434,176	115,325	101,471	88.4	0.12	13,244	11.6	0.12
Insurance								
Insured	106,279,655	161,665	141,965	88.2	0.11	18,824	11.8	0.11
Uninsured	20,282,002	34,830	32,893	94.8	0.15	1,728	5.2	0.15

Source: Contract Report (March 2010). NORA Morbidity and Disability: The National Health Interview Survey (NHIS) 1997–2007. Department of Epidemiology and Public Health, University of Miami School of Medicine

The estimates from this table are based on a question from the National Health Interview Survey that asked respondents "During the PAST 12 MONTHS have you had SURGERY or other surgical procedures either as an inpatient or an outpatient? This includes both major surgery and minor procedures such as setting bones or removing growths."

[1] Sample size from the National Health Interview Survey for the years 1997–2007
[2] Percent (prevalence) estimated from the National Health Interview Survey for the years 1997–2007
[3] Response categories include (1) less than High School graduate, (2) High School graduate or GED, and (3) Some college or higher education.

Table 40. Prevalence of surgery during the past 12 months estimated for workers 18 years and older, Agriculture, Forestry, and Fishing sector, National Health Interview Survey, 1997–2007

Subgroup	US Estimated Worker Population	NHIS sample size[1]	1 year or greater			Past 12 months		
			Number	Percent[2]	Standard error	Number	Percent[2]	Standard error
All subgroups	2,694,267	4,378	4,021	91.6	0.54	337	8.4	0.54
Gender								
Male	2,088,446	3,367	3,133	92.7	0.57	219	7.3	0.57
Female	605,820	1,011	888	87.7	1.20	118	12.3	1.20
Race								
White	2,462,020	3,908	3,577	91.4	0.57	311	8.6	0.57
Black	95,149	184	169	91.0	2.55	15	9.0	2.55
Other	137,098	286	275	96.1	1.31	11	3.9	1.31
Ethnicity								
Non-Hispanic	2,014,159	2,839	2,550	89.8	0.69	279	10.2	0.69
Hispanic	680,108	1,539	1,471	96.8	0.48	58	3.2	0.48
Age group								
18–24	389,835	544	506	91.2	1.89	34	8.8	1.89
25–64	2,120,076	3,508	3,245	92.4	0.53	249	7.6	0.53
65 and older	184,356	326	270	82.6	2.15	54	17.4	2.15
Education[3]								
Less than HS	865,745	1,669	1,595	96.2	0.55	66	3.8	0.55
High school	843,218	1,254	1,130	89.4	1.08	116	10.6	1.08
More than HS	962,165	1,407	1,251	89.2	0.92	154	10.8	0.92
Insurance								
Insured	1,787,027	2,692	2,398	89.3	0.71	285	10.7	0.71
Uninsured	894,314	1,671	1,608	96.1	0.62	52	3.9	0.62

Source: Contract Report (March 2010). NORA Morbidity and Disability: The National Health Interview Survey (NHIS) 1997–2007. Department of Epidemiology and Public Health, University of Miami School of Medicine

The estimates from this table are based on a question from the National Health Interview Survey that asked respondents "During the PAST 12 MONTHS have you had SURGERY or other surgical procedures either as an inpatient or an outpatient? This includes both major surgery and minor procedures such as setting bones or removing growths."

[1] Sample size from the National Health Interview Survey for the years 1997–2007
[2] Percent (prevalence) estimated from the National Health Interview Survey for the years 1997–2007
[3] Response categories include (1) less than High School graduate, (2) High School graduate or GED, and (3) Some college or higher education.

Table 41. Prevalence of hospital emergency room visit during the past 12 months estimated for workers 18 years and older, All NORA sectors, National Health Interview Survey, 1997–2007

Subgroup	US Estimated Worker Population	NHIS sample size[1]	No Visits			1 or more Visits		
			Number	Percent[2]	Standard error	Number	Percent[2]	Standard error
All subgroups	126,898,030	196,924	161,854	82.4	0.11	35,070	17.6	0.11
Gender								
Male	68,530,792	97,768	81,835	83.4	0.14	15,933	16.6	0.14
Female	58,367,238	99,156	80,019	81.2	0.15	19,137	18.8	0.15
Race								
White	105,313,053	157,040	130,438	82.9	0.12	26,602	17.1	0.12
Black	14,056,560	27,262	20,754	76.6	0.32	6,508	23.4	0.32
Other	7,528,417	12,622	10,662	85.5	0.39	1,960	14.5	0.39
Ethnicity								
Non-Hispanic	111,862,532	163,004	133,260	82.0	0.12	29,744	18.0	0.12
Hispanic	15,035,498	33,920	28,594	84.8	0.27	5,326	15.2	0.27
Age group								
18–24	16,959,193	21,858	16,571	75.8	0.36	5,287	24.2	0.36
25–64	105,946,456	167,739	139,210	83.4	0.11	28,529	16.6	0.11
65 and older	3,992,381	7,327	6,073	82.8	0.51	1,254	17.2	0.51
Education[3]								
Less than HS	14,798,890	26,367	21,288	80.2	0.31	5,079	19.8	0.31
High school	36,048,733	54,264	43,936	81.0	0.19	10,328	19.0	0.19
More than HS	75,434,176	115,325	95,860	83.5	0.13	19,465	16.5	0.13
Insurance								
Insured	106,279,655	161,665	132,978	82.6	0.12	28,687	17.4	0.12
Uninsured	20,282,002	34,830	28,527	81.4	0.27	6,303	18.6	0.27

Source: Contract Report (March 2010). NORA Morbidity and Disability: The National Health Interview Survey (NHIS) 1997–2007. Department of Epidemiology and Public Health, University of Miami School of Medicine
The estimates from this table are based on a question from the National Health Interview Survey that asked respondents "During the PAST 12 MONTHS HOW MANY TIMES have you gone to a HOSPITAL EMERGENCY ROOM for your health?"
[1] Sample size from the National Health Interview Survey for the years 1997–2007
[2] Percent (prevalence) estimated from the National Health Interview Survey for the years 1997–2007
[3] Response categories include (1) less than High School graduate, (2) High School graduate or GED, and (3) Some college or higher education.

Table 42. Prevalence of hospital emergency room visit during the past 12 months estimated for workers 18 years and older, Agriculture, Forestry, and Fishing sector, National Health Interview Survey, 1997–2007

Subgroup	US Estimated Worker Population	NHIS sample size[1]	No Visits			1 or more Visits		
			Number	Percent[2]	Standard error	Number	Percent[2]	Standard error
All subgroups	2,694,267	4,378	3,757	85.4	0.61	621	14.6	0.61
Gender								
Male	2,088,446	3,367	2,907	85.8	0.67	460	14.2	0.67
Female	605,820	1,011	850	84.0	1.32	161	16.0	1.32
Race								
White	2,462,020	3,908	3,373	85.9	0.64	535	14.1	0.64
Black	95,149	184	135	73.2	3.78	49	26.8	3.78
Other	137,098	286	249	85.5	2.87	37	14.5	2.87
Ethnicity								
Non-Hispanic	2,014,159	2,839	2,383	83.9	0.73	456	16.1	0.73
Hispanic	680,108	1,539	1,374	89.9	1.00	165	10.1	1.00
Age group								
18–24	389,835	544	456	82.8	2.12	88	17.2	2.12
25–64	2,120,076	3,508	3,023	85.7	0.66	485	14.3	0.66
65 and older	184,356	326	278	87.4	1.56	48	12.6	1.56
Education[3]								
Less than HS	865,745	1,669	1,469	87.3	1.01	200	12.7	1.01
High school	843,218	1,254	1,037	82.6	1.15	217	17.4	1.15
More than HS	962,165	1,407	1,212	86.1	0.98	195	13.9	0.98
Insurance								
Insured	1,787,027	2,692	2,288	85.0	0.73	404	15.0	0.73
Uninsured	894,314	1,671	1,454	86.0	1.13	217	14.0	1.13

Source: Contract Report (March 2010). NORA Morbidity and Disability: The National Health Interview Survey (NHIS) 1997–2007. Department of Epidemiology and Public Health, University of Miami School of Medicine
The estimates from this table are based on a question from the National Health Interview Survey that asked respondents "During the PAST 12 MONTHS HOW MANY TIMES have you gone to a HOSPITAL EMERGENCY ROOM for your health?"
[1] Sample size from the National Health Interview Survey for the years 1997–2007
[2] Percent (prevalence) estimated from the National Health Interview Survey for the years 1997–2007
[3] Response categories include (1) less than High School graduate, (2) High School graduate or GED, and (3) Some college or higher education.

Table 43. Prevalence of current smokers estimated for workers 18 years and older, All NORA sectors, National Health Interview Survey, 1997–2007

Subgroup	US Estimated Worker Population	NHIS sample size[1]	Current			Former			Never		
			Number	Percent[2]	Standard error	Number	Percent[2]	Standard error	Number	Percent[2]	Standard error
All subgroups	126,898,030	196,924	47,553	23.8	0.17	37,470	19.6	0.13	110,816	56.6	0.19
Gender											
Male	68,530,792	97,768	25,797	25.7	0.21	21,014	21.7	0.17	50,345	52.6	0.23
Female	58,367,238	99,156	21,756	21.5	0.20	16,456	17.2	0.17	60,471	61.3	0.24
Race											
White	105,313,053	157,040	38,967	24.4	0.18	32,365	21.1	0.14	84,879	54.5	0.20
Black	14,056,560	27,262	6,099	21.6	0.39	3,376	12.1	0.24	17,590	66.3	0.41
Other	7,528,417	12,622	2,487	18.6	0.49	1,729	13.6	0.37	8,347	67.8	0.59
Ethnicity											
Non-Hispanic	111,862,532	163,004	40,999	24.5	0.18	32,851	20.4	0.14	88,237	55.0	0.20
Hispanic	15,035,498	33,920	6,554	18.3	0.30	4,619	13.8	0.27	22,579	67.8	0.39
Age group											
18–24	16,959,193	21,858	6,014	27.6	0.44	1,725	7.8	0.21	14,028	64.5	0.47
25–64	105,946,456	167,739	40,686	23.6	0.17	32,893	20.7	0.14	93,211	55.6	0.19
65 and older	3,992,381	7,327	853	11.3	0.45	2,852	41.3	0.71	3,577	47.5	0.71
Education[3]											
Less than HS	14,798,890	26,367	8,394	34.3	0.43	4,189	16.3	0.30	13,625	49.5	0.45
High school	36,048,733	54,264	17,036	31.6	0.27	10,194	19.6	0.22	26,703	48.7	0.30
More than HS	75,434,176	115,325	21,871	18.0	0.17	22,953	20.3	0.16	70,009	61.7	0.21
Insurance											
Insured	106,279,655	161,665	35,373	21.4	0.17	32,895	20.9	0.14	92,534	57.6	0.20
Uninsured	20,282,002	34,830	12,077	36.1	0.37	4,525	13.0	0.23	18,018	50.8	0.40

Source: Contract Report (March 2010). NORA Morbidity and Disability: The National Health Interview Survey (NHIS) 1997–2007. Department of Epidemiology and Public Health, University of Miami School of Medicine

The estimates from this table are based on a question from the National Health Interview Survey that asked respondents "Is the individual a never smoker, former smoker, or current smoker (based on the questions: Have you smoked at least 100 cigarettes in your entire life? Do you now smoke cigarettes every day, some days, or not at all?)"
[1] Sample size from the National Health Interview Survey for the years 1997–2007
[2] Percent (prevalence) estimated from the National Health Interview Survey for the years 1997–2007
[3] Response categories include (1) less than High School graduate, (2) High School graduate or GED, and (3) Some college or higher education.

Table 44. Prevalence of current smokers estimated for workers 18 years and older, Agriculture, Forestry, and Fishing sector, National Health Interview Survey, 1997–2007

Subgroup	US Estimated Worker Population	NHIS sample size[1]	Current			Former			Never		
			Number	Percent[2]	Standard error	Number	Percent[2]	Standard error	Number	Percent[2]	Standard error
All subgroups	2,694,267	4,378	1,037	23.1	0.79	809	19.0	0.69	2,500	57.9	0.96
Gender											
Male	2,088,446	3,367	839	23.9	0.90	662	20.0	0.77	1,836	56.0	1.06
Female	605,820	1,011	198	20.3	1.39	147	15.5	1.34	664	64.2	1.69
Race											
White	2,462,020	3,908	892	22.5	0.86	734	19.3	0.75	2,254	58.2	1.04
Black	95,149	184	62	32.4	3.92	27	13.6	2.82	93	54.0	4.36
Other	137,098	286	83	26.4	3.08	48	17.5	3.09	153	56.1	3.84
Ethnicity											
Non-Hispanic	2,014,159	2,839	705	24.1	0.95	617	21.4	0.80	1,498	54.6	1.06
Hispanic	680,108	1,539	332	20.2	1.55	192	12.1	1.06	1,002	67.8	1.90
Age group											
18–24	389,835	544	143	27.4	2.58	43	9.6	1.75	352	62.9	2.79
25–64	2,120,076	3,508	864	23.6	0.88	648	19.2	0.77	1,971	57.2	1.03
65 and older	184,356	326	30	7.5	1.48	118	37.1	2.97	177	55.4	3.01
Education[3]											
Less than HS	865,745	1,669	456	28.1	1.67	258	16.2	1.12	943	55.7	1.89
High school	843,218	1,254	330	25.2	1.37	227	18.7	1.16	690	56.2	1.57
More than HS	962,165	1,407	239	16.5	1.14	319	21.8	1.26	842	61.7	1.60
Insurance											
Insured	1,787,027	2,692	521	18.4	0.88	594	22.2	0.85	1,560	59.4	1.08
Uninsured	894,314	1,671	511	32.3	1.59	215	12.9	0.98	930	54.9	1.72

Source: Contract Report (March 2010). NORA Morbidity and Disability: The National Health Interview Survey (NHIS) 1997–2007. Department of Epidemiology and Public Health, University of Miami School of Medicine
The estimates from this table are based on a question from the National Health Interview Survey that asked respondents "Is the individual a never smoker, former smoker, or current smoker (based on the questions: Have you smoked at least 100 cigarettes in your entire life? Do you now smoke cigarettes every day, some days, or not at all?)"
[1] Sample size from the National Health Interview Survey for the years 1997–2007
[2] Percent (prevalence) estimated from the National Health Interview Survey for the years 1997–2007
[3] Response categories include (1) less than High School graduate, (2) High School graduate or GED, and (3) Some college or higher education.

Table 45. Prevalence of current alcohol drinkers estimated for workers 18 years and older, All NORA sectors, National Health Interview Survey, 1997–2007

Subgroup	US Estimated Worker Population	NHIS sample size[1]	Current			Former			Never		
			Number	Percent[2]	Standard error	Number	Percent[2]	Standard error	Number	Percent[2]	Standard error
All subgroups	126,898,030	196,924	134,393	70.2	0.25	22,860	11.6	0.12	35,763	18.2	0.22
Gender											
Male	68,530,792	97,768	71,167	74.0	0.26	11,361	11.8	0.14	12,883	14.2	0.23
Female	58,367,238	99,156	63,226	65.7	0.30	11,499	11.5	0.14	22,880	22.8	0.27
Race											
White	105,313,053	157,040	111,944	73.0	0.27	17,899	11.5	0.13	24,126	15.5	0.23
Black	14,056,560	27,262	15,073	56.5	0.48	3,708	13.3	0.25	7,872	30.2	0.50
Other	7,528,417	12,622	7,376	57.0	0.62	1,253	9.9	0.35	3,765	33.1	0.63
Ethnicity											
Non-Hispanic	111,862,532	163,004	113,759	71.2	0.27	19,517	11.9	0.13	26,504	16.9	0.23
Hispanic	15,035,498	33,920	20,634	62.6	0.40	3,343	9.8	0.22	9,259	27.5	0.40
Age group											
18–24	16,959,193	21,858	14,751	66.9	0.50	1,013	4.5	0.17	5,610	28.6	0.48
25–64	105,946,456	167,739	115,756	71.3	0.25	20,289	12.4	0.13	28,406	16.3	0.22
65 and older	3,992,381	7,327	3,886	55.8	0.75	1,558	21.4	0.60	1,747	22.8	0.59
Education[3]											
Less than HS	14,798,890	26,367	14,320	56.7	0.42	3,885	15.1	0.29	7,511	28.2	0.39
High school	36,048,733	54,264	34,718	66.0	0.34	7,374	13.8	0.20	10,904	20.2	0.32
More than HS	75,434,176	115,325	84,953	74.9	0.26	11,490	9.9	0.13	17,099	15.2	0.23
Insurance											
Insured	106,279,655	161,665	112,405	71.3	0.26	18,808	11.7	0.13	27,414	17.1	0.22
Uninsured	20,282,002	34,830	21,736	64.6	0.40	4,015	11.6	0.23	8,242	23.8	0.37

Source: Contract Report (March 2010). NORA Morbidity and Disability: The National Health Interview Survey (NHIS) 1997–2007. Department of Epidemiology and Public Health, University of Miami School of Medicine
The estimates from this table are from the National Health Interview Survey that asked respondents three questions related to historical and current alcohol use patterns (In your ENTIRE LIFE, have you had at least 12 drinks of any type of alcoholic beverage? In ANY ONE YEAR, have you had at least 12 drinks of any type of alcoholic beverage? In the PAST YEAR, how often did you drink any type of alcoholic beverage?)"
[1] Sample size from the National Health Interview Survey for the years 1997–2007
[2] Percent (prevalence) estimated from the National Health Interview Survey for the years 1997–2007
[3] Response categories include (1) less than High School graduate, (2) High School graduate or GED, and (3) Some college or higher education.

Table 46. Prevalence of current alcohol drinkers estimated for workers 18 years and older, Agriculture, Forestry, and Fishing sector, National Health Interview Survey, 1997–2007

Subgroup	US Estimated Worker Population	NHIS sample size[1]	Current			Former			Never		
			Number	Percent[2]	Standard error	Number	Percent[2]	Standard error	Number	Percent[2]	Standard error
All subgroups	2,694,267	4,378	2,773	65.8	1.01	608	14.0	0.63	878	20.3	0.86
Gender											
Male	2,088,446	3,367	2,195	67.6	1.07	486	14.4	0.70	578	18.0	0.89
Female	605,820	1,011	578	59.6	2.01	122	12.6	1.23	300	27.8	1.79
Race											
White	2,462,020	3,908	2,507	66.3	1.07	523	13.7	0.68	778	19.9	0.90
Black	95,149	184	93	57.2	3.69	41	22.0	3.27	39	20.8	2.96
Other	137,098	286	173	61.5	3.42	44	12.9	2.46	61	25.6	3.08
Ethnicity											
Non-Hispanic	2,014,159	2,839	1,889	68.0	1.12	438	15.0	0.78	446	17.0	0.87
Hispanic	680,108	1,539	884	59.3	2.00	170	10.8	1.15	432	29.9	1.85
Age group											
18–24	389,835	544	344	68.6	2.79	30	4.2	0.86	154	27.2	2.62
25–64	2,120,076	3,508	2,283	67.1	1.05	492	14.7	0.73	634	18.2	0.85
65 and older	184,356	326	146	44.9	3.53	86	26.1	2.75	90	29.0	3.18
Education[3]											
Less than HS	865,745	1,669	939	58.3	1.84	242	14.7	1.11	434	27.0	1.62
High school	843,218	1,254	774	63.3	1.70	186	15.1	1.11	260	21.5	1.41
More than HS	962,165	1,407	1,040	74.5	1.41	177	12.4	0.98	172	13.1	1.10
Insurance											
Insured	1,787,027	2,692	1,737	66.9	1.16	410	14.6	0.78	489	18.5	0.96
Uninsured	894,314	1,671	1,027	63.5	1.71	195	12.7	1.09	387	23.9	1.45

Source: Contract Report (March 2010). NORA Morbidity and Disability: The National Health Interview Survey (NHIS) 1997–2007. Department of Epidemiology and Public Health, University of Miami School of Medicine
The estimates from this table are from the National Health Interview Survey that asked respondents three questions related to historical and current alcohol use patterns (In your ENTIRE LIFE, have you had at least 12 drinks of any type of alcoholic beverage? In ANY ONE YEAR, have you had at least 12 drinks of any type of alcoholic beverage? In the PAST YEAR, how often did you drink any type of alcoholic beverage?)"
[1] Sample size from the National Health Interview Survey for the years 1997–2007
[2] Percent (prevalence) estimated from the National Health Interview Survey for the years 1997–2007
[3] Response categories include (1) less than High School graduate, (2) High School graduate or GED, and (3) Some college or higher education.

Table 47. Prevalence of obesity estimated for workers 18 years and older, All NORA sectors, National Health Interview Survey, 1997–2007

Subgroup	US Estimated Worker Population	NHIS sample size[1]	Underweight BMI < 18.5			Healthy Weight BMI=18.5-24.9			Overweight BMI ≥ 25.0 < 30.0			Obese BMI ≥ 30.0		
			Number	Percent[2]	Standard error	Number	Percent[2]	Standard error	Number	Percent[2]	Standard error	Number	Percent[2]	Standard error
All subgroups	126,898,030	196,924	3,098	1.6	0.04	74,938	39.0	0.17	68,981	36.5	0.15	43,705	22.8	0.15
Gender														
Male	68,530,792	97,768	606	0.7	0.04	30,686	31.4	0.21	42,958	44.4	0.21	21,898	23.5	0.19
Female	58,367,238	99,156	2,492	2.8	0.07	44,252	48.3	0.24	26,023	26.9	0.19	21,807	21.9	0.19
Race														
White	105,313,053	157,040	2,492	1.6	0.04	61,178	39.5	0.18	55,242	36.8	0.16	33,144	22.1	0.16
Black	14,056,560	27,262	274	0.9	0.07	7,834	29.8	0.37	9,703	37.0	0.35	8,591	32.3	0.38
Other	7,528,417	12,622	332	3.2	0.22	5,926	50.2	0.68	4,036	32.1	0.61	1,970	14.5	0.45
Ethnicity														
Non-Hispanic	111,862,532	163,004	2,761	1.7	0.04	63,618	39.7	0.18	55,835	35.9	0.16	35,858	22.6	0.16
Hispanic	15,035,498	33,920	337	1.0	0.07	11,320	34.2	0.37	13,146	40.9	0.33	7,847	24.0	0.35
Age group														
18–24	16,959,193	21,858	801	3.9	0.17	11,904	55.8	0.43	5,499	25.9	0.40	3,075	14.4	0.31
25–64	105,946,456	167,739	2,217	1.3	0.04	60,474	36.5	0.18	60,437	37.9	0.16	39,204	24.2	0.16
65 and older	3,992,381	7,327	80	1.1	0.14	2,560	34.7	0.68	3,045	44.0	0.69	1,426	20.3	0.58
Education[3]														
Less than HS	14,798,890	26,367	356	1.8	0.15	8,662	35.3	0.40	9,925	37.6	0.39	6,436	25.3	0.37
High school	36,048,733	54,264	826	1.6	0.07	19,057	36.3	0.28	19,180	36.6	0.25	13,418	25.5	0.25
More than HS	75,434,176	115,325	1,906	1.6	0.05	46,919	41.1	0.22	39,561	36.2	0.19	23,671	21.1	0.18
Insurance														
Insured	106,279,655	161,665	2,396	1.5	0.04	61,339	38.7	0.19	57,018	36.9	0.16	36,078	22.9	0.16
Uninsured	20,282,002	34,830	695	2.2	0.13	13,426	40.7	0.36	11,843	34.7	0.34	7,531	22.4	0.31

Source: Contract Report (March 2010). NORA Morbidity and Disability: The National Health Interview Survey (NHIS) 1997–2007. Department of Epidemiology and Public Health, University of Miami School of Medicine
The estimates from this table are based on a questions from the National Health Interview Survey that asked respondents about their weight without shoes (pounds) and height in inches.
[1] Sample size from the National Health Interview Survey for the years 1997–2007
[2] Percent (prevalence) estimated from the National Health Interview Survey for the years 1997–2007
[3] Response categories include (1) less than High School graduate, (2) High School graduate or GED, and (3) Some college or higher education.

Morbidity and disability among workers 18 years and older in the Agriculture sector, 1997–2007

Table 48. Prevalence of obesity estimated for workers 18 years and older, Agriculture, Forestry, and Fishing sector, National Health Interview Survey, 1997–2007

Subgroup	US Estimated Worker Population	NHIS sample size[1]	Underweight BMI < 18.5			Healthy Weight BMI=18.5-24.9			Overweight BMI ≥ 25.0 < 30.0			Obese BMI ≥ 30.0		
			Number	Percent[2]	Standard error	Number	Percent[2]	Standard error	Number	Percent[2]	Standard error	Number	Percent[2]	Standard error
All subgroups	2,694,267	4,378	55	1.2	0.18	1,500	36.3	0.99	1,740	41.0	1.02	880	21.5	0.76
Gender														
Male	2,088,446	3,367	28	0.8	0.17	1,061	33.0	1.06	1,454	44.6	1.11	685	21.5	0.84
Female	605,820	1,011	27	2.7	0.59	439	48.1	2.05	286	28.0	1.71	195	21.2	1.61
Race														
White	2,462,020	3,908	50	1.3	0.20	1,333	36.4	1.07	1,556	41.0	1.08	785	21.3	0.80
Black	95,149	184	1	0.6	0.60	62	31.8	4.18	69	36.7	3.94	49	30.9	3.96
Other	137,098	286	4	1.1	0.81	105	37.8	3.83	115	43.5	3.91	46	17.6	3.01
Ethnicity														
Non-Hispanic	2,014,159	2,839	45	1.4	0.22	1,078	38.5	1.15	1,072	38.5	1.18	582	21.6	0.92
Hispanic	680,108	1,539	10	0.8	0.30	422	29.4	1.72	668	48.8	1.91	298	20.9	1.28
Age group														
18–24	389,835	544	9	1.5	0.55	283	58.6	2.77	154	29.9	2.58	62	10.0	1.54
25–64	2,120,076	3,508	43	1.2	0.21	1,106	32.7	1.03	1,434	42.2	1.14	765	23.9	0.88
65 and older	184,356	326	3	0.6	0.38	111	31.6	3.07	152	50.1	3.32	53	17.7	2.26
Education[3]														
Less than HS	865,745	1,669	20	1.5	0.40	499	33.4	1.55	677	41.5	1.64	350	23.6	1.36
High school	843,218	1,254	14	0.9	0.25	420	33.8	1.66	511	42.3	1.86	271	23.0	1.58
More than HS	962,165	1,407	20	1.2	0.29	563	40.9	1.60	542	39.3	1.59	257	18.6	1.11
Insurance														
Insured	1,787,027	2,692	33	1.0	0.20	911	35.2	1.12	1,097	41.7	1.14	573	22.1	0.87
Uninsured	894,314	1,671	21	1.7	0.42	583	38.5	1.66	639	39.8	1.69	303	20.0	1.34

Source: Contract Report (March 2010). NORA Morbidity and Disability: The National Health Interview Survey (NHIS) 1997–2007. Department of Epidemiology and Public Health, University of Miami School of Medicine
The estimates from this table are based on a questions from the National Health Interview Survey that asked respondents about their weight without shoes (pounds) and height in inches.
[1] Sample size from the National Health Interview Survey for the years 1997–2007
[2] Percent (prevalence) estimated from the National Health Interview Survey for the years 1997–2007
[3] Response categories include (1) less than High School graduate, (2) High School graduate or GED, and (3) Some college or higher education.

Table 49. Prevalence of not meeting CDC recommended leisure time levels of physical activity estimated for workers 18 years and older, All NORA sectors, National Health Interview Survey, 1997–2007

Subgroup	US Estimated Worker Population	NHIS sample size[1]	Meets Guideline			Does Not Meet Guideline		
			Number	Percent[2]	Standard error	Number	Percent[2]	Standard error
All subgroups	126,898,030	196,924	60,942	34.1	0.22	121,354	65.9	0.22
Gender								
Male	68,530,792	97,768	32,283	36.0	0.25	57,891	64.0	0.25
Female	58,367,238	99,156	28,659	31.9	0.25	63,463	68.1	0.25
Race								
White	105,313,053	157,040	50,402	35.2	0.23	94,906	64.8	0.23
Black	14,056,560	27,262	7,030	28.4	0.44	18,289	71.6	0.44
Other	7,528,417	12,622	3,510	29.9	0.59	8,159	70.1	0.59
Ethnicity								
Non-Hispanic	111,862,532	163,004	52,997	35.3	0.23	97,494	64.7	0.23
Hispanic	15,035,498	33,920	7,945	25.3	0.35	23,860	74.7	0.35
Age group								
18–24	16,959,193	21,858	7,828	39.2	0.50	12,523	60.8	0.50
25–64	105,946,456	167,739	51,416	33.6	0.22	103,728	66.4	0.22
65 and older	3,992,381	7,327	1,698	25.8	0.63	5,103	74.2	0.63
Education[3]								
Less than HS	14,798,890	26,367	4,718	21.1	0.36	19,715	78.9	0.36
High school	36,048,733	54,264	13,347	27.4	0.31	36,585	72.6	0.31
More than HS	75,434,176	115,325	42,721	40.0	0.24	64,408	60.0	0.24
Insurance								
Insured	106,279,655	161,665	52,241	35.4	0.22	97,328	64.6	0.22
Uninsured	20,282,002	34,830	8,570	27.2	0.37	23,752	72.8	0.37

Source: Contract Report (March 2010). NORA Morbidity and Disability: The National Health Interview Survey (NHIS) 1997–2007. Department of Epidemiology and Public Health, University of Miami School of Medicine
The estimates from this table are based on four question from the National Health Interview Survey that permits one to assess whether respondents met CDC Healthy People 2010 recommendations for leisure time physical activity (i.e., engaged in light or moderate activity ≥ 30 minutes ≥ 5 times per week or rigorous activity ≥ 20 minutes ≥ 3 times per week or both. The four questions sought responses on (1) frequency of light/moderate activity (times per week); (2) duration of light/moderate activity (in minutes); (3) frequency of vigorous activity; and (4) duration of vigorous activity. See Adams PF, Barnes PM. Summary health statistics for the U.S. population: National Health Interview Survey, 2004. National Center for Health Statistics. Vital Health Stat 10 (229). 2006. DHHS Publication No. (PHS) 2006-1557, Series 10, No. 229.
[1] Sample size from the National Health Interview Survey for the years 1997–2007
[2] Percent (prevalence) estimated from the National Health Interview Survey for the years 1997–2007
[3] Response categories include (1) less than High School graduate, (2) High School graduate or GED, and (3) Some college or higher education.

Table 50. Prevalence of not meeting CDC recommended leisure time levels of physical activity estimated for workers 18 years and older, Agriculture, Forestry, and Fishing sector, National Health Interview Survey, 1997–2007

Subgroup	US Estimated Worker Population	NHIS sample size[1]	Meets Guideline			Does Not Meet Guideline		
			Number	Percent[2]	Standard error	Number	Percent[2]	Standard error
All subgroups	2,694,267	4,378	1,018	26.5	0.92	2,975	73.5	0.92
Gender								
Male	2,088,446	3,367	744	25.4	1.02	2,305	74.6	1.02
Female	605,820	1,011	274	30.1	1.80	670	69.9	1.80
Race								
White	2,462,020	3,908	916	26.4	0.96	2,656	73.6	0.96
Black	95,149	184	39	25.6	3.71	134	74.4	3.71
Other	137,098	286	63	28.8	3.68	185	71.2	3.68
Ethnicity								
Non-Hispanic	2,014,159	2,839	798	30.2	1.10	1,772	69.8	1.10
Hispanic	680,108	1,539	220	16.0	1.21	1,203	84.0	1.21
Age group								
18–24	389,835	544	152	34.4	2.82	354	65.6	2.82
25–64	2,120,076	3,508	806	25.7	0.97	2,381	74.3	0.97
65 and older	184,356	326	60	19.0	2.40	240	81.0	2.40
Education[3]								
Less than HS	865,745	1,669	235	17.2	1.31	1,302	82.8	1.31
High school	843,218	1,254	294	26.0	1.50	847	74.0	1.50
More than HS	962,165	1,407	484	35.8	1.58	794	64.2	1.58
Insurance								
Insured	1,787,027	2,692	702	28.9	1.11	1,764	71.1	1.11
Uninsured	894,314	1,671	313	21.8	1.46	1,199	78.2	1.46

Source: Contract Report (March 2010). NORA Morbidity and Disability: The National Health Interview Survey (NHIS) 1997–2007. Department of Epidemiology and Public Health, University of Miami School of Medicine
The estimates from this table are based on four question from the National Health Interview Survey that permits one to assess whether respondents met CDC Healthy People 2010 recommendations for leisure time physical activity (i.e., engaged in light or moderate activity $\geq$ 30 minutes $\geq$ 5 times per week or rigorous activity $\geq$ 20 minutes $\geq$ 3 times per week or both. The four questions sought responses on (1) frequency of light/moderate activity (times per week); (2) duration of light/moderate activity (in minutes); (3) frequency of vigorous activity; and (4) duration of vigorous activity. See Adams PF, Barnes PM. Summary health statistics for the U.S. population: National Health Interview Survey, 2004. National Center for Health Statistics. Vital Health Stat 10 (229). 2006. DHHS Publication No. (PHS) 2006-1557, Series 10, No. 229.
[1] Sample size from the National Health Interview Survey for the years 1997–2007
[2] Percent (prevalence) estimated from the National Health Interview Survey for the years 1997–2007
[3] Response categories include (1) less than High School graduate, (2) High School graduate or GED, and (3) Some college or higher education.

Table 51. Prevalence of lifetime HIV test estimated for workers 18 years and older, All NORA sectors, National Health Interview Survey, 1997–2007

Subgroup	US Estimated Worker Population	NHIS sample size[1]	Yes			No		
			Number	Percent[2]	Standard error	Number	Percent[2]	Standard error
All subgroups	126,898,030	196,924	76,067	37.8	0.20	114,789	62.2	0.20
Gender								
Male	68,530,792	97,768	34,778	35.4	0.25	59,762	64.6	0.25
Female	58,367,238	99,156	41,289	40.6	0.24	55,027	59.4	0.24
Race								
White	105,313,053	157,040	56,355	35.4	0.21	95,852	64.6	0.21
Black	14,056,560	27,262	14,858	55.5	0.48	11,578	44.5	0.48
Other	7,528,417	12,622	4,854	37.8	0.58	7,359	62.2	0.58
Ethnicity								
Non-Hispanic	111,862,532	163,004	62,707	37.6	0.21	95,190	62.4	0.21
Hispanic	15,035,498	33,920	13,360	38.8	0.44	19,599	61.2	0.44
Age group								
18–24	16,959,193	21,858	8,019	33.0	0.44	13,325	67.0	0.44
25–64	105,946,456	167,739	67,082	39.5	0.22	95,482	60.5	0.22
65 and older	3,992,381	7,327	966	13.4	0.49	5,982	86.6	0.49
Education[3]								
Less than HS	14,798,890	26,367	8,753	32.3	0.42	16,760	67.7	0.42
High school	36,048,733	54,264	18,821	33.5	0.29	33,719	66.5	0.29
More than HS	75,434,176	115,325	48,268	40.9	0.23	63,743	59.1	0.23
Insurance								
Insured	106,279,655	161,665	62,010	37.5	0.22	94,601	62.5	0.22
Uninsured	20,282,002	34,830	13,916	39.3	0.38	19,940	60.7	0.38

Source: Contract Report (March 2010). NORA Morbidity and Disability: The National Health Interview Survey (NHIS) 1997–2007. Department of Epidemiology and Public Health, University of Miami School of Medicine
The estimates from this table are based on a question from the National Health Interview Survey that asked respondents "Have you ever been tested for HIV?"
[1] Sample size from the National Health Interview Survey for the years 1997–2007
[2] Percent (prevalence) estimated from the National Health Interview Survey for the years 1997–2007
[3] Response categories include (1) less than High School graduate, (2) High School graduate or GED, and (3) Some college or higher education.

Table 52. Prevalence of lifetime HIV test estimated for workers 18 years and older, Agriculture, Forestry, and Fishing sector, National Health Interview Survey, 1997–2007

Subgroup	US Estimated Worker Population	NHIS sample size[1]	Yes			No		
			Number	Percent[2]	Standard error	Number	Percent[2]	Standard error
All subgroups	2,694,267	4,378	1,065	24.7	0.75	3,153	75.3	0.75
Gender								
Male	2,088,446	3,367	727	22.1	0.79	2,509	77.9	0.79
Female	605,820	1,011	338	33.6	1.84	644	66.4	1.84
Race								
White	2,462,020	3,908	917	23.6	0.78	2,850	76.4	0.78
Black	95,149	184	73	43.0	4.81	102	57.0	4.81
Other	137,098	286	75	31.8	3.31	201	68.2	3.31
Ethnicity								
Non-Hispanic	2,014,159	2,839	758	26.0	0.87	1,981	74.0	0.87
Hispanic	680,108	1,539	307	20.7	1.54	1,172	79.3	1.54
Age group								
18–24	389,835	544	120	21.5	2.18	411	78.5	2.18
25–64	2,120,076	3,508	920	26.7	0.85	2,462	73.3	0.85
65 and older	184,356	326	25	8.0	1.51	280	92.0	1.51
Education[3]								
Less than HS	865,745	1,669	316	20.2	1.38	1,296	79.8	1.38
High school	843,218	1,254	293	21.8	1.30	920	78.2	1.30
More than HS	962,165	1,407	452	31.6	1.33	902	68.4	1.33
Insurance								
Insured	1,787,027	2,692	673	24.2	0.85	1,919	75.8	0.85
Uninsured	894,314	1,671	391	25.9	1.47	1,221	74.1	1.47

Source: Contract Report (March 2010). NORA Morbidity and Disability: The National Health Interview Survey (NHIS) 1997–2007. Department of Epidemiology and Public Health, University of Miami School of Medicine
The estimates from this table are based on a question from the National Health Interview Survey that asked respondents "Have you ever been tested for HIV?"
[1] Sample size from the National Health Interview Survey for the years 1997–2007
[2] Percent (prevalence) estimated from the National Health Interview Survey for the years 1997–2007
[3] Response categories include (1) less than High School graduate, (2) High School graduate or GED, and (3) Some college or higher education.

Table 53. Prevalence of not receiving an influenza vaccination during the past 12 months estimated for workers 18 years and older, All NORA sectors, National Health Interview Survey, 1997–2007

Subgroup	US Estimated Worker Population	NHIS sample size[1]	Yes			No		
			Number	Percent[2]	Standard error	Number	Percent[2]	Standard error
All subgroups	126,898,030	196,924	40,401	20.9	0.15	154,881	79.1	0.15
Gender								
Male	68,530,792	97,768	17,898	18.7	0.18	79,022	81.3	0.18
Female	58,367,238	99,156	22,503	23.5	0.21	75,859	76.5	0.21
Race								
White	105,313,053	157,040	33,373	21.5	0.17	122,428	78.5	0.17
Black	14,056,560	27,262	4,574	16.6	0.29	22,399	83.4	0.29
Other	7,528,417	12,622	2,454	20.4	0.50	10,054	79.6	0.50
Ethnicity								
Non-Hispanic	111,862,532	163,004	35,693	21.9	0.16	125,950	78.1	0.16
Hispanic	15,035,498	33,920	4,708	13.7	0.27	28,931	86.3	0.27
Age group								
18–24	16,959,193	21,858	2,770	12.9	0.29	18,883	87.1	0.29
25–64	105,946,456	167,739	33,669	20.8	0.16	132,706	79.2	0.16
65 and older	3,992,381	7,327	3,962	57.1	0.68	3,292	42.9	0.68
Education[3]								
Less than HS	14,798,890	26,367	3,876	14.6	0.30	22,262	85.4	0.30
High school	36,048,733	54,264	10,007	18.6	0.22	43,797	81.4	0.22
More than HS	75,434,176	115,325	26,356	23.3	0.19	88,109	76.7	0.19
Insurance								
Insured	106,279,655	161,665	37,134	23.2	0.17	123,190	76.8	0.17
Uninsured	20,282,002	34,830	3,205	9.2	0.19	31,343	90.8	0.19

Source: Contract Report (March 2010). NORA Morbidity and Disability: The National Health Interview Survey (NHIS) 1997–2007. Department of Epidemiology and Public Health, University of Miami School of Medicine
The estimates from this table are based on a question from the National Health Interview Survey that asked respondents "During the PAST 12 MONTHS, have you had a flu shot? A flu shot is usually given in the fall and protects against influenza for the flu season."
[1] Sample size from the National Health Interview Survey for the years 1997–2007
[2] Percent (prevalence) estimated from the National Health Interview Survey for the years 1997–2007
[3] Response categories include (1) less than High School graduate, (2) High School graduate or GED, and (3) Some college or higher education.

Table 54. Prevalence of not receiving an influenza vaccination during the past 12 months estimated for workers 18 years and older, Agriculture, Forestry, and Fishing sector, National Health Interview Survey, 1997–2007

Subgroup	US Estimated Worker Population	NHIS sample size[1]	Yes			No		
			Number	Percent[2]	Standard error	Number	Percent[2]	Standard error
All subgroups	2,694,267	4,378	608	14.2	0.61	3,738	85.8	0.61
Gender								
Male	2,088,446	3,367	427	12.7	0.65	2,915	87.3	0.65
Female	605,820	1,011	181	19.4	1.39	823	80.6	1.39
Race								
White	2,462,020	3,908	554	14.5	0.65	3,325	85.5	0.65
Black	95,149	184	24	12.4	2.61	160	87.6	2.61
Other	137,098	286	30	10.3	2.24	253	89.7	2.24
Ethnicity								
Non-Hispanic	2,014,159	2,839	487	16.6	0.75	2,336	83.4	0.75
Hispanic	680,108	1,539	121	7.1	0.78	1,402	92.9	0.78
Age group								
18–24	389,835	544	43	9.0	1.60	498	91.0	1.60
25–64	2,120,076	3,508	400	11.8	0.59	3,081	88.2	0.59
65 and older	184,356	326	165	53.0	2.89	159	47.0	2.89
Education[3]								
Less than HS	865,745	1,669	182	11.6	1.00	1,474	88.4	1.00
High school	843,218	1,254	185	14.7	1.02	1,059	85.3	1.02
More than HS	962,165	1,407	237	16.2	1.07	1,166	83.8	1.07
Insurance								
Insured	1,787,027	2,692	499	18.2	0.79	2,176	81.8	0.79
Uninsured	894,314	1,671	108	6.3	0.70	1,548	93.7	0.70

Source: Contract Report (March 2010). NORA Morbidity and Disability: The National Health Interview Survey (NHIS) 1997–2007. Department of Epidemiology and Public Health, University of Miami School of Medicine
The estimates from this table are based on a question from the National Health Interview Survey that asked respondents "During the PAST 12 MONTHS, have you had a flu shot? A flu shot is usually given in the fall and protects against influenza for the flu season."
[1] Sample size from the National Health Interview Survey for the years 1997–2007
[2] Percent (prevalence) estimated from the National Health Interview Survey for the years 1997–2007
[3] Response categories include (1) less than High School graduate, (2) High School graduate or GED, and (3) Some college or higher education.

Table 55. Prevalence of never receiving a pneumococcal vaccination estimated for workers 60 years and older, All NORA sectors, National Health Interview Survey, 1997–2007

Subgroup	US Estimated Worker Population	NHIS sample size[1]	Yes			No		
			Number	Percent[2]	Standard error	Number	Percent[2]	Standard error
All subgroups	8,947,375	15,437	4,516	29.8	0.45	10,921	70.2	0.45
Gender								
Male	4,903,958	7,622	2,085	28.4	0.59	5,537	71.6	0.59
Female	4,043,417	7,815	2,431	31.5	0.63	5,384	68.5	0.63
Race								
White	7,884,204	13,110	4,033	31.1	0.49	9,077	68.9	0.49
Black	715,325	1,732	376	21.7	1.23	1,356	78.3	1.23
Other	347,846	595	107	16.7	1.69	488	83.3	1.69
Ethnicity								
Non-Hispanic	8,360,710	13,982	4,300	30.9	0.47	9,682	69.1	0.47
Hispanic	586,665	1,455	216	13.9	1.13	1,239	86.1	1.13
Age group								
60–64	5,060,713	8,296	1,516	18.9	0.51	6,780	81.1	0.51
65 and older	3,886,662	7,141	3,000	44.0	0.70	4,141	56.0	0.70
Education[3]								
Less than HS	1,385,505	2,718	662	26.2	1.08	2,056	73.8	1.08
High school	2,850,046	4,865	1,402	29.1	0.78	3,463	70.9	0.78
More than HS	4,651,458	7,753	2,432	31.4	0.62	5,321	68.6	0.62
Insurance								
Insured	8,391,603	14,396	4,395	30.9	0.48	10,001	69.1	0.48
Uninsured	544,635	1,018	119	12.4	1.19	899	87.6	1.19

Source: Contract Report (March 2010). NORA Morbidity and Disability: The National Health Interview Survey (NHIS) 1997–2007. Department of Epidemiology and Public Health, University of Miami School of Medicine
The estimates from this table are based on a question from the National Health Interview Survey that asked respondents "Have you ever had a pneumonia shot? This shot is usually given once or twice in a person's lifetime and is different from the flu shot. It is also called the pneumococcal vaccine."
[1] Sample size from the National Health Interview Survey for the years 1997–2007
[2] Percent (prevalence) estimated from the National Health Interview Survey for the years 1997–2007
[3] Response categories include (1) less than High School graduate, (2) High School graduate or GED, and (3) Some college or higher education.

Table 56. Prevalence of never receiving a pneumococcal vaccination estimated for workers 60 years and older, Agriculture, Forestry, and Fishing sector, National Health Interview Survey, 1997–2007

Subgroup	US Estimated Worker Population	NHIS sample size[1]	Yes			No		
			Number	Percent[2]	Standard error	Number	Percent[2]	Standard error
All subgroups	312,192	534	165	30.8	2.23	369	69.2	2.23
Gender								
Male	241,064	414	127	30.6	2.47	287	69.4	2.47
Female	71,128	120	38	31.4	4.31	82	68.6	4.31
Race								
White	290,830	478	158	32.1	2.33	320	67.9	2.33
Black	16,202	39	5	14.4	6.95	34	85.6	6.95
Other	5,161	17	2	12.5	8.64	15	87.5	8.64
Ethnicity								
Non-Hispanic	290,509	474	159	32.4	2.35	315	67.6	2.35
Hispanic	21,684	60	6	9.4	4.39	54	90.6	4.39
Age group								
60–64	132,974	216	41	20.1	2.96	175	79.9	2.96
65 and older	179,219	318	124	38.8	2.89	194	61.2	2.89
Education[3]								
Less than HS	92,810	180	46	27.5	3.89	134	72.5	3.89
High school	133,138	210	69	32.4	3.64	141	67.6	3.64
More than HS	85,805	143	50	32.0	3.67	93	68.0	3.67
Insurance								
Insured	288,588	484	160	31.9	2.32	324	68.1	2.32
Uninsured	23,468	49	5	17.6	7.69	44	82.4	7.69

Source: Contract Report (March 2010). NORA Morbidity and Disability: The National Health Interview Survey (NHIS) 1997–2007. Department of Epidemiology and Public Health, University of Miami School of Medicine
The estimates from this table are based on a question from the National Health Interview Survey that asked respondents "Have you ever had a pneumonia shot? This shot is usually given once or twice in a person's lifetime and is different from the flu shot. It is also called the pneumococcal vaccine."
[1] Sample size from the National Health Interview Survey for the years 1997–2007
[2] Percent (prevalence) estimated from the National Health Interview Survey for the years 1997–2007
[3] Response categories include (1) less than High School graduate, (2) High School graduate or GED, and (3) Some college or higher education.

References

Behrens V, Seligman P, Cameron L, Mathias CG, Fine L [1994]. The prevalence of back pain, hand discomfort, and dermatitis in the US working population. Am J Public Health 84(11):1780–5.

Biddlecom AE, LeClere FB, Hardy AM, Hendershot GE [1992]. National study of knowledge of AIDS, testing patterns, and self-assessed risk among health care workers. J Acquir Immune Defic Syndr 5(11):1131–6.

Botman SL, Jack SS [1995]. Combining National Health Interview Survey Datasets: issues and approaches. Stat Med 14(5–7):669–77.

Brackbill R, Frazier T, Shilling S [1994a]. Smoking characteristics of US workers, 1978–1980. Am J Ind Med 13(1):5–41.

Brackbill RM, Cameron LL, Behrens V [1994b]. Prevalence of chronic diseases and impairments among US farmers, 1986–1990. Am J Epidemiol 139(11):1055–65.

Caban AJ, Lee DJ, Fleming LE, Gómez-Marin O, LeBlanc W, Pitman T [2005]. Obesity in US workers: The National Health Interview Survey, 1986 to 2002. Am J Public Health 295(9):1614–22.

Caban-Martinez AJ, Lee DJ, Fleming LE, Arheart KL, Leblanc WG, Chung-Bridges K, Christ S, Pitman T [2007a]. Dental care access and unmet dental care needs among U.S. workers: The National Health Interview Survey, 1997 to 2003. J Am Dent Assoc 138(2):227–30.

Caban-Martinez AJ, Lee DJ, Fleming LE, LeBlanc WG, Arheart KL, Chung-Bridges K, Christ SL, McCollister KE, Pitman T [2007b]. Leisure-time physical activity levels of the US workforce. Prev Med 44(5):432–6.

CDC [2000]. Measuring Healthy Days. Population Assessment of Health-Related Quality of Life. Atlanta, GA: Centers for Disease Control and Prevention. [http://www.cdc.gov/hrqol/pdfs/mhd.pdf]. Date accessed: October 17, 2011.

Christ SL, Lee DJ, Fleming LE, Leblanc WG, Arheart KL, Chung-Bridges K, Caban AJ, McCollister KE. [2007]. Employment and occupation effects on depressive symptoms in older americans: does working past age 65 protect against depression? J Gerontol B Psychol Sci Soc Sci 62(6):S399–403.

Cooper SP, Buffler PA, Lee ES, Cooper CJ [1993]. Health characteristics by longest held occupation and industry of employment: United States, 1980. Am J Ind Med 24(1):25–39.

Engstrom JL, Paterson SA, Doherty A, Trabulsi M, Speer KL [2003]. Accuracy of self-reported height and weight in women: an integrative review of the literature. J Midwifery Womens Health 48(5):338–45.

Fleming LE, Gómez-Marin O, Zheng D, Ma F, Lee D [2003]. National Health Interview Survey mortality among US farmers and pesticide applicators. Am J Ind Med 43(2):227–33.

Fleming LE, LeBlanc W, Pitman P, Caban A, Gómez-Marín O, Lee D, Zheng D, Dulce J [2004]. Monograph: Occupation, Disability and Self Reported Health: The National Health Interview Survey 1986–1994. [http://www.umiamiorg.com/publications/monograph/thenationalhealthinterviewsurveymonograph.pdf]. Date accessed: October 17, 2011.

Fleming LE, Pitman P, LeBlanc W, Caban A, Gómez-Marín O, Lee D, Zheng D, Dulce J [2005]. Monograph: Occupation and Mortality: The National Health Interview Survey (NHIS) 1986–1994. [http://www.umiamiorg.com/publications/monograph/mortalitymonograph.pdf]. Date accessed: October 17, 2011.

Fleming LE, Pitman P, LeBlanc W, Lee D, Chung Bridges K, Caban Martinez A, Gómez-Marín O, Christ S, McCollister K, Arheart K, Ferraro K [2007a]. Monograph: Occupations and Health Disparities: The National Health Interview Survey 1997–2004. [http://www.umiamiorg.com/publications/monograph/Health%20Disparities%20Monograph.pdf]. Date accessed: October 17, 2011.

Fleming LE, Lee DJ, Martinez AJ, Leblanc WG, McCollister KE, Bridges KC, Christ SL, Arheart KL, Pitman T [2007b]. The health behaviors of the older US worker. Am J Ind Med 50(6):427–37.

Gómez-Marin O, Fleming LE, Lee DJ, LeBlanc W, Zheng D, Ma F, Jané D, Pitman T, Caban A Jr. [2004]. Acute and chronic disability among U.S. farmers and pesticide applicators: the National Health Interview Survey (NHIS). J Agric Saf Health 10(4):275–85.

Gómez-Marin O, Fleming LE, Caban A, Leblanc WG, Lee DJ, Pitman T [2005]. Longest held job in US occupational groups: the National Health Interview Survey. J Occup Environ Med 47(1):79–90.

Guo H, Tanaka S, Halperin W, Cameron L [1999]. Back pain prevalence in US industry and estimates of lost workdays. Am J Public Health 89(7):1029–1035.

Hurwitz EL, Morgenstern H [1997]. Correlates of back problems and back-related disability in the United States. J Clin Epidemiol 50(6):669–81.

Kuczmarski MF, Kuczmarski RJ, Najjar M [2001]. Effects of age on validity of self-reported height, weight, and body mass index: findings from the Third National Health and Nutrition Examination Survey, 1988–1994. J Am Diet Assoc 101(1):28–34.

La Rosa JH [1988]. Women, work, and health: employment as a risk factor for coronary heart disease. Am J Obstet Gynecol 158(6 Pt 2):1597–602.

Lee DJ, Fleming LE, Gomez-Marin O, Leblanc W [2004]. Risk of hospitalization among firefighters: the national health interview survey, 1986–1994. Am J Public Health 294(11):1938–9.

Lee DJ, Fleming LE, Gómez-Marín O, LeBlanc WG, Arheart KL, Caban AJ, Christ SL, Chung-Bridges K, Pitman T. [2006a]. Morbidity ranking of US workers employed in 206 occupations: The National Health Interview Survey (NHIS) 1986–1994. J Occup Environ Med 48(2):117–134.

Lee DJ, Fleming LE, Leblanc WG, Arheart KL, Chung-Bridges K, Christ SL, Caban AJ, Pitman T. [2006b]. Occupation and lung cancer mortality in a nationally representative U.S. Cohort: The National Health Interview Survey (NHIS). J Occup Environ Med 48(8):823–32.

Lee DJ, Fleming LE, Arheart KL, LeBlanc WG, Caban AJ, Chung-Bridges K, Christ SL, McCollister KE, Pitman T [2007a]. Smoking rate trends in U.S. occupational groups: the 1987 to 2004 National Health Interview Survey. J Occup Environ Med 49(1):75–81.

Lee DJ, Fleming LE, McCollister KE, Caban AJ, Arheart KL, LeBlanc WG, Chung-Bridges K, Christ SL, Dietz N, Clark JD 3rd. [2007b]. Health care provider smoking cessation advice among US worker groups. Tob Control 16(5):325–8.

McCollister KE, Arheart KL, Lee DJ, Fleming LE, Davila EP, Christ SL, Caban-Martinez AJ, West J, Clark JE, Erard MJ [2010]. Declining Health Insurance Access Among US Hispanic Workers: Not all Jobs are Created Equal. Am J Ind Med 53(2)163–70.

NCHS [1989]. National Center for Health Statistics Vital and Health Statistics Report Series 2, No. 110. Design and estimation for the National Health Interview Survey, 1985–94. By Massey JT, Moore TF, Parsons VL, Tadros W. Hyattsville, MD: U.S. Department of Health and Human Services, Public Health Service, Centers for Disease Control and Prevention, National Center for Health Statistics. DHHS Publication No. (PHS) 89-1384. [http://www.cdc.gov/nchs/data/series/sr_02/sr02_110.pdf].

NCHS [1990]. National Center for Health Statistics Vital and Health Statistics Report Series 10, No. 175. Types of injuries by selected characteristics: United States, 1985–87. By Collins JG. Hyattsville, MD: U.S. Department of Health and Human Services, Public Health Service, Centers for Disease Control and Prevention, National Center for Health Statistics. DHHS Publication No. (PHS) 91-1503. [http://www.cdc.gov/nchs/data/series/sr_10/sr10_175.pdf].

NCHS [1993a]. National Center for Health Statistics. Industry and Occupation coding for Death Certificates 1993. NCHS instruction manual, Part 19. Hyattsville, MD: U.S. Department of Health and Human Services, Centers for Disease Control and Prevention, National Center for Health Statistics.

NCHS [1993b]. National Center for Health Statistics Vital and Health Statistics Report Series 10, No. 186. Health Conditions among the currently employed: United States, 1988. By Park, C. H., Wagener, D. K., Winn, D. M., Pierce, J. P. Hyattsville, MD: U.S. Department of Health and Human Services, Public Health Service, Centers for Disease Control and Prevention, National Center for Health Statistics. DHHS Publication No. (PHS) 93-1514. [http://www.cdc.gov/nchs/data/series/sr_10/sr10_186.pdf].

NCHS [2000]. National Center for Health Statistics Vital and Health Statistics Report Series 2, No. 130. Design and estimation for the National Health Interview Survey, 1995–2004. By Botman SL, Moore TF, Moriarty CL, Parsons VL. Hyattsville, MD: U.S. Department of Health and Human Services, Centers for Disease Control and Prevention, National Center for Health Statistics. DHHS Publication No. (PHS) 2000-1330. [http://www.cdc.gov/nchs/data/series/sr_02/sr02_130.pdf].

NCHS [2002a]. National Center for Health Statistics Vital and Health Statistics Report Series 10, No. 205. Summary health statistics for U.S. adults: National Health Interview Survey, 1997. By Blackwell DL, Collins JG, Coles R. Hyattsville, MD: U.S. Department of Health and Human Services, Centers for Disease Control and Prevention, National Center for Health Statistics. DHHS Publication No. (PHS) 2002-1533. [http://www.cdc.gov/nchs/data/series/sr_10/sr10_205.pdf].

NCHS [2002b]. National Center for Health Statistics Vital and Health Statistics Report Series 10, No. 209. Summary health statistics for U.S. adults: National Health Interview Survey, 1998. By Pleis JR, Coles R. Hyattsville, MD: U.S. Department of Health and Human Services, Centers for Disease Control and Prevention, National Center for Health Statistics. DHHS Publication No. (PHS) 2003-1537. [http://www.cdc.gov/nchs/data/series/sr_10/sr10_209.pdf].

NCHS [2003a]. National Center for Health Statistics Vital and Health Statistics Report Series 10, No. 212. Summary health statistics for U.S. adults: National Health Interview Survey, 1999. By Pleis JR, Coles R. Hyattsville, MD: U.S. Department of Health and Human Services, Centers for Disease Control and Prevention, National Center for Health Statistics. DHHS Publication No. (PHS) 2003-1540. [http://www.cdc.gov/nchs/data/series/sr_10/sr10_212.pdf].

NCHS [2003b]. National Center for Health Statistics Vital and Health Statistics Report Series 10, No. 215. Summary health statistics for U.S. adults: National Health Interview Survey, 2000. By Pleis JR, Schiller JS, Benson V. Hyattsville, MD: U.S. Department of Health and Human Services, Centers for Disease Control and Prevention, National Center for Health Statistics. DHHS Publication No. (PHS) 2004-1543. [http://www.cdc.gov/nchs/data/series/sr_10/sr10_215.pdf].

NCHS [2004a]. National Center for Health Statistics Vital and Health Statistics Report Series 10, No. 218. Summary health statistics for U.S. adults: National Health Interview Survey, 2001. By Lucas JW, Schiller JS, Benson V. Hyattsville, MD: U.S. Department of Health and Human Services, Centers for Disease Control and Prevention, National Center for Health Statistics. DHHS Publication No. (PHS) 2004-1546. [http://www.cdc.gov/nchs/data/series/sr_10/sr10_218.pdf].

NCHS [2004b]. National Center for Health Statistics Vital and Health Statistics Report Series 10, No. 222. Summary health statistics for U.S. adults: National Health Interview Survey, 2002. By Lethbridge-Cejku M, Schiller JS, Bernadel L. Hyattsville, MD: U.S. Department of Health and Human Services, Centers for Disease Control and Prevention, National Center for Health Statistics. DHHS Publication No. (PHS) 2004-1550.
[http://www.cdc.gov/nchs/data/series/sr_10/sr10_222.pdf].

NCHS [2005]. National Center for Health Statistics Vital and Health Statistics Report Series 10, No. 225. Summary health statistics for U.S. adults: National Health Interview Survey, 2003.By Lethbridge-Cejku M, Vickerie J. Hyattsville, MD: U.S. Department of Health and Human Services, Centers for Disease Control and Prevention, National Center for Health Statistics. DHHS Publication No. (PHS) 2005-1553. [http://www.cdc.gov/nchs/data/series/sr_10/sr10_225.pdf].

NCHS [2006a]. National Center for Health Statistics Vital and Health Statistics Report Series 10, No. 228. Summary Health Statistics for U.S. Adults: National Health Interview Survey, 2004. By Lethbridge-Cejku M, Rose D, Vickerie J. Hyattsville, MD: U.S. Department of Health and Human Services, Centers for Disease Control and Prevention, National Center for Health Statistics. DHHS Publication No. (PHS) 2006-1556.
[http://www.cdc.gov/nchs/data/series/sr_10/sr10_228.pdf].

NCHS [2006b]. National Center for Health Statistics Vital and Health Statistics Report Series 10, No. 232. Summary Health Statistics for U.S. adults: National Health Interview Survey, 2005. By Pleis JR, Lethbridge-Cejku M. Hyattsville, MD: U.S. Department of Health and Human Services, Centers for Disease Control and Prevention, National Center for Health Statistics. DHHS Publication No. (PHS) 2008-1560. [http://www.cdc.gov/nchs/data/series/sr_10/sr10_232.pdf].

NCHS [2007]. National Center for Health Statistics Vital and Health Statistics Report Series 10, No. 235. Summary Health Statistics for U.S. adults: National Health Interview Survey, 2006. By Pleis JR, Lethbridge-Cejku M. Hyattsville, MD: U.S. Department of Health and Human Services, Centers for Disease Control and Prevention, National Center for Health Statistics. DHHS Publication No. (PHS) 2008-1563. [http://www.cdc.gov/nchs/data/series/sr_10/sr10_235.pdf].

NCHS [2008]. National Center for Health Statistics National Health Interview Survey (NHIS) Public Use Data Release. NHIS Survey Description. Variance Estimation and Other Analytic Issues, pp. 97–108. [ftp://ftp.cdc.gov/pub/Health_Statistics/NCHS/Dataset_Documentation/NHIS/2007/srvydesc.pdf]. Date accessed: October 17, 2011).

Nelson DE, Emont SL, Brackbill RM, Cameron LL, Peddicord J, Fiore MC [1994a]. Cigarette smoking prevalence by occupation in the United States. A comparison between 1978 to 1980 and 1987 to 1990. J Occup Med 36(5):516–25.

Nelson DE, Giovino GA, Emont SL, Brackbill R, Cameron LL, Peddicord J, Mowery PD [1994b]. Trends in cigarette smoking among US physicians and nurses. JAMA 271(16):1273-5.

NIOSH [1980]. Industrial Characteristics of Persons Reporting Morbidity during the Health Interview Surveys Conducted in 1969–1974. By Kaminski R, Spirtas R. Cincinnati, OH. U.S. Department of Health and Human Services, Center for disease Control, National Institute for Occupational Safety and Health, DHHS (NIOSH) Publication No. 80–123.

Research Triangle Institute [2004]. Software for Survey Data Analysis (SUDAAN) Version 8.0.2. Research Triangle Park, NC: Research Triangle Institute.

Soderholm SC [2006]. National Occupational Research Agenda. Cross-sector research in the second decade. Presented at the 2006 NORA Symposium. Washington, D.C.. April 2006. [http://www.cdc.gov/niosh/nora/symp06/pdfs/cross06present.pdf]. Date accessed: October 17, 2011.

Spencer EA, Appleby PN, Davey GK, Key TJ [2002]. Validity of self-reported height and weight in 4808 EPIC-Oxford participants. Public Health Nutr 5(4):561–5.

Sterling TD, Weinkam JJ [1989]. Comparison of smoking-related risk factors among black and white males. Am J Ind Med 15(3):319–33.

Sterling T, Weinkam J [1990]. The confounding of occupation and smoking and its consequences. Soc Sci Med 30(4):457–67.

Tanaka S, Wild DK, Seligman PJ, Halperin WE, Behrens VJ, Putz-Anderson V [1995]. Prevalence and work-relatedness of self-reported carpal tunnel syndrome among U.S. workers: analysis of the Occupational Health Supplement data of 1988 National Health Interview Survey. Am J Ind Med 127(4):451–70.

Wagener DK, Winn DW [1991]. Injuries in working populations: black-white differences. Am J Public Health 81(11):1408–14.

Zwerling C, Whitten PS, Davis CS, Sprince NL [1997]. Occupational injuries among workers with disabilities: the National Health Interview Survey, 1985–1994. JAMA 278(24):2163–6.

Zwerling C, Whitten PS, Davis CS, Sprince NL [1998]. Occupational injuries among older workers with visual, auditory, and other impairments. A validation study. J Occup Environ Med 40(8):720–3.

Zwerling C, Whitten PS, Sprince NL, Davis CS, Wallace RB, Blanck P, Heeringa SG [2003]. Workplace accommodations for people with disabilities: National Health Interview Survey Disability Supplement, 1994–1995. J Occup Environ Med 45(5):517–25.

Appendices

Appendix 1.
Detailed Matrix of Morbidity and Disability Questions from the NHIS asked consistently 1997-2007

Variable	NHIS Question	NHIS Possible Responses	NHIS variable Name	Study Definition	Study Missing Data (N)
Demographics					
Gender	Are you male or female?	Male, Female	SEX	Male, female	None
Age	How old are you? (years)	Age in years	AGE	Continuous, Categorized: 1=18-24 years 2=25-64 3=65+	None
Race	What races do you consider yourself to be?	NHIS recode variable: white, black, other. Other includes other race than white or black such as includes Indian American, Alaska native, native Hawaiian, other Pacific Islander, Asian, Indian, Chinese, Filipino, other race, multiple race.	RACE	1=White 2=Black 3=All Other	None
Ethnicity	Do you consider yourself to be Hispanic or Latino? Hispanic includes: Puerto Rican, Cuban, Dominican, Mexican, Central/South American, other Latin American, other Hispanic	Hispanic, non-Hispanic	HISPAN_I	1=Non-Hispanic 2=Hispanic	None
Insurance	Are you covered by health insurance or any other health care plan?	Yes, No	PHICOV(97-99),NOTCOV(00-07)	1=Insured 2=Not insured	429
Education	What is the highest level of education that you have completed?	1st, 2nd, third, 4th, fifth, 6th, 7th, 8th, 9th, 10th, 11th, 12th no diploma, GED, high school diploma, some college (no degree), associate degree, bachelors, masters, doctorate degree	EDUC	< 12 years; 12 years; >12 years	968
Health Status					
Health Last Year	Compared with 12 MONTHS AGO, would you say your health is (better, worse, or about the same)?	1) Better, 2) Worse, 3) about the same	AHSTATYR	1) Better, 2) Worse, 3) about the same	349
Self Rated Health	Would you say health in general is excellent, very good, good, fair, or poor?	1) excellent, very good, good 2) fair or poor	HEALTH	0=excellent, very good, good 1=fair or poor	84

Appendix 1.
Detailed Matrix of Morbidity and Disability Questions from the NHIS asked consistently 1997-2007

Variable	NHIS Question	NHIS Possible Responses	NHIS variable Name	Study Definition	Study Missing Data (N)
Bed Day (Cat)	During the PAST 12 MONTHS, that is, since [12 month ref date], ABOUT how many days did illness or injury keep you in bed for more than half of the day? (Include days while an overnight patient in a hospital).	Number of times	BEDDAYR	Continuous and categorical: 1=0 days 2=1 day 3=2+ days	1506
Lost Work Day (CAT)	During the PAST 12 MONTHS, that is, since [12 month ref date], ABOUT how many days did you miss work at a job or business because of illness or injury (do not include maternity leave)?	Number of times	WKDAYR	Continuous and as categorical: 1=0 days 2=1 day 3=2-5 days 4=6+ days	1942
Disability and limitations in activity					
Special Equipment	Do you now have any health problem that requires you to use special equipment, such as a cane, a wheelchair, a special bed, or a special telephone?	Yes, No	SPECEQ		152
Any functional Limitations	NHIS recode based on all the 12 NHIS questions on activity limitations	Any functional limitation (e.g. did not answer "not all") versus not limited in any way	FIA1AR	Yes if said limitation to any of 12 questions, No if otherwise	383
Hearing Impairment	Which statement best describes your hearing (without a hearing aid): good, a little trouble, a lot of trouble, deaf?	Good, a little trouble, a lot of trouble, deaf	AHEARST	1=hearing impaired if a little or a lot of trouble hearing, or deaf. 0=Not hearing impaired	59
Visual Impairment	Based on two questions: o Do you have trouble seeing, even when wearing glasses or contact lenses? and o Are you blind or unable to see at all?	Yes, No	AVISION	1=visual impaired if answered yes to any of the two questions 0=not visually impaired	98
Morbidity					

Appendix 1.
Detailed Matrix of Morbidity and Disability Questions from the NHIS asked consistently 1997-2007

Variable	NHIS Question	NHIS Possible Responses	NHIS variable Name	Study Definition	Study Missing Data (N)
Cancer	Have you EVER been told by a doctor or other health professional that you had cancer or a malignancy of any kind? (yes/no)	Yes, No	CANEV	1=Yes 0=No	122
Hypertension	Have you EVER been told by a doctor or other health professional that you have had hypertension, also called high blood pressure?	Yes, No	HYPEV	1=Yes 0=No	189
Heart Disease	Have you EVER been told by a doctor or other health professional that you had heart disease?. Based on NHIS questions of specific diseases: ○ Coronary heart disease ○ Angina ○ Heart attack ○ Any kind of heart condition or heart disease	Each of the 4 questions have responses of Yes or No	CHDEV ANGEV MIEV HRTEV	1= answered yes to having been told had, coronary heart disease, angina, heart attack, or any other heart condition. 0=otherwise	64
Asthma	Have you EVER been told by a doctor or other health professional that you had asthma?	Yes, No	AASMEV	1=Yes 0=No	126

Appendix 1.
Detailed Matrix of Morbidity and Disability Questions from the NHIS asked consistently 1997-2007

Variable	NHIS Question	NHIS Possible Responses	NHIS variable Name	Study Definition	Study Missing Data (N)
Severe Psychological Distress	Is the individual depressed? Based on 6 NHIS questions: "During the past 30 days how often did you feel...?" o so sad that nothing could cheer you up? o nervous? o restless or fidgety? o hopeless? o that everything was an effort? o worthless?	For each of the 6 NHIS variables, responses are: 1=All of the time, 2=most of the time, 3=some of the time, 4=a little of the time, 5=none of the time	SAD NERVOUS RESTLESS HOPELESS EFFORT WORTHHLS	Score 0-24 based on sum of the 6 depression questions of number of days with symptoms (e.g. need cheering up, nervous, restless/fidgety, hopeless, too much effort, worthless, in the past 30 days. A cutoff of <13 will be used to define severe psychological distress (Pratt et al. 2007).	1693
Diabetes	Have you EVER been told by a doctor or other health professional that you had diabetes or sugar diabetes?	Yes, No	DIBEV	1=Yes 0=No	1566
Health care utilization or access					
Seen Primary Health care Provider	During the past 12 months, have you seen a primary health care provider (any of the following): o Ob/GYN o general doctor	o Seen/talked to a Ob/GYN: Yes, No o Seen/talked to a general doctor: Yes/No	AHCSYR7, AHCSYR9	0=seen Ob/GYN and/or general doctor 1=otherwise	None
Dental	About how long has it been since you last saw or talked to a dentist? Include all types of dentists, such as orthodontists, oral surgeons, and all other dental specialists, as well as dental hygienists.	Never, < 6 months, 6 months – 1 yr, >1 yr but no more than 2 years, > 2 years but no more than 5 years, >5 years	ADENLONG	0=within the past year 1=greater than a year	1854

Appendix 1.
Detailed Matrix of Morbidity and Disability Questions from the NHIS asked consistently 1997-2007

Variable	NHIS Question	NHIS Possible Responses	NHIS variable Name	Study Definition	Study Missing Data (N)
Surgery	During the PAST 12 MONTHS, have you had SURGERY or other surgical procedures either as an inpatient or an outpatient? This includes both major surgery and minor procedures such as setting bones or removing growths.	1) Yes 2) No	ASRGYR	1=Yes 0=No	1098
Emergency Room Visit	During the PAST 12 MONTHS, HOW MANY TIMES have you gone to a HOSPITAL EMERGENCY ROOM for your health?	Number of times	AHERNOY2	1=Yes 0=No	None
Health risk factors or behaviors					
Smoking	Is the individual a never smoker, former smoker, or current smoker? Based on the NHIS questions: o Have you smoked at least 100 cigarettes in your entire life? o Do you now smoke cigarettes every day, some days, or not at all?	o Yes, No o Everyday, some days, not at all	SMKEV SMKNOW	1=Never smoker, if the person said no to the question of ever smoker " Have you smoked at least 100 cigarettes in your entire life? 2=Former smoker, if answered yes to "ever smoker" but no to the question " Do you now smoke cigarettes every day, some days or not at all? 3=Current smoker, if the person classified as ever smoker and said smoke cigarettes every day or some days	1085

Appendix 1.
Detailed Matrix of Morbidity and Disability Questions from the NHIS asked consistently 1997-2007

Variable	NHIS Question	NHIS Possible Responses	NHIS variable Name	Study Definition	Study Missing Data (N)
Drinking	Is the individual a risky drinker? Based on the NHIS questions: o In your entire life, have you had at least 12 drinks of any type of alcoholic beverage? o In the past year, how often did you drink alcoholic beverages? o In the past year, on those days that you drank, on the average, how many drinks did you have?	o Yes, No o Number of times o Number of drinks	ALCLIFE ALC12MO ALCCAMT	Yes if an individual reported: 1) an average consumption of >14 alcoholic beverages for men or > 9 alcoholic beverages for women and 2) reported >12 binge drinking episodes; a binge episode is 5+ drinks in one episode. (Coups et al., 2004) These are based on a combination of questions regarding frequency and amount of alcohol consumption in the past 12 months.	62,531
Body Mass Index (cat)	NHIS recode variable	NHIS Recoded variable based on NHIS variables: o Self-reported weight without shoes (pounds) (AWEIGHTP) o Self-reported total height in inches (AHEIGHT)	BMI	Continuous and categorical: 1=Underweight (<18.5) 2=healthy weight (18.5-24.9) 3=overweight (≥25.0<30.0) 4=obese (>=30)	6202

Appendix 1.
Detailed Matrix of Morbidity and Disability Questions from the NHIS asked consistently 1997-2007

Variable	NHIS Question	NHIS Possible Responses	NHIS variable Name	Study Definition	Study Missing Data (N)
Leisure Time Physical Activity	Did the individual meet CDC Health People 2010 recommendations for leisure time physical activity (i.e. engaged or light-moderate activity for ≥ 30 minutes ≥ 5 times/week or "vigorous activity" ≥ 20 minutes ≥ 3 times per week or both). (Adams et al 2006). Based on NHIS questions: o Frequency of light/ moderate activity (times per week)? o Duration of light/ moderate activity (in minutes)? o Freq vigorous activity (times per week)? o Duration of vigorous activity (in minutes)?	o Times per week & Minutes per session o Times per week & Minutes per session	MODFREQW MODMIN VIGFREQW VIGMIN	1=yes, did meet recommendations 0=No, did not meet recommendations	14,628
HIV/AIDS Test	The next questions are about the test for HIV. Have you ever been tested for HIV?	Yes, No	AIDSTST	1=Yes 0=No	6068
Influenza Vaccine	During the past 12 months, have you had a flu shot? A flu shot is usually given in the fall and protects against influenza for the flu season.	Yes, No	SHTFLUYR	1=Yes 0=No	1642
Pneumococcal Vaccine	Have you ever had a pneumonia shot? This shot is usually given only once or twice in a person's lifetime and is different from the flu shot. It is also called the pneumococcal vaccine.	Yes, No	SHTPNUYR	1=Yes 0=No Only asked for those 60 years of age or older.	181,487

Appendix 2.

Description of Conversion of 1986–2004 National Health Interview Survey (NHIS) Industries into NORA Sectors

NORA Sectors (http://www.cdc.gov/niosh/programs/)

- Sector 1 - Agriculture, Forestry, Fishing
- Sector 2 - Construction
- Sector 3 - Healthcare and Social Assistance
- Sector 4 - Manufacturing
- Sector 5 - Mining
- Sector 6 - Services
- Sector 7 - Transportation, Warehousing, Utilities
- Sector 8 - Wholesale and Retail Trade

There is no issue in conversion from NHIS Industries into the NORA Sectors from 2005 NHIS onward since NHIS uses the NAICS Codes.

However, for 1986–2004 NHIS, the NHIS Industry codes do not translate directly into NORA Sectors, and a conversion is necessary (see attached figure which depicts the conversion process). The conversion from NHIS-recoded census industry codes into NORA Sector codes was accomplished using the NHIS Industry13 Recode to define Sectors 1,2,4,5,7,and 8 as follows:

- Sector 1 - Agriculture, Forestry and Fisheries (Industry 13 NHIS code 1)
- Sector 5 - Mining (Industry 13 NHIS code 2)
- Sector 2 - Construction (Industry13 NHIS code 3)
- Sector 4 - Manufacturing (Industry13 NHIS code 4)
- Sector 7 - Transport, Communication, Other Public Utilities (Industry13 NHIS code 5)
- Sector 8 - Wholesale Trade (Industry13 NHIS code 6)
- Sector 8 - Retail Trade (Industry13 NHIS code 7)

To define NORA Sectors 3 and 6, the following conversion was used:

- Sector 6 - Finance, Insurance, Real Estate (Industry13 NHIS code 8)
- Sector 6 - Business and Repair Services (Industry13 NHIS code 9)
- Sector 6 - Personal Services (Industry13 NHIS code 10)
- Sector 6 - Entertainment and recreation Services (Industry13 NHIS code 11)
- Sector 6 - Professional/Related Services (Industry13 NHIS code 12 [excluding Industry 41 NHIS codes 80, 81, and 84])
- Sector 3 - Professional/Related Services (Industry13 NHIS code 12 only for Industry 41 NHIS codes 80, 81, and 84)
- Sector 6 - Public Administration (Industry13 NHIS code 13)

Using the Industry41 NHIS code 84 to place workers in the Healthcare and Social Assistance sector has the undesirable result of also including Museums/art galleries/zoos, Labor Unions, and Membership organizations, n.e.c. industries. These people should be assigned to the Services Sector (NORA Sector 6). The 1986–1994 NHIS data sets provide a more detailed industry code that allows the identification of these groups (detail codes 872, 873, and 881 are designated by an asterisk (*)). For the **1986-1994 data sets**, this would involve changing approximately 2,000 out of approximately 63,000 Healthcare Sector workers into Service Sector workers (3%). Since this detailed industry code is publicly available in the NHIS data sets, this was done (see below).

For the **1995–2004 NHIS data sets**, this detailed industry information is not publicly available due to NCHS confidentiality concerns. The Services sector workers, who are inadvertently captured by this categorization of workers in Healthcare and Social Assistance sector, remain in the Healthcare and Social Assistance sector group for the estimates and analyses used for the 1997–2007 report.

Specific explanation of detailed industry codes for 1986–1994 data:

Three NHIS Census Industry Code (CIC) Recodes were used to define the Healthcare and Social Assistance NORA Sector 3: Industry41 code 80; Industry41 code 81; and Industry41 code 84. These subset of industries, are ordered below with corresponding NHIS Census Industrial Codes (CIC), Industry titles and 1987 Standardized Industry Codes (SIC) (SIC codes in parentheses).

Industry41	CIC	Industry Title (1987 Standardized Industry Codes)
Recode 80	831	Hospitals (806)
Recode 81	812	Offices and clinics of physicians (801, 803)
Recode 81	820	Offices and clinics of dentists (802)
Recode 81	821	Offices and clinics of chiropractors (8041)
Recode 81	822	Offices and clinics of optometrists (8042)
Recode 81	830	Offices and clinics of health practitioners, n.e.c. (8043, 8049)
Recode 81	832	Nursing and personal care facilities (805)
Recode 81	840	Health services, n.e.c. (807, 808, 809)
Recode 84	861	Job training and vocational rehabilitation services (833)
Recode 84	862	Child day care services (part 835)
Recode 84	863	Family child care homes (part 835)
Recode 84	870	Residential care facilities, without nursing (836)
Recode 84	871	Social services, n.e.c. (832, 839)
Recode 84	872	Museums, art galleries, and zoos (84)*
Recode 84	873	Labor unions (863)*
Recode 84	880	Religious organizations (866)
Recode 84	881	Membership organizations, n.e.c. (861, 862, 864, 865, 869)*

(861): Business associations
(862): Professional membership organizations
(864): Civic, social, fraternal organizations
(865): Political associations
(869): Membership organizations, n.e.c.; e.g., Travel motor clubs, Humane societies, Farm business organizations, Athletic associations

References:
The Relationship between the 1990 Census and Census 2000 Industry and Occupation Classification Systems, Technical Paper #65. Prepared By Thomas S. Scopp Under Special Contract with the U.S. Census Bureau, October 30, 2003
Map of 1987 SIC to 2002 NAICS:
http://www.census.gov/epcd/naics02/S87TON02.HTM

Appendix 3: Conversion of 1986–2004 National Health Interview Survey (NHIS) Industries into NORA Sectors (flowchart)

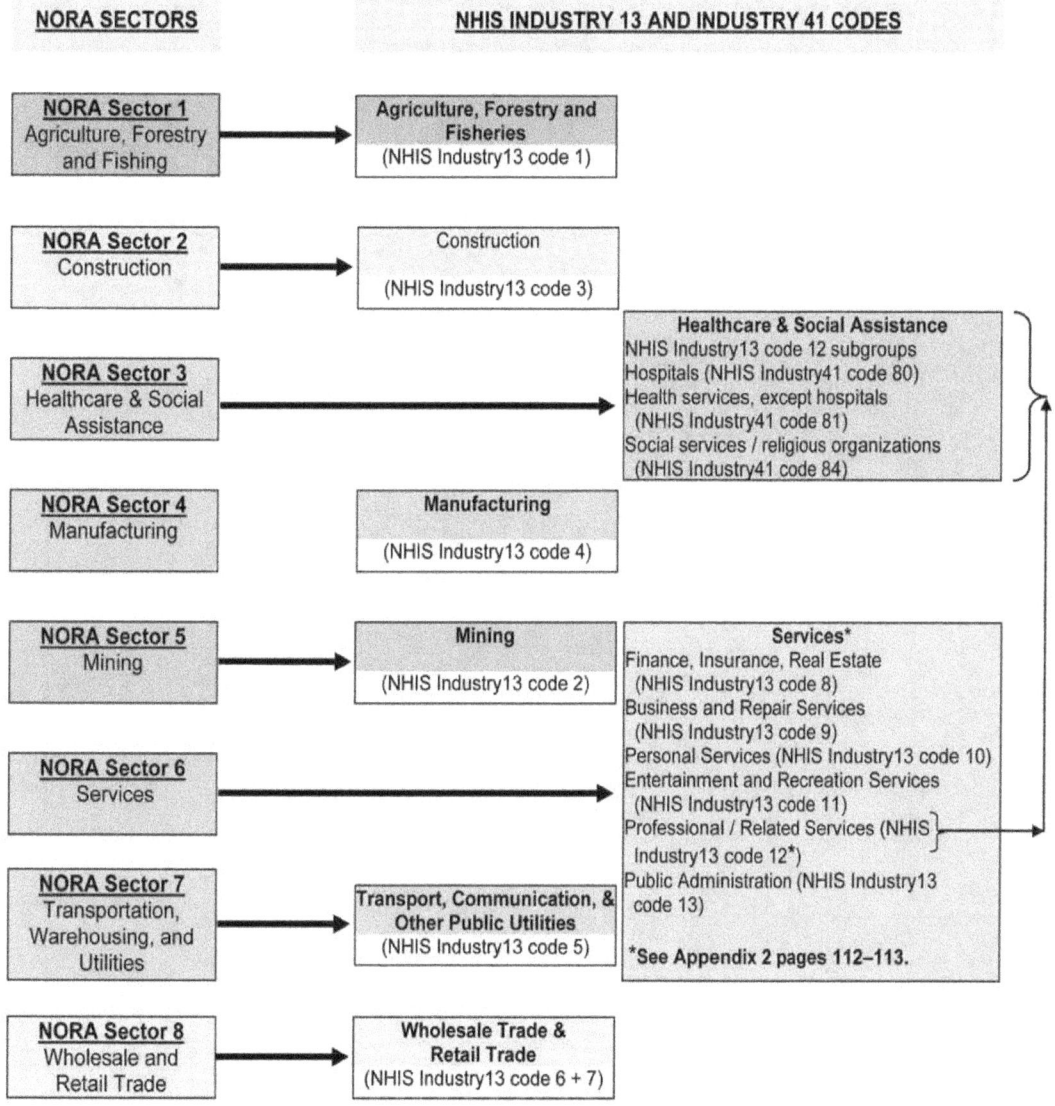